CLOSE
PURSUIT

CLOSE
PURSUIT

A Week in the Life of an
NYPD Homicide Cop

CARSTEN STROUD

VIKING

VIKING
Penguin Books Canada Limited, 2801 John Street, Markham, Ontario, Canada L3R 1B4
Penguin Books, Harmondsworth, Middlesex, England
Viking Penguin Inc., 40 West 23rd Street, New York, New York 10010 U.S.A.
Penguin Books Australia Ltd., Ringwood, Victoria, Australia
Penguin Books (N.Z.) Ltd., Private Bag, Takapuna, Auckland 9, New Zealand

First published by Penguin Books Canada Limited, 1987

Printed and bound in the United States of America

Canadian Cataloguing in Publication Data

Stroud, Carsten, 1946-
  Close pursuit.
ISBN 0-670-80837-7
1. New York (N. Y.). Police Dept. I. Title.
HV8148.N5S76 1986   363.2'09747'1   C85-098666-4

for

Phillip Cardillo,
Juan Andino,
Irma Lozado,
and
Anthony Venditti

ACKNOWLEDGMENTS

I have a lot of people to thank for this book but I can only name a few of them here.

MORTON MINT, who believed in it first.

STEPHEN RUBIN, who put his money on a dark horse.

BEVERLY LEWIS, who made a good book a better book.

BETSY CENEDELLA, whose care and research kept me from making a total fool of myself.

The COLBERTS, NANCY, STAN, & DAVID, who made it all happen in the first place.

LINDA MAIR, my wife, who went the distance with style and wit, as she does in every story.

And finally, to all the Eddie Kennedys in the NYPD—thanks. Take care.

CONTENTS

NOTES ON THE MATERIAL

Early in the research for this book I was spending a lot of time sitting around in my apartment on East 38th Street, going quietly bonkers waiting for various New York Police Department detectives to return my calls. I got into the habit of cruising through the boroughs in a rented Plymouth, drinking black coffee and listening to the cross-talk on my police radio. One Friday night I was pushing my way through the standard traffic jam on 42nd Street, trying to guess how many neon lights there were between Seventh and Eighth Avenues. It was a dense and humid night, early in the spring but showing some real heat down on street level, the air thick enough to slide on, reeking of diesel oil and popcorn, the way midtown does on a Friday night. A call came over my radio for the foot patrol officers—they call them Portables in the NYPD. There was a fight going on in a porno theater at Eighth and 43rd. To my right I could see four of these officers, three solid-looking guys and a wiry female cop who looked a little like Patti LuPone. They were jogging west along the block, answering the call. The woman was talking into her handset and I could hear her voice on my radio, a little breathless, talking as she ran, saying that she and three other Portables were on their way. It seemed a couple of squad cars were also responding. Well, this was nothing special for a midtown Friday night, but, as I said, it was either do this or go home and talk to Elmore, my house plant, so I decided to follow them over in the Plymouth.

In the night, in the right light, I look a bit like a plainclothes cop, just under six feet and a little on the beefy side, hard-case moustache and I don't smile a lot, so when the Portables met up with six other uniform cops outside the porno theater, I just eased myself into the group and went inside with them. For kicks, more or less. Which, as it turned out, was exactly what I got.

The theater was massive and packed with people, and black as a dragon's colon except for the screen, where the film was still running. The place smelled like a dragon's colon too. My feet stuck to the floor as I ran along the back row behind the cops. They split up and went both ways down the aisles toward what looked like a small riot going on in the front row. People were screaming and shouting. Somebody was getting the better of somebody else and being pretty noisy about it. Whatever was going on in the film had something to do with sex but it looked more like a full-color close-up of a car accident. Over the screams and the shouts from a crowd of people fighting each other down in the first row, just black outlines against the screen, you could hear the heavy breathing and the sighs of the couple making love in the film, and the crackle of police radios and heavy feet pounding down the aisles and the jingle of police gear on their belts. I was still at the top of the aisle, holding the radio, when a big black guy came racing up out of the dark. Behind him I could just make out a couple of coplike figures chasing him. It dawned on me that this was not a good place to be standing, looking vaguely official and holding a portable police radio, so I decided to get out of the guy's way. I was still trying to do that, shoving at the crowd behind me, when he flew right into me and we both went down.

Now I was not at all sure what it was my feet had been sticking to on the floor of this porno theater but I could imagine, so as we got all tangled up and went down, I did my best to see to it that the black guy was on the bottom. Let him worry about what was on the floor. He hit the ground with a meaty thump and his breath came out all at once and I found myself more or less kneeling on his chest, trying to get up again. This hand grabbed me by the hair and I felt my head being jerked back hard. There was a red exit light shining just above us and I could see this very angry black woman with her blouse unbuttoned and her teeth clenched. She was hissing at me in some foreign language and I got the impression that the guy I was kneeling on was somebody important to her, but before I could get off my knees she poked me, hard, in the right eye with her thumb.

This smarted a bit and I was wearing contact lenses so the next few seconds were a little hazy. The next clear recollection I had, I was on one hand and two knees on the floor, holding my right eye. The black guy was back on his feet and tugging at the arm of the black woman. I could hear cop boots pounding up the aisle and the jingle of handcuffs and the couple on the screen gasping and crying out in the same rhythm.   I tried to get to my feet and just as I did, the black woman hissed something at me and then she stepped back and kicked me with a pointy-toed shoe in the soft part of my right side just beneath the rib cage. I stopped looking for my contact lens at this stage and settled down onto the floor again, making a sound like a slow leak in a truck tire.

When I got back to my apartment on East 38th Street it was four in the morning and there was a message on the machine for me from a detective I'd been trying to reach for a week. I called him at work and he told me he'd heard I had just gotten myself beaten up by a black hooker and how would I like to go out for a drink and tell him about it because he hadn't had a good laugh in a couple of weeks. Of course I said yes.

This is what you have to go through to get a cop to talk to you in this town.

Not that I'm complaining. After all, news is one thing. Most detectives know that it's a reporter's job to ferret out stories and generally harass the NYPD to find out things the department would rather you didn't know. That's what journalists do, and God bless them. But that's not what I was after.

What I wanted was something more elusive, certainly more intrusive, and, finally, none of my damned business. I wanted the essence of the thing, the psychic landscape of homicide work in New York City, how it felt and what it did to them, what they were afraid of and what they hated. What kind of dreams they had. Personal stuff.

I have an editor in Toronto who says that it is the business of writers to ask questions whose answers they have no right to. That's literally what I was doing.

It took about two years of background and six months in the city, but I finally got a few working detectives in the NYPD to open up. I went to crime scenes, interrogations, autopsies, arrests. I met some wives and children. I saw a lot of squad-room life, and I got a view of New York that will stay with me forever. As much as any outsider can be, I was allowed into the club and I was told the truth as they saw it. It is an uncompromising truth, frequently ugly and racist, often violent and cruel. As one detective used to say to me, whenever I was looking a little green around the edges or taking things too hard, it is what it is. As far as they were concerned, I could either accept it and live with it, or I could go back to my place, open up a Beck's, and watch TV with the sound off.

All the access I got was unofficial—kindnesses and trust extended to me by serving officers and detectives in various sectors of the force. Without their help and guidance this book would not have been written.

For that reason, I have changed names and altered the details wherever it was necessary to protect the identity of my sources. There may also be places in the book where procedures described vary from formal procedures. I wrote them as I saw them. I make no apology for this. The book is not an exercise in investigative journalism. There have been many superb investigative books written about the NYPD, starting with *Target Blue* by Robert Daley, and *Black Police, White Society* by Stephen H. Leinen. Nick Pileggi and Mark Daly are doing good work in this area for *New York* Magazine. A New York Homicide lieutenant by the name of Vernon Geberth has written a brilliant text on the techniques of homicide work, called *Practical Homicide Investigation*. Reporters from print and television dissect the triumphs and failures of the NYPD on a regular basis, and some of this work is superb. A lot of it isn't. A lot of it is shallow and exploitive, or reflexively, thoughtlessly liberal and fuzzy-minded.

I'm good at emotion, at atmosphere and sensation. I'm not as ready to pronounce one element of the NYPD vile and another element heroic as I might be if I were a full-time player in the local journalistic games. I'm an outsider, a Canadian, and it seems the better part of wisdom for me to step carefully here. I have a lot of background in police work. I've written about the police and worked next to them for almost ten years, in one capacity or another. I know them pretty well, in Canada, in Mexico and Central America. And the most difficult and indecipherable police force I've ever run into is the subject of this book: the NYPD.

I lived as close to the NYPD as I could for six months and although I have made some friends and some enemies, I see now that a lifetime could be spent trying to get a clear and valid picture of the force. New York City is, in many ways, a unique environment, with its own ethics and rules, its own code. The NYPD reflects this dichotomy, at once profane and vulgar and brutal, and yet with something in it that is noble and true and fine. Like America, I suppose, and like all of us, waiting for the dawn with one foot in hell. The book is about homicide work in New York City. This is what the streets are like, and these are the people as I see them. This is how they live, and this is what they dream about. If you care about these things, you will care about this book.

CHAPTER I

DREAM SEQUENCE

This little black kid is running, he's got one knee out of the fabric and every time his right leg comes up the cap shows like the top swivel of a camshaft rod, down it goes again and up comes the other. Kennedy is watching this from his car and he can see that the kid isn't running for fun: His blue-black skin is streaming wet and pulled back tight and his mouth is wide and gasping, the bony little body stretching out for every yard of sidewalk. Kennedy can see the kid coming from two blocks away but the scene is compressed: just a small nigger kid racing toward Kennedy, straight into the slanting sundown so that the dusty yellow light is glinting off the kid's cheeks and his eyes are almost closed, he's flying up this street with a solid wall of grills and smashed headlights and rusting fenders on his left and the tenement stoops and the garbage on his right. Kennedy can hear the pam pam pam pa-pam *of the kid's shoes and see the dust puff up each time the toe comes down. Kennedy's own heart is working and his breath is short and chuffing, keeping a pace with the kid. He feels he ought to get out of the car, get down there on the street but he's in a post here, can't leave that or the whole number's blown. In his mind he's saying come on come on, kid, move move. The kid seems to hear this, Christ knows how, and he gets some speed from somewhere and now he can see Kennedy in the car, something to run to, so his eyes change and some of the panic is going from his face . . .*

. . . THERE! There that's the son of a bitch, Kennedy's belly muscles jump and the skin across his shoulders tightens up. A

sharp-faced white guy with bottle-blue eyes, half-hidden, he's got a black satin jacket, come on, kid, run, but the guy's between them, between Kennedy and the kid, the man's too close. Kennedy sees all this in the time it takes for the kid's leg to come forward, toe out, heel drops and takes the shock and the dust comes up. Kennedy reaches for the door latch, he can see the thick gold ring on his heavy hand, and he starts to get out.

Now he's out on the sidewalk and down on a knee, he's yelling to the kid and his arms are wide like he's a catcher or a saint. Kennedy can feel the sidewalk grit digging into his knee through the gray wool of his slacks. Maybe the gun, should he have the gun out? No, this is a street kid, he'll think it's for him, he knows I'm a cop but the gun will slow him up. Kennedy calls again, he can feel the places in his arms where the kid will hit, he can feel the skinny body and the weight of it as he takes him in and picks him up off the ground, his left hand locked around his right wrist, he'll swing the kid straight into the car and then go for the asshole down the street. He lives this future-second five times and each time the kid makes it to him his chest fills up with a lightness so liquid he can feel tears start. Safe safe and home. Now a car door slams from up the block behind him, he's back in real time, the kid is still closing fast, and the lieutenant is severely pissed here, Kennedy can hear that. Kennedy, you fuckin' dildo, what the fuck are you doing? Kennedy turns to call back. It's okay, I'm just going to save this kid, sir. When he looks back there's a flicker of black satin fifty yards down the block and the street is empty.

Never get out of the boat. Crazy bastard in that movie was right. Kennedy gets up into a running stumble, his right hand going back to the holster where he fumbles at the Chief. The radio! It's on the seat—no time. He gets the butt in his palm and tugs, hearing some lining rip where he snags the hammer, but he just pulls it through and now it's Kennedy who's racing down the block in his goddam Florsheim Eagles, the shock going pom pom pompom. He's old, that's clear, no speedster like the kid. Doorways are flashing by on his left, and now there are people in the streets as if they'd risen up from the ground and they swivel to watch him as he goes by with his jacket billowing out and his tie flapping. Kennedy sees them as a flurry of lidded eyes, grim black faces, faded jeans and shiny head scarves, ritual tattoos, fucking home boys with skin the color of bunker oil and the threat coming off them in waves. Christ, they hate us, thinks Kennedy, can't they see what the hell's going on here? He wants to stop and explain it, to make them understand but he keeps going with his heart ripping up his chest, pounding on his framework like a fighter working a bag.

He clears the curb, a car cuts left in a glitter of chrome and a whiff of hot vapor. Kennedy doesn't look back and he's in the air as he hits the next block. Which door? Which ruined fucking pile? Here! No, here? How far down? A shattered wall comes up fast on his left, here's the yellow Pinto he saw the kid near. He stops, heaving, and puts a shoulder to the wall, passing his gun hand across his eyes. This is the door, he knows that. Up the street and down, the people are crowding the upper windows, leaning on pillows, hanging their legs over the roof lines, holding cans of Coors, staring at him with half-closed eyes, quietly hating him as only the blacks can. He turns away and looks into the hole in the wall. Backup? He's alone and that's that, fuck the backup. He flips out the cylinder and watches as a single drop of sweat comes off his face and lands on one of the brass circles, and the stamped letters W-W 38 SP swell and waver in the droplet. He snaps the cylinder shut and takes a ragged breath. Shit. The doorway smells like a grave.

He tries to go in fast and to the right, get out of the silhouette and get some stone up against his back like they taught him at Rodman's Neck, but he hooks a spike in the shoulder of his jacket and tumbles into the dark like a mailbag full of bad news, his gun up in front of him wavering and his other hand sinking up to the wrist in something cold and slick. Now the smell is on him. In him. A ferocious exhalation of rotting mattresses, old piss, mold and age, dead wood and rodent passions, things that crawl and things that leave a trail. The shadows in here are shot through with pale-yellow beams from the cracks in the walls. All six floors have burned and fallen into each other long ago, collapsing onto the ground floor, leaving a huge hollow space full of dust motes and scents, and the thought comes to Kennedy that he hasn't been to Mass in seven months. Like a chapel in hell, he thinks, and the urge to get up and get out is so strong he can feel his thigh muscles tensing. Oh, kid, what the fuck are we doing here?

Five long seconds go by without a sound from the street and without a bullet out of the darkness, so Kennedy pushes himself up and takes another step. The smell gets worse. He can see better now, he can see the walls running wet. The middle of the summer, and the place is still wet. There's a heap in the middle of the floor where a tangle of pipes and timbers rises up in a monkey puzzle of crazy angles. Another step and the floor gives way slowly and then comes back, as if he were walking over the body of something asleep and breathing. Well, we don't want to wake that fucker, thinks Kennedy, grinning. What's that line? We don't want to be here when it gets hungry. Woody Allen is saying this to some item he's trying to hustle. He laughs out loud, takes another step, his left foot lands on nothing and now he's down to the hip, something's got him by the ankle, and here comes that feeling everybody braces for but nobody can handle, when an injury comes your way you never even tried to imagine. A spike, a pipe, a shattered plank, whatever it is it's deep deep in his thigh. Kennedy shrieks like a girl here—a woman's cry, it goes seventy feet straight up into the dripping roof and loses itself in a blanket of dark fur and leathery wings. A slow rustle comes back down, tiny claws flex, and now the air is full of shrill crystalline piping. Kennedy freezes, looks up at the roof line and back down at his leg where it disappears into the dirt and garbage, all panic gone and thinking with perfect clarity: Kennedy, you fucking dildo, you are going to die in this fucking hole. He hears a step, there's a shimmer of black satin, blue eyes, now for a shining moment the place is full of blue light. A second blow comes up against his ear, his head rocks back. This fucker can kick! The back of his head comes off a brick but by then he's out.

CHAPTER 2

CARNIVORES

Kennedy's cat woke him up at five on Monday morning by bringing him an imperfectly killed bat and dropping it on his pillow. Kennedy was still in the dream, at the point where he has gone through a hole in the floor of this burnout up in the Bronx and he's got the spike stuck in his thigh muscle. Kennedy's cat knows this part because every time Kennedy dreams it he jerks and shivers on the bed and Dudley has to get off and get out, just to find some peace. Dudley doesn't mind this too much, since it is Dudley's pleasure to go forth into the long Manhattan nights to fornicate and/or fight with anything pretty enough or stupid enough to get in his way. He goes out through a two-foot hole in the screening that he went to no end of trouble to claw open the second week he and Kennedy started rooming together. It's a short hop to the awning of an Italian café. Then over to the threadbare elm at the curbside and onto the streets. The streets go everywhere a jet-black thirteen-pound one-eyed tomcat could ever want to go. Whenever Dudley hit the street—usually around midnight and nothing showing but that big yellow eye with the bright red gleam way down inside it—whenever he hit the street the word got around fast. Pigeons under the eaves stopped talking things over with their mates; big brown rats in the garbage bins went down flat and slitted up their eyes; candy-assed peke-a-poos stopped yapping and headed for the nearest friendly doorman. The rust-colored Rottweiler who took care of the Italian café after hours moved to the front window and thanked whatever dog-gods there are that he had some plate glass in front of him. He had more or less decided that this particular cat was a major shitstorm of bad dog-news after they'd gone a few rounds in the Dumpster out back six months ago. He still had the slits in his nose and he'd have them forever. Last night Dudley's foray had bagged him a pair of brown bats who had been stunting and soaring around the street lamp outside the café, exulting in whatever it is that bats exult in, and the leap out of the dark had taken both of them down into the gutter in a tangle of black fur and leathery wings, blood and white bones. The Rottweiler picked up the supersonic chittering from the street. So did the rats and the pigeons in the sky.

The sun gets into Kennedy's room in a kind of triple play, Tinker to Evers to Chance, striking a slanted facet of a local high-rise and ricocheting down into the canyon floor. There it hits six perfectly placed panes of glass on the Florida room of a brownstone on the south side of the street and shoots up through the Venetian blinds at the bedroom window of Kennedy's flat on the north side. Finally it strikes a bullet-starred Budweiser mirror on the opposite wall which Kennedy is too lazy or too stubborn to move, and it would hit Kennedy right in the eyes if he hadn't learned to sleep with a pillow over his face.

So there was just enough light for Kennedy to get a pretty good look at what it was that Dudley had dropped onto his pillow. Kennedy bounded out of the bed so fast that Dudley lost his concentration for a nanosecond, just long enough for the not-quite-dead bat to slither out from under the tomcat's paw and take off, hell-for-leather, toward the nearest exit.

Kennedy was doing pretty much the same thing at half the speed, but since the bat had twice the distance to cover, and since they had both decided that the nearest exit was the door into the bathroom, well, it didn't take a degree in ballistics to figure out that they were going to end up in the same place in about three seconds. Dudley, who considered himself something of an authority in these matters, and who was by now only too aware of Kennedy's negative reaction to raw bat for breakfast, decided to bring this unhappy affair to a timely end and launched himself off the foot of the bed with a view to intercepting the bat in midflight.

Heroic though this leap certainly was, Dudley from time to time failed to allow for the fact that he had only one eye and was therefore at a disadvantage when it came to judging distances in stressful situations. He fell rather short of his airborne intercept, landing instead on the broad expanse of Kennedy's naked back at roughly the same time that Kennedy and the bat reached the bathroom door.

Kennedy, feeling something dreadfully sharp and energetic sinking tiny terrible claws into his body, went into a low crouch and spun madly about in the doorway, visions of rabid bats and ten-inch needles flickering in his mind. As he came around he managed to get himself in a virtual nose-to-snout confrontation with the flying bat.

Eye-to-beady-red-eye, it came to Kennedy that the moment was right for a little gunplay, and he lurched back through the doorway in the direction of his ankle holster lying beside the bed. Dudley, still aboard and slightly confused by all the spinning and leaping, dug in and went along for the ride.

Meanwhile the bat executed a double Immelmann and a barrel rollout and flew straight back the way he had come, fetching up, breathless and panicked, on top of the Venetian blinds over the bedroom window.

Dudley, seeing this maneuver, pushed off against Kennedy's back and scrambled across the floor toward the window while Kennedy, off-balance, stumbled into the night table, snagging his Smith & Wesson and bringing it up into a firing position just as the alarm clock on the falling night table hit the floor in a shower of blue sparks and set fire to a corner of the down comforter that Kennedy's ex-girlfriend had left behind.

Kennedy had the bat in his sights and was squeezing the trigger when the fire got his attention. By the time he had beaten out the flames, Dudley had taken out the bat. He was in the corner doing something undeniably fatal to it and Kennedy sat for a while at the foot of the bed, watching him do it. After about three minutes of this, Kennedy brought the gun back up and leveled the sights on a spot just behind Dudley's right shoulder-joint. He held this position for another thirty seconds, letting his breath out slowly, in a slightly ragged way, keeping his index finger outside the trigger guard. His mind delivered a series of apparently unrelated facts having to do with the building materials of his bedroom wall, the penetrating power of his semi-wadcutter .38 special load, the value of Dudley's company, his relationship with the CO of the 19th Precinct, just a few blocks away, and the possibility of removing bloodstains from the wallpaper on Dudley's far side. His hand shook very little during this period. The smoke from the brief fire on his down cover rose, in patterns of ovals and deltas and sinuous curls, up through the shaft of sunlight coming in through the window until it reached the ceiling, where it flattened out, spreading itself along the plaster in a posture suggestive of mild expectancy and polite interest in the tableau beneath it. Dudley settled onto his belly and ate quietly, even daintily, not looking at Kennedy but with his right ear laid back along his skull and a certain tautness in his lines. The phone rang. It was Stokovich.

An hour later Detective Eddie Kennedy got out of a gypsy cab at the intersection of Avenue C and East 4th in Alphabet City. A Radio Motor Patrol car, an RMP, with two officers—a black policewoman and an older white cop—was waiting for him. The two cops, looking bored, were drinking coffee out of a Mickey Mouse thermos. Another uniform, a young foot patrolman, was sitting on the curb holding his head in his hands. All three of them straightened up a bit as Kennedy walked over with his badge out.

About ten feet from this boy, inside a yellow crime-scene ribbon, the body of a young male lay in that curiously boneless disarray of the truly and suddenly dead. His head was lying in a lake of brown blood, and a delta of blood had formed in the pits and cracks along the sidewalk, running toward the curb in a system of canals and rivulets, looking like an aerial photograph of Mars. Kennedy asked the older of the RMP officers whether or not the body had been checked for vital signs. The man chuckled into his coffee and said the body had rigor and lividity and was as dead as it gets. The black policewoman nodded, unsmiling, and held herself apart from the talk. Kennedy took out his pocket Kodak and loaded a new film cassette into it.

While he was doing this, Dudley was lapping water out of the apartment toilet, feeling a little drowsy, and watching the way slender threads of rich red bat's blood were drifting down into the deep. Being a cat, he could not see the blood as red. He saw it instead as a slow undulation of dark-gray lines against a shimmering field of pale-white. It was the scent that held him, so powerful and detailed, so layered and shaded and full of nuance.

First Rule: Never Get Out of the Boat. Kennedy stood at the

edge of the ribbon and looked across the distance at the body. Poor bastard. So what the hell do we have here? He had spent a little while talking to the First Officer, the kid now looking ghostly in the back of the RMP. He'd been at the tail of his shift when Central got a call: male Hispanic voice; time in, 0437 hours; this date. "You go to 'La Colonización,' you dumb fucks, you get a *maricon* to play with. *Hasta!*" "La Colonización" was hard to miss. The body was right underneath it.

It's a mural painted on the side wall of a ruined market on the northwest corner of C and East 4th. It's fifty feet long, perhaps ten feet high. There's a long expanse of Caribbean shoreline, an eggshell beach bordered by palms and loaded with tropical fruit: mangoes and bananas, papayas, avocados, coconuts—nature's riches. The sea rolls in through shades of tourmaline and deep-purple to emerald and pale-green, the lightest blue. Three sailing ships have just cleared the horizon. The *Niña*, the *Pinta*, and the *Santa Maria*. "La Colonización." You have to step back a few yards to get the joke: The pretty thing is on a ruined building, next door to a vacant lot full of bricks and rubble.

Across the street there are more bombed-out and empty buildings. The place looks like Beirut, as if running battles were fought here every Saturday night. The next block is worse. In the whole area, bounded by 14th Street, First Avenue, East Houston, and the FDR Drive, there are hundreds of five- and six-story buildings that went up in the thirties and have been allowed to fall down ever since the near-bankruptcy of New York in 1975. It's also home to roughly 100,000 people who live either in the Jacob Riis and Lillian Wald projects off Avenue D or here and there in flats and basements in the brownstones. There isn't a block without a burnout or a pit full of ruin—protected, for some demented reason, by brand-new wire fencing, as if there were a problem with rubble-thievery. Whatever isn't fenced off or burned down is covered with iron bars and graffiti. The man who invented the spray can ought to be dragged down to Alphabet City and put to work with a toothbrush and some Ajax. There isn't a space unmarked from ankle-high to the top of the first-floor windows.

If you can ignore the scars, you can see that the proportions of these old brownstones are perfect; a nice rhythm has been set up between the corniced windows and the brickwork. There's symmetry here, and craftsmanship in the cut-stone lintels, the gargoyles and the mullions, and in the wholeness of the execution. Italianate and well-proportioned in design, the whole area was scaled down and set out in wide streets and avenues. The men who built Alphabet City are all dead now. So is Alphabet City.

The solid citizens who live here now, and there are a lot of them, stay here because there's no place else to go. Black and Hispanic in the main, the population also includes some whites and Orientals, and even a few tough trendoids from the East Village and SoHo who have been forced into the region by gentrification. This area is clearly destined for the same thing. The landlords who own these buildings have only to wait about ten years and the property will triple in value, and then the white-painters and the fan-window crowd will buy in by the phalanx. In the meantime, it's a free-fire zone and heroin heaven.

Kennedy had been working this area for about three years, ever since he was transferred from the South Bronx at his own request. It still made him nervous.

There's a rule called 24/24 in the Homicide lexicon. It means that the most important hours in the investigation of any murder are the last twenty-four hours in the victim's life and the first twenty-four hours after his body has been discovered. The secret of the killing lies in this time zone. Go back beyond that and the forces that led to his death are too diffuse, and after the first twenty-four hours the witnesses are starting to forget things; the tissues are drying out; the weapons are being destroyed. Clothes are being burned and stories are being agreed upon. Under the circumstances, Kennedy felt a sense of urgency. The trick was to ignore that. Kennedy's first partner used to say, "The stiff will still be dead in the morning." The one thing a Homicide cop has that no other cop can count on is time to do it right. But he gets no second chance.

Kennedy's system had been worked out over the years, and much of it has passed into formal NYPD Academy training. It was second nature to him by now, a kind of Zen attitude that came over him in the first minutes of a case, giving him the stillness and the focus he needed to see what there was to see and to know it when he saw it.

Kennedy kept a pack of steno notepads in the top drawer of his dresser. When he'd gotten the call from his lieutenant, the

first thing he'd done was to take one of these new pads along with
him. He flipped it open now and started writing in it.

He wrote out the time of Stokovich's call—0516 hours—and
the date. Beneath this he wrote out the means by which he had
received the call. He wrote down *landline,* which is NYPD jargon
for a telephone call. He identified his boss in this way:

Lieutenant Bruno Stokovich, NYPD.
C.O., Midtown Central Detective Area Task Force.

Then he started to describe the scene from the moment he had
arrived, starting with the First Officer report. The First Officer is
the first policeman on the scene, the person whose job it is to make
the preliminary investigation of the crime. In most cases this
amounts to nothing more than making certain the victim is really
dead, helping him if he isn't, and keeping the elements and the
crowds off the crime-scene area until the detectives and the Patrol
Supervisor get there.

In this case, the streets had been deserted when the officer
had reached the scene. He had moved the man's shirt aside so he
could put a couple of fingers on the hollow place where the ribs
meet the breastbone. There had been no movement. He had left
the shirt up and he could see a wide area of purple stain under
the skin, like a port-wine spill. He had also attempted to raise
the man's wrist. It was slightly stiff. Rigor was setting in. The
officer had had no doubt the victim was dead. He had marked
him so in his memo book, and called in for some assistance.
Communications had relayed the call to the desk officer at the
local precinct and an RMP had been dispatched to assist in pro-
tecting the site.

The young cop had referred to his memo book several times,
and Kennedy had made certain that the officer's entries were
complete and accurate. The chain of evidence started from the
moment the First Officer arrived at the killing, and Kennedy had
lost cases because the sequence of events or the evidential chain
had been broken by inconsistent or careless entries. He spoke to
the young man for a long time, until he was satisfied that his
report was correct and complete.

Since the streets had been deserted and the weather clear—
the sun just rising and the day still cool—the cop had left the body

uncovered and stepped carefully backward out of the crime scene, retracing his footsteps as if he were walking on ice.

Kennedy noted this, and took another look at the cop. He couldn't have been older than twenty-one. Solid but half-formed, the way suburban kids are. Maybe an athlete in high school. Probably recruited from Jersey or up in Yonkers and still a little stunned by Manhattan. But the kid had done well. Kennedy had vivid memories of crime scenes where he'd arrived to find a couple of gold braids from downtown standing inside the ribbon, passing evidence around like a pretzel tray at a retirement racket. The kid had even made a note of his path into and back out of the crime scene. The other two cops, who had arrived in the RMP, had never gone inside it at all.

So the scene was still clean. It was a pleasant surprise. Kennedy finished his first notations and put the steno pad into his jacket pocket.

It was now 0637 hours. The block would be crowded soon, with kids on vacation and people getting up to go to their jobs. Monday in Manhattan came on fast. He thought for a second.

"Hey, sonny!"

The First Officer got up off the curb and came over to Kennedy. "Yes, sir?" His broad young face was a mixture of nausea and avidity. It was a look Kennedy knew well.

"We're going to leave him here a bit. Let the crowds get a look. You call the Medical Examiner? The Crime Scene Unit? Yeah? Okay, I want one of your Anti-Crime guys out here in fifteen minutes. Who's good?"

The kid thought about it for a minute.

"You want someone with Spanish?"

"No, I want Pushtu. Yeah, Spanish."

"Stradazzi. Looks like a greaser too. But he's not on until the next shift."

"Yes? Look, young fellow, you get on your portable here and you call your Patrol Sergeant—who's he today?"

"Bergman. Nathan Bergman? Sergeant Bergman, sir."

"Long fucking name, hah? Yeah, I know that dildo. What's your problem with him?"

"Problem, sir? I got no beef with Sergent Bergman."

"Bullshit. You got an overtime beef with him. Guy's got the

Administrative Guide tattooed on his ass. Give me the radio."
Kennedy took the Motorola handset and pressed the call button.

"One-oh-four to Central, K?"

"One-oh-four? No landline, one-oh-four?"

"Negative, Central. I'm in the field. Can you get me Sergeant
Bergman, at the Eighth? We need an Officer Stradazzi out here.
ACU man. Tell Bergman Detective Kennedy is asking. Badge
number four-two-four-seven. Tell him I say please."

The woman on Dispatch laughed once. "Roger, one-oh-four.
You're with Nine Frank?"

The driver of the RMP nodded at Kennedy.

"Yeah, Nine Frank. Still on that call. I'll want a tape of that
call on this run. You have a call back?"

"Negative, one-oh-four. No call back. You'll have to call me
on a landline for the rest."

"Yeah. Tell Pendleton I'll be in today."

"Roger, one-oh-four."

Kennedy handed the set back to the kid. "When Stradazzi
gets on to you— What time you off, kid?"

"It's Harris, sir. Brian Harris? I'm off at oh-eight-hundred,
sir. But if you need me to stay. . . ?"

"I need you to stay. When this ACU guy gets on to you, I
want him out here in the crowd. What's the color today?"

"The color, sir?"

"Will you can the 'sir' crap? Call me Eddie. I'll call you Brian,
okay? Good. I mean the code color for your SCU guys. You
know, if it's Tuesday I must be wearing a lime-green headband.
That shit."

Harris's face opened up. "Oh, yes, sir. The color for last shift
was blue. But it's not headbands now—it's a belt. At least I think
it was a belt." He went for his memo book but Kennedy stopped
him.

"Yeah. Well, I want to know the color for right now, and see
that your guy's wearing it when he wanders out here. I *don't* want
him walking up to me and asking me what should he do, right?
I'm going to let this stiff cook for a bit until we draw a crowd.
Maybe we can tag the asshole before lunch."

"Oh, I see. You mean he works the area. Sees what he can
hear? What he can see, I mean."

"Brilliant, Harris. You should be a cop. You take the RMP and pick him up if you have to."

"Oh, sir—Eddie. I can't pick up an MOS in a department car unless it's official. Patrol Guide regulation number one-sixteen—"

Kennedy held himself in. "Harris, how long you been out of the Academy? An hour? I'm supervising this investigation and I can send you to Albany for cigarettes if I want. I need a good ear on that street right now and you're gonna go get him. Now go!"

As Harris pelted away toward the squad car, one hand on his hat, the other holding up his belt, Kennedy let himself curse the ten million ways in which department regs made his life hell. It seemed that every stage of every investigation had to be pushed through or around a mountain of bureaucratic bull. The Patrol Sergeant wasn't really to blame for being reluctant to cut into his overtime allowances. Patrol Sergeants had to answer to the desk officer, who had to answer to Ops Coordinator, who jumped whenever the Exec woke up and asked for coffee, and the Exec got the heebies whenever the Precinct Commander had a skin rash, and the Precinct Commander got skin rashes because he had to keep the Duty Captain for the Borough happy, which cannot be done, because the Duty Captain is worried sick about what the Zone Commander is going to say about the overtime rates when he finds out, and the Zone Commander spends most of his office hours agonizing about the things the Patrol Borough Commander will say to *him*. And of course the Patrol Borough Commander lives for the day when he can take his monthly report to the Chief of Patrol, who is God, and say, with just the right mixture of pride and humility, that he is smack-dab into the black side of his Payroll Estimate for the month. Whereupon the Chief of Patrol will smile a sweet smile and silently thank the gods that he doesn't have to explain to the Commissioner just exactly why it is that his department is *still* costing the city too goddam much.

Which explains why young Officer Harris didn't want to ask anybody back at the precinct for overtime pay, and why Eddie Kennedy spends many of his off-duty hours at Brew's drinking Miller Lite out of an Old-Fashioned glass and pretending it's Chivas Regal, which he used to drink back in the days before he got an ulcer.

Kennedy had already taken several shots of the whole crime scene from outside the ribbon. He now stepped over the ribbon and entered the crime area itself. The first thing he looked at was the body.

It's an oddity of life that most people who fantasize about working on a big-city homicide squad, or who pretend to do it for CBS or NBC, don't seem to realize that at the heart of every homicide investigation is a dead body, and the essence of the job is to be able to confront that body in all its grim carnality, its stolid and perfect distance, and its sensory intimacy. You walk up to the thing and you step in its blood and juices, you smell it and you feel it, and your job is to get down onto the ground with it and to slip underneath the skin and inhabit the skull and make its last seconds live and live again. Every cop maintains that detachment is the key, but the truth is that he gives up a section of his soul to every corpse and he dies a little death at the beginning of every case. If he were truly detached he could never see what has to be seen. The key to the thing is intimacy without emotion. Even the ones who have that quality never keep it for long. A few years on the job, and you're either out of homicide or well into the process of freezing solid forever. For cops, homicide work is the top of the ladder. You become a boss and drive a desk, you go to the FBI or Drug Enforcement or the Department of Investigation. Now and then you kill a glass of Johnnie Walker Black with a .357 chaser and your widow has to call in a workman to get your brains off the wood paneling.

What the hell is going on today? Kennedy was thinking. Bitching about the bosses and ragging the harness guys and doing pretty much zip about this poor son of a bitch leaking his vital essences into the street. Kennedy took six more shots with his pocket Kodak as he moved carefully inward toward the body up against the wall. He took these shots for his personal record; he always used a whole roll of film on each case and he tried to get his shots in before the Crime Scene Unit wagon got there. The CSU photographer takes the official shots, and the forensic technicians bag whatever samples or scrapings or detritus the supervising detective asks them to bag. But the process changes things; maybe it even changes the invisible lines of psychic force that hang over a body like spider webs. Once you walk through the crime scene you can never get it to feel the same again, any more than you could put a spider web back together so the spider wouldn't know.

Kennedy got to within two feet of the body, which up to now had played such a little part in the game. He pulled up the legs of his pure wool slacks and set his Florsheim Eagles down like bone china in two clear patches. The street and the block and the whole damned city slowed down and stopped so Eddie could hear the ghost of a heartbeat coming from the dead man. It gave him a chill, but he knew this frisson from a long way back. You always got it at this moment. You thought: Shit, the guy's not dead, and you saw a chest rise and fall or you heard the heartbeat. It was part of focussing. It passed as soon as Kennedy took a breath. This guy was dead, dead enough to start that mushroom-on-a-wet-basement-wall scent. This asshole gets up again without help and I'm out of here at flank speed, thought Kennedy.

The man was maybe in his twenties, dressed in tattered Reeboks, no socks, army fatigues with worn cuffs held in tight by two yellow elastic bands. He had long skinny legs. There was a hole in one knee of his pants, and the skin under it was the color of walnut except where it had been scraped away. The scrape was raw and empty, just an abrasion through the top skin and down into the fat beneath it. There was no blood. Kennedy could make out the torn ends of a few capillaries. He had gotten that scrape around the same time he died—within a few minutes perhaps. Up past the knees there was a slice in one of the big patch pockets. Something in that? A mugging? Look at that in a second. Oh my, look at this. The man's crotch was wet, and there was a strong smell coming from the area. He'd let go of everything when he died, or just before. Thank god for M.E.'s. Let them sort out the guy's underwear. His pants were held up with a garrison belt closed by a tarnished brass buckle. The buckle had a Marine Corps badge on it. Maybe a vet? Check with the VA. His T-shirt was pulled out of his belt and had ridden up his chest, exposing a sunken belly. The belly had patches of wine-colored stain, just like that Harris kid had said. Some of the patches had solid lines of demarcation and the belly was mottled. Harris had said he'd pulled the shirt aside so he could check the man's signs, so maybe that was how the shirt came out. One thing sure. The guy hadn't died here. The port-wine stains were post-mortem lividity. That came from the effect of gravity on the blood after the heart stopped pumping. The blood settled into the lowest portions of the body. If this guy had died here under the painting he'd have PML on his buttocks, except where the weight of his body had pressed the blood out. It showed up as two white patches surrounded by purple. And he'd have it in places on his back, between the shoulder blades. He sure wouldn't have it on his belly like that. So he'd been killed somewhere else and dumped here.

Moving up the body, still not touching it, Kennedy noted in passing that there were defense cuts in the victim's left hand: a series of parallel wounds in his fingertips and in the palm. The defense cuts were open, empty of blood, and the skin around them was waxy and pale. There were no rings or bracelets on the body, but there was a tattoo of a teardrop on the man's left cheek.

Marielito? Maybe one of the exiles expelled by Castro from Mariel Harbor back in 1980? Some of the Marielitos were hardened criminals and they affected this kind of criminal society marking, such as tears or crosses or knives tattooed on the hands or the cheeks. The last time Kennedy had seen marks like this he'd been working in the Bronx. Marielito gangs were causing a lot of trouble up around the 46th Precinct. But the Hell's Angels owned Alphabet City, and they were unlikely to let a Marielito hit take place down here unless they were doing the hitting. The man's right eye was wide open and the ball itself was protruding slightly from the socket. The cornea was milky. Kennedy pulled out a pair of thin plastic gloves and slipped them on. He put his right hand up against the chest close to the armpit and held it there for a few seconds.

Still some warmth there. He looked up at the sky. It was fully morning; the sun was shining at an oblique angle down into the streets. The top half of the mural was in the sun now. The day was going to be hot, even this late into September. What had the night been like? Hot and humid even up in the East Eighties. So it would be a cookhouse down here on the Lower East Side. Wherever this man had died, it had probably been hot. The underarm was still warm. The variables were numberless when you were trying to guess the time of death. The victim was skinny, and sometimes rigor set in faster in skinny people. Some fat people never went through rigor. Kennedy pushed the man's jaw and touched his neck. The muscles here were like boards. Well along into rigor. The eyes were milky. There was no give to the eyeball. He guessed the man had been dead for no more than five to ten hours.

Things got more complicated up around the face and neck. There was a deep wound in the right-hand side of the neck, exposing the cartilage and neck muscles. The severed stump of an artery showed clearly. The wound had pulled open along the lines of cleavage, the tensions placed on various sections of the surface skin by muscle groups or skeletal structure. The cleavage lines at the side of the neck run in a more or less horizontal pattern, and the cut had been made from behind the ear almost to the collar bone. A bitch of a cut, thought Kennedy. Question is, did he get it before or after he died? Let the Medical Examiner sort that out. The blood had dried brown and thick around the blue-black hair. He could see the unmistakable signs of a large penetrating wound in the body's right temple area. That accounted for the popped eye. Intracranial pressure and hydraulic shock from a large-caliber bullet, probably. But Kennedy had seen similar wounds made by hammers, police batons, even a gin bottle. A slug was a good bet, though. He couldn't make out an exit-wound site without moving the body, and he didn't want to do that until the CSU and the Assistant Medical Examiner had gotten here.

Come to think of it, where the hell was the Assistant DA? A Monday morning, at this hour—what was it, almost 0700?—shit, they'd send that dildo Sorvino! Otherwise known as The Duck. Well, Sorvino wouldn't be here until after 0800. He'd wait until then to deal with him.

So, he'd got a male victim, possible mid-twenties, possible Hispanic, so far no ID. Got a major incision-type wound, not a stabbing wound, in the carotid area of the neck. Also a possible large-caliber bullet wound in the right temple area. Possible defense cuts, one abrasion visible on left knee. Post-mortem lividity and degree of rigor suggested a probable time of death from maybe 2000 hours last night to around 0100 hours this morning. One last thing here.

Kennedy put a knee down gingerly and leaned across the body as far as he could without putting a hand on the brick wall or touching it in any way. With his right hand he managed to lift the victim's head up very slightly. There was dried blood pooled in the curve of his ear, but the sidewalk under the skull was relatively free of blood. "Bingo," said Kennedy.

"What the hell are you doing, Kennedy?"

Kennedy knew the voice. He resisted the urge to drop the man's head, and instead set it down gently. He had to push it a bit at the end, to counter the effects of rigor. Then he swiveled on his toes without rising. A large shape was blocking out the sunlight, standing in the aura with hands on hips. A familiar pose.

"Morning, Lieutenant. You're still up?"

Stokovich didn't move out of the way. "You through with the touchy-feely, Kennedy? You screwing up another crime scene? Where's the Command Post? Who's your Recorder?"

Kennedy got up slowly and stepped backward out of the crime scene. Stokovich waited until he had cleared the ribbon, and then he brushed by him and walked straight on in and crouched down beside the body. Kennedy stayed outside and watched Stokovich's broad back stretching the windowpane check of his business suit. He was heavyset, with an unruly shock of prematurely white hair. The back of his neck folded down over the stiff white collar of his tailor-made shirts. My my my, Lieutenant Bruno Stokovich, ruler of the Task Force. A lawyer with a degree in criminology, citations up the ying-yang, puts in more time running lectures at John Jay College of Criminal Justice than anybody else in the Midtown area. Hands like a pair of fat hairless pit bulls. That's Stokovich, the biggest pit bull in the five boroughs and the most profane son of a bitch ever to draw breath. It had taken Kennedy a few months to realize that underneath Bruno Stokovich's gruff facade there was an even rougher interior. He was pushing to become one of the homicide stars in the NYPD, and after that he was headed right into Headquarters. He had an eye on the Chief of Detectives' position, and if Mr. Nicastro didn't watch out, he'd have it too. Look at the bastard, squatting in there like a bull in a lottery pen, putting his fat pink dogs all over the body. Kennedy turned away and walked back to the RMP. The two harness cops were still there, looking supremely bored.

"Did Harris get Stradazzi yet? We have some signs of life here." Kennedy looked down East 4th. People were showing up on the stoops. A few doors away an elderly black woman was struggling down the front stairs with a garbage bag. Past her a group of teenagers were gathering by a basketball court. It wouldn't take them long to notice that something was going on down here at the corner.

The older white cop, whose plate read Haggerty, sighed and burped and generally conveyed his lack of interest. The black policewoman spoke up when it was clear that Haggerty wasn't going to. Kennedy noted the tension between them.

"Central says Stradazzi took a cab. Harris is back at the station getting shit from Bergman for letting you fuck him over on the airwaves. Bergman don't want Harris to pull no overtime and he says you can't override the Patrol Supervisor *and* you got to go through the ACU Supervisor to get an ACU guy in the crowd. *And* the Duty Captain was standing by the desk when Harris got in so he's coming out to oversee the investigation. *And—*"

"The Duty Captain? Bozeman?"

The black woman closed her eyes halfway and let a kind of cynical tide roll across her mahogany face. Kennedy waited her out. You had to walk carefully with black policewomen, especially the younger ones. Give them any rough talk at all and you were facing somebody from the Equal Employment branch and the Internal Affairs Department was shuffling through your performance records.

"Yes, sir." She let the "sir" roll out just enough to give it a touch of insubordination. "The Duty Captain is Captain Bozeman and he's on his way right now. Also he wants to know why there's no EMS ambulance here."

"Harris said he called a bus, but that Central couldn't promise him a bus until oh-eight-hundred. He made the guy Deceased Confirmed Dead at Scene. Why hassle Emergency Medical Services?"

"Bozeman say you don't have no bus, you don't have no bust. Procedures according to the Patrol Guide regs—"

Kennedy held up a hand. She was dropping into that sing-song tone and Kennedy was finding it harder and harder to be polite to her. If she'd been white and male, he'd have scorched the bastard and sent him off in the RMP to find a bus. But she was black and female and that gave her all the aces. He couldn't win that fight and he'd learned not to try. One thing the black female PW knows is her goddam rights.

"Okay. Put a call in for a bus ASAP Emergency. Let's get an
official DCDS on this one. Now you, Officer Stokes?"

She pulled that long low up-from-under look again. He could
see her thinking that she wasn't going to take no shit duty from no
mick dick. Kennedy swallowed his temper and asked her in as
neutral a tone as he could find if she would kindly open her memo
book and start making a record of every event and every person
who showed up at the scene.

"I'm going to make you Recorder. I'll need you to keep on
top of the comings and goings. Mark down the fact that Lieutenant Stokovich is on the scene and currently up to his French cuffs
in the body. No no, you know what I mean. Just keep track of this
stuff, will you? There's a good girl."

Her head came up sharply at that, but Kennedy was away
from the car and walking back toward Stokovich. He figured the
lieutenant was probably coming up with pretty much the same
ideas from the corpse. He was almost there when a blue Ford
pulled up and the Assistant Medical Examiner got out.

Kennedy watched him shake himself out. He was glad to see
him. The M.E. brushed down his charcoal two-piece suit, buffed
his shoes one at a time on the back of each pant-leg, and yawned
mightily in the sunlight. Kennedy felt a huge grin coming.

Marcuse looked over at Kennedy and pushed his half-frames
up onto his wide pink forehead.

"Eddie, my boy! You're up early. I thought you'd still be up
in the Catskills plundering nature's bounty and generally spreading venereal disease and lowering the land values." Marcuse was
watching Stokovich poke about in the crime scene as he said this.
By a tacit agreement, neither said anything about it. Kennedy
took the old man's hand. It felt stiff and brittle, and there was
arthritis in the knuckles. Marcuse was getting old.

Marcuse, perhaps sensing Kennedy's reaction, tugged the
hand away a little too quickly. The glasses flopped down onto his
nose.

"Let's see if we can drag Lestrade off the carcass, shall we?
Step aside there, you great ugly thing. Let me see what they've
done to the poor laddie."

Kennedy stopped him. "Give us a while, Doc. We haven't
had the CSU in yet. Go get a coffee from Nine Frank. Okay?"

Marcuse sighed and walked over to the squad car. Stokovich came back out just as the Crime Scene Unit wagon arrived.

"CSU guys are here. You wanna brief 'em, Eddie? I've got Robinson coming over, and I think Farrell is off that floater job. You want me to give you this one?"

"I thought you already gave me this one. You got me out of bed at five in the fucking morning."

"Yeah? I hear you were playing with your cat. How is that crazy fucker, anyway?" Stokovich and Dudley had met once, at a pre-racket racket Kennedy had thrown for one of his buddies in the old Seven Zone, and Stokovich had shown up to do some campaigning. The buddy's name was Fogarty, and Fogarty was making quite a name for himself in the Organized Crime Task Force, a joint FBI, IRS, Justice Department, and NYPD operation headquartered over on West 57th. It looked like Fogarty was going to ride the Agniello della Croce confessions up to the thirteenth floor. Chief of Detectives Nicastro was saying nice things about Fogarty, so Stokovich wanted Fogarty to say nice things about *him* to Nicastro. Anyway, the thing had gone a little sour when Stokovich got the idea that it would be amusing to use Kennedy's electric razor to shave the initials of the Seventh Zone Homicide Squad into Dudley's back. Kennedy had stayed out of the thing. Stokovich and a mope from Justice who was at the time learning the ropes from Fogarty tried to corner Dudley in the kitchen. It wasn't the best idea Stokovich had ever had.

While Bruno was talking to him, Kennedy tried to get a look at the lieutenant's left wrist. The sleeve was too long. Damn, but he loved those heavy gold cuff links. Maybe he wore his sleeves too long to cover up the marks Dudley had given him. Thinking about that made Kennedy glad he hadn't shot his cat this morning.

"You in there, Eddie?"

"Yes, sir, I'm here. Sorry, I was thinking about Farrell. He beat that one?"

"Yeah. Victim was a hooker from Hunts Point. Looks like the hooker was doing a hose job on one of the truckers up at the market—guy gets a hand up underneath the broad's skirt and finds out he's got a boy gobbling on his machinery. Beat the hooker to death. Threw him in the drink off Baretto Point."

"Baretto Point? How the hell'd the guy float all the way down to the Thirty-fourth Street heliport?"

Stokovich shrugged. "Beats me, Eddie. Anyway, what you got on your sheet right now? You got the Adeline Muro thing?"

"Yeah, but that's beginning to look a little messy. Serology shows there were two secretors involved, right? Two blood types? A two-on-one breakaway. A cameo belonging to her turned up in a bust uptown but they turned the guy loose for some dumb reason. And we've got the Gypsies—looks like they were in on that stabbing over on Van Dam. You've got me doing the Green Book too. You could say I got a full sheet."

"Hey, Eddie . . . you take the city's money."

This was typical homicide talk. Investigators in every Task Force carried massive caseloads, each one spinning away in time, and they scurried from one to the other like a juggler on the Ed Sullivan show keeping his plates spinning on the top of a row of canes. The record of all those cases—the time, date, location, and major circumstances of every homicide the Task Force had been handed that year—was kept in a clothbound ledger, the Green Book. Entries got made in varying hands, in blue ball-point, stamped SOLVED in red ink or noted as OPEN or PENDING. The Green Book was reviewed and updated by any squad man with the time.

Kennedy looked at Stokovich for a long second, trying not to let the prodding set him off. Anyway, the man was right. And the Adeline Muro case was special, a particularly nasty bit of business, now over a week old and still a scar in his memory.

"Yes, sir. I do the city's work. And I have a lot of it. Gypsies, the Muro thing. The Green Book, and this poor bastard over here. What I want, I think we ought to get up to the Bronx after Mokie Muro. That's what I'd rather do, tell you the truth. This kid'll still be dead in the morning but who the fuck knows *where* Mokie Muro's gonna be? You ask me, I say he's hanging out with the Ching-a-lings. You want to make me happy, send me up there."

Stokovich was silent for a moment. Kennedy watched the crowd sidelong, as if he were unconcerned. In the last few minutes the word had spread all around the area. Close to a hundred people were gathering here and there across the street, straining and staring, talking fast between themselves in soft Cuban Spanish, and the "Swain" jargon blacks use on the streets was carrying in the still air. The sunlight had moved down across "La Colonización" until it reached the dead man. It seemed to Kennedy that the

sprawled figure caught in the hot yellow light, hard up against the
theatrical background, was there for precisely that reason: to
be seen, in the morning, in the sunlight. If that was true,
then he had been killed as an example, and the example was
meant to be seen by the very people who were now gathering
around. Somebody in that collection of closed black faces and
Spanish eyes knew the dead man. Maybe he knew the killers too.
Kennedy took the camera out again. The cassette was only
half-used.

Stokovich looked up as he sensed Kennedy's attention drifting.

"You figure the perps are in the crowd?" He said it softly,
casually.

"It occurred to me. He's been moved here. I figure they
moved him to set an example."

Stokovich looked around in an offhand way. "So tell the CSU
guys to take shots of the crowd, sort of by the way. Don't make a
thing out of it. Why don't you get one of the ACU guys from the
Eighth to get out there and mingle?"

Kennedy had been looking for his man. He didn't know if
Stradazzi was on the street yet. He had spotted three possible
undercover guys. What was the color today?

Stokovich was waiting for an answer.

"Good idea, sir. I'll get right on it."

Stokovich nodded. "Look, Eddie. You're gonna have to wait
for Quantico to get back to us on the mutilations in the Muro case
before we can spare a team for citywide. You take this shmuck
here, and I'll get Fratelli to chase those Armenians, okay? Maybe
you can close this one by the end of the shift, hah?"

Kennedy looked at his watch. It was 0800 hours. His workday
officially started at 0800 hours this week.

"I'm into overtime by fifteen-hundred hours, sir."

"Don't give me that shit, Kennedy. Go get your car!"

The boss went the way he'd come, conveying a sense of
urgency—a man full of purpose. When he pulled off he did it fast,
and he liked to use the siren. People got out of his way.

As the lieutenant pulled away through the crowd in his new
blue Chrysler, Eddie Kennedy felt a look coming from the by-
standers. A scruffy little man with long black curly hair and a
twitchy way about him was wandering around in front of a knot of

Hispanic males. Something about the guy set off a small clear bell in Kennedy's mind.

So, Harris got me my ACU man, thought Kennedy. Good act. Looks like a junkie from here. Plaid work shirt, do-rag, pointy-toed shoes, pants too short, and baby-blue socks. Don't tell me baby-blue socks are the ACU code color for the day. Only in Manhattan would they tell a guy to wear baby-blue socks so his fellow officers don't blow his nuts off one day when he comes pelting down the alleyway with his piece out answering some cop's Signal Thirteen.

Kennedy spent the next hour overseeing the work of the Crime Scene Unit. Working on his hunches and his observations of the area, Kennedy had widened the crime scene perimeters to include a large section of the street in front of the mural, the roof of the market itself, and a stretch of the sidewalk for forty feet in either direction. He had no solid reason for doing this, but the larger the net the better your chances of catching something. The head of the CSU for this shift was a lanky redheaded cop with blue-white skin and a general air of gloom. He looked mildly dead. Kennedy's private name for the Forensic technician was Spider, but his real name was Sergeant Alastair Kearny, and he claimed descent from Stephen Kearny, the U.S. Army general who got the Mexican War off to a fine start by annexing Texas for President Polk. Alastair therefore considered it his moral and family duty to loathe all things vaguely Andalusian, which he did with a nicely judged sense of egalitarianism, hating all Hispanic races equally and without passion, serving up a distillation of venom in a half-hearted way, wearily and with little hope that his enmity would be felt as acutely as he would wish.

There were three men in Kearny's team this morning: the photographer, with his 4 × 5, and a couple of technicians to do the formal sketch, make every measurement imaginable and relate each one to the compass points, and to collect any and all objects, samples, scrapings, and particles that might be on or around the body. It was Kennedy's job to isolate and identify items of special interest to the investigation, based on his almost intuitive sense of the scene. It was in judgments such as these that the skills and talent of a homicide detective made the most difference. Crime Scene Units would, if asked, spend three days at the scene taking scrapings from anything and everything that had ever come within a block of the place. Good homicide detectives helped to focus this search without being too cavalier about possible clues.

While Kearny was setting up, Kennedy went over to South Frank and poured himself a cup of coffee in the Recorder's seat. Officer Stokes was standing over by the ribbon, taking notes with a grim intensity. Well, she might not be a sweetheart, but Kennedy figured that her generalized dislike of all things white would insure that she got it all down in print. Haggerty, the older cop who had been on the scene when Kennedy arrived, showed every sign of being a short-timer whittling his stick down and doing as little as possible to risk his pension. Taking on an assignment as Recorder at a crime scene meant risk. He'd have to do overtime, he'd have to do the work, he'd have to get it right, and one way or another he'd have to go to court or see the Assistant District Attorney, and along every step of the way there was ample opportunity to screw up royally. Better to let the uppity shine they'd stuck him with do the tricky stuff. Serve her right, she fucks it up. Kennedy had read all that in the gray defeated contours of Haggerty's face and come to more or less the same conclusion. Let Stokes do it. At least she'd get it right.

Kennedy leaned back into the black vinyl, propped a foot up on the dashboard, and tried to figure out just where and when he'd got the hook in him over this miserable little killing. It came to him in a minute. They were too fucking cute. Whoever killed this boy was a smartass. If he'd just shot the boy where he stood and walked away, the Department would have had a rat's chance of finding him, and less chance of getting the DA to push the case. But noooo, as Belushi used to say, but noooo . . . he had to get cute about it. Kill the kid, leave him lying around on his belly somewhere, dropping skin flakes and physical evidence all over the carpet, and then scoop him up and drive him over to "La Colonización" and dump him in the street. In Kennedy's street, too. And Kennedy has to get up at five in the morning, on a Monday, and dragass down to this shithole and do his dance just so the smartass could sit at a window somewhere around here, sit there in his purple jockey shorts and his gold earrings, and stuff himself with cold tacos and Coors while he laughed at Kennedy around a mouthful of chili rellenos. *And* he makes a call to

Communications just in case the patrol guys manage to overlook a leaking stiff in the roadway.

Of course there were a couple of puzzles here. Just to make the thing intriguing. For instance, post-mortem lividity fixes, in average room temperature, about eight hours after death. Gravity will pull the blood into the low places of the body; gravity will make it leak out of the nose and the eyes, out of the mouth. But after a while the blood gets too thick to move, and you can hang the corpse up by its big toe without changing the post-mortem lividity one bit. So Kennedy had made the time of death at five to ten hours into last night. But the lividity was fixed, which meant the body had to have stayed in its original position for at least eight hours, give or take one. Right? Right.

So, where did all the blood come from? Kennedy leaned forward in the seat. He could see the boy's head from here, lying in a sludge of dark-brown blood. The problem was, how did they get enough blood out of him to carry in a bucket and dump on him here? And how did they stop it from congealing during the eight hours that the body was lying in whatever it was it was lying in?

Well, that was why God made medical examiners. Kearny was making his way over, stepping high and bringing his lanky long legs down in a series of barely coordinated extensions, looking for all the world like a depressed daddy-longlegs.

Marcuse was asleep in the blue Ford, his head propped up on the driver's backrest, his gold-wire frames sitting up on his forehead. Kearny pounded on the window glass as he went by. Marcuse jerked up. From the way his mouth was moving, Kennedy assumed he was a little cranky. Kearny noticed none of this. He never did.

"Well, Eddie. We've got the little greaser six ways from Sunday. I've got Dorfmann bagging the kid's hands. I'm not so sure those are legit defense cuts, though. They look a little stagy. Too regular, y'know what I mean? Like they been arranged in neat little rows. Most of your defense cuts, they're all over the wrists and hands, every which way, this n' that, y'know? So anyway I got a bunch of shit and you gotta sign for this. Here's a rough sketch. Get the formal sketch later. Measured the place like crazed weasels. Want me to chalk the site?"

Kennedy laughed. "Chalk the site? What is this, *Kojak*? Kearny,

I don't chalk outdoor sites. I never have, and I never will. The spray-paint brigade will fuck it up as soon as we break for tiffin. You got a real thing about chalk, don't you?"

Kearny looked hurt. "Detective's Guide, everybody says 'chalk the site.' So I chalk the site. Don't be like that, Eddie. It don't look good on you. You're too short."

Kennedy laughed again, a short sharp snort. "Kearny, you want to chalk the site, I think you should chalk the site. I really do. And I'm sorry I haven't had you chalking every damned crime scene I've ever worked on. I tell you what—we'll go back down the list. We'll go back to every crime scene you and me have ever worked on. Damn it, we'll chalk every one of them this afternoon! Hah?"

Kearny's face set deeper and deeper into the lines of a martyred saint. "I'm saying a novena for your black Irish soul, Detective Kennedy, and little good it'll do you, damned as you are. We'll be running along now. Got work on Christopher Street. You sign all these, and we'll be in with the shots directly."

"Color *and* black-and-white?"

Kearny rolled his eyes, nodded, and stalked away to the wagon. Marcuse, the Assistant Medical Examiner, was already working on the body, delicately, painstakingly, but with swift and certain motions in spite of those knotted hands. Marcuse was a joy to watch. Kennedy had once broken up at a Benihana grill when it came to him in the middle of eating some shredded kobi slices that Marcuse could have gotten work anywhere as the blade man at a sushi bar. *Thwock thwock thwock.* Slick slick slick. Aha! Here's the cause of death. You want ginger too?

Kennedy left him to it and concentrated on bringing his notes up to date. So far, he'd done it all. It made quite a list. Under his initial entries, he had added:

- exact time of arrival
- the precise location and closest street address
- weather and street conditions
- lighting conditions
- personnel interviews
- names, ranks, badge numbers, of every official
- time of arrival of each official
- extensive notes of First Officer's interview

- location of victim
- confirmed deceased Dead at Scene
- how the death was confirmed
- how he personally verified that pronouncement
- his estimate of the extent of the crime scene
- the names, ranks, and badge numbers of the CSU team
- his instructions to the CSU team
- steps taken to insure crime scene integrity
- the Recorder's name, rank, and badge number
- when and how he notified Communications of his Command Post location (Right now, it was an RMP.)
- name of the M.E. responding
- name of the Assistant DA (when he gets here)
- name, rank, and badge number of any additional investigators (So far, he hadn't asked for any.)
- complete documentation of the crime scene operations
- his personal observations
- his means of insuring the continuity of evidence
- his methods for securing physical evidence
- how he established a "chain of evidence custody"
- who his "searching officer" was (Kennedy put his own name here.)
- the apparent cause of death

That brought Kennedy around to Marcuse. It was Kennedy's private hunch that the cause of death was that wound in the carotid, and that the head wound was more stage dressing. Marcuse was still hunched over the body. He was taking so long with it that Kennedy began to think the matter would have to wait for the formal autopsy. He hoped Marcuse could do it this morning.

When he glanced at his watch he got a small jolt. It was a little after nine-thirty in the morning. He still had to decide on a canvass of the neighborhood. One would certainly be necessary, but it wasn't always a good idea to do it right away. For one thing, the crowd was still pretty avid, and the way the straights and the shits were mixed up over there, no sensible citizen would freely give a cop good information with all sorts of criminal elements standing around and memorizing faces. Better to pull in some of the afternoon shift, and some of the second platoon guys from the 8th. Give them a good briefing after Kennedy had the M.E.'s

report and after he'd managed to get some kind of handle on
the thing. No, no canvass right now. It could wait until the
dinner hour, when everybody'd be at home and more inclined
to talk. Stokovich loved to throw a canvass into the Jacob Riis
Houses at three in the morning. Kennedy figured Bruno got off
on the stir, and on freaking out the citizenry. Also it looked
great when the Duty Captain pulled up with his gold-shield
chauffeurs and saw all those uniforms buzzing around and the
lieutenant right there in the middle of it, looking grim and
professional.

Trouble was, nobody who has to get out of bed at three in the
morning will give the guy at the door anything but the bum's
rush. Kennedy always staged his canvasses at a decent hour, and
he made sure the people doing the asking had a real interest in
the case.

A lot of the Patrol guys down here in Lower Manhattan liked
to work for Kennedy. Eddie was always careful to send in commendation reports on any patrol officer who did good work, or
who showed some insight and effort. The secret of getting these
usually bored-brainless cops to put some heart in it was to make
damned certain that the ones who did got some credit for it.
Credit for good uniform work was what had gotten Kennedy his
gold shield in the first place.

No, no canvass now. And here's Marcuse with a face like
a Chippewa hatchet. Kearny bother him that much? No.

Marcuse took a Styrofoam coffee cup and poured two fingers
of brandy into it from a brown bottle marked FORMALDEHYDE. It
was Marcuse's little joke.

"Well, Detective Kennedy . . . it's a hard day when the
criminals of this city get to acting out their television fantasies on
the actual streets of the town."

"Yeah? You think the thing's a setup?"

"Lacking only the script girl and a faggot with a bullhorn
screeching at the citizenry. Young fellow's been dead, I'd say
maybe eight hours, maybe more."

"The lividity? Fixed?"

"Are you sure you're Irish? So clearly do you think, I find
myself doubting it more and more. Yes, well, the lividity, extent
of rigor, weight, body type, skin color, etcetera, and so forth. He's

fair drained, as well. But I don't think that's his blood running all over the place—no I indeed do not."

Kennedy didn't either, but the idea was to listen to your M.E. Not outscore him.

"No, I do not. Even if he'd been drained into a bucket they'd have had the devil's own time keeping the blood from congealing, breaking down, clotting. If I read this correctly, I'd say it's not human blood at all. Steer's blood, or some such."

"Or taken from a more recent corpse?"

"Always a possibility. We'll see."

"Can you do it soon?"

"The autopsy? You'll attend?"

"Yes. I'm 'chain of evidence,' right?"

"Bruno not giving you a lackey today?"

"I'll get one. When do you want me there?"

Marcuse pulled his left hand down the side of his face, an unsettling gesture in the old man.

"We'll have the attendants in now. It's nine forty-five? Barring a crowd . . . Let's say we set it up for noon? I'll have Mervyn set out some sandwiches?"

Boris, thought Kennedy. A definite Boris Karloff.

"Thanks, Charlie. But no snacks, hah?"

Marcuse leered at him.

"Then let's get a sheet over the chappie. I hear Bozeman's on his way over. You don't want that asshole from *Live at Five* talking the Duty Captain into posing with his foot on the youngster's chest, do you?"

Christ, the Duty Captain. Kennedy had forgotten all about Bozeman.

"Has anybody heard from him? Or from the DA's office, for that matter? Where the hell's Sorvino?"

Marcuse sighed theatrically, and patted Kennedy's shoulder. "Not my cross to bear, son. I'll see you at noon. Sure about those snackies?"

Kennedy said yes, he was sure.

The Assistant District Attorney for the shift was an ambitious kid named Genno Sorvino. He stayed exactly eleven minutes, long enough to put his Bass Weejuns into the blood, fiddle with the paper bags tied around the corpse's hands, give a few random and contradictory orders to various officials who were not in any way under his authority, strike a few manly poses for the benefit of the gaggle of teenagers at the corner, and to warn Eddie Kennedy that the DA took a harsh view of this sort of random street crime and he, Genno Sorvino, was personally going to make it his business to see that some real work got done on things like this instead of the usual cop complacency, and furthermore . . .

But the *Live Eye* cameras showed up then, so Kennedy didn't have to listen to any more. It came to him that Sorvino had timed that very nicely.

CHAPTER 3

GORMENGHAST

When they trucked away the body it spoiled things for the crowd. Kennedy sat in the back of the RMP with Stokes and Haggerty and watched the attendants wrap the victim up in a clean white sheet, which was used to tuck him into a body bag. The body bag was zipped up in seconds. As soon as the metal snap hit home, something came out of the crowd, an invisible exhalation, almost ectoplasmic. It floated above the crowd the way the smoke from Kennedy's bedspread had hovered over the room. After a long time, a hot dry wind came in off the East River and blew it east and north, into the megaliths and stelae of lower midtown. Giving up this vapor took the heart out of the people. They broke up into smaller groups, disintegrated further, slipping away along the side streets and across the empty lots toward their cold-water apartments and their stifling studios, where the heat that had moved in back in May, in the first days of The Drought, was now curled up in the corners of the ceiling. The hallways and the stairwells hold the heat the way they hold the smells. No breezes come here. On daybeds still damp from last night's sweat, they think about nothing over and over again while the evening comes on softly. At night there would be an RMP from the 8th standing guard over the crime scene, and another squad car would replace it at midnight.

Kearny had come up zero on positive ID of the deceased, so Kennedy had released the body to the M.E.'s attendants, seen to it that every trace of the crime-scene search was picked up and bagged, and checked out Stokes's journal of the morning's comings and goings against his own record. She was precise, accurate, and she could even write neatly. He was glad he'd gotten her to do the job, even if she was a mildly insubordinate bitch. Kennedy would always trade an amiable incompetent for a surly professional—black, white, or windowpane plaid like Bruno's suit. Just as long as The Job got done.

Stokes and Haggerty helped Kennedy perform a modified grid search of the crime-scene perimeter. Kennedy hadn't expected much. It was fun, however, to watch Haggerty huffing and chuffing on his knees through the litter in the curbside gutters. It was just possible that Officer Stokes got the slightest boot out of this, too, but you wouldn't know it from the flat half-lidded look she was walking around under.

There just isn't a chillier chill than the chill a black woman can put on you, Kennedy mused, picking through the bloodstains with a wooden shish-kabob skewer. He kept a few of these in his coat pocket in case he had to put his hands into places of which his mother wouldn't approve. They found nothing worth noting, nothing that rang any kind of alarm bell in Kennedy's mind. Kennedy liked to imagine that he could think like his cat in matters of this sort. Let all the colors slide down out of the landscape, let the scene go all flat and two-dimensional, find a still place for his thoughts, and leave them there. Stop thinking. Hold his breath. Wait for something to move out there. Wait for somebody's nerves to resonate. Dudley could do that sort of thing half-asleep.

"Hey, Stokes! You got a cat?"

Stokes didn't even look up. "No, sir, I don't have no cat. I don't even like cats. Sir."

Kennedy wasn't surprised. She didn't look like the cat type. Neat little creature, though. Short and solid, with a reasonable set of hips on her. Kennedy shook his head and grinned into the blood pool. You're a long way from heaven, Eddie Kennedy.

"Stokes, Haggerty, let's can this. Take me to the station. I need a car."

He also needed to talk to Stradazzi. Right now, the Anti-Crime Unit man was Kennedy's best bet. Nobody spoke in the RMP until Kennedy asked Haggerty to stop at a Photomat on 23rd Street. Kennedy knew a girl there who would have his Instamatic cassette processed and ready within the hour. He needed those shots for the autopsy at noon. The CSU shots wouldn't be ready until tomorrow morning.

When Stokes and Haggerty let Kennedy off at the station, Stradazzi was standing at the desk. "You've got to be Kennedy," he said, putting out a filthy hand. "I'm Marco Stradazzi. I got something for you."

"Yeah?" said Kennedy. "I sort of hoped you would."

Marco Stradazzi was a compact little wop with sloping shoulders and big hands and a sardonic sideways pull to his smile that made him look twice his age. He said he'd been on the force about three years and that Anti-Crime Unit work in Alphabet City came to him naturally, since he was the only member of his family who wasn't into something illegal. In the part of Jersey where he was born, the family thought of him as mildly embarrassing. He told Kennedy all this as they walked across the station-house hall under the color portraits of Ronald Reagan, Ed Koch, Mario Cuomo, Benjamin Ward, and various Deputy Chiefs in blue and gold.

Most of the patrol cops were out on The Job. Sergeant Bergman stayed on the phone as they left. Kennedy figured he was listening to the weather tape. It was easier to send secondhand shit to a gold shield than it was to serve it up across the counter. There were three types of cop, as far as Kennedy had been able to determine: bandits who were brilliant on the street and terrible in the station; stand-up officers who played by the rules as much as they could; and drones like Bergman, corporate functionaries who lived by the Patrol Guide and told themselves that police work was easy if you had nice handwriting and knew exactly whom to cut and whom to curry. People like Bergman were the blood and bones of Headquarters, as far as Kennedy was concerned. And this sharp little ACU guy? So far it looked like Marco Stradazzi was a bandit. Stradazzi had taken a phone call from his ACU supervisor at around 0715 hours, caught a cab all the way in from Long Island City, and slipped into his character in the locker room downstairs. His character was "Ramon," ex-psychiatric case *summa cum yo-yo* from Bellevue with a minor in blue sky and toot. No one in the neighborhood was surprised to see Ramon stumbling around at the shooting this morning. The deserted building across from the mural was a shooting gallery for a lot of the Cuban and Puerto Rican junkies, so his cover was perfect.

Kennedy could see that Marco Stradazzi had enjoyed himself this morning. If his information was good, Kennedy would try to make sure he got a bar for it—Meritorious Police Duty, if something solid came out of it.

Kennedy and Stradazzi went up to the Task Force squad room. Six gray metal desks stood in a row across from a line of dark-green metal filing cabinets. A special holding cell, painted dull-brown, was set into one of the walls. Most of the wall space was covered with duty rosters, special Department notices, Legal Bureau bulletins, calendars, all of them taped to the green-painted cinder blocks or pinned into various corkboards. No one was in the squad room, since the week before had been busy and most of the eight-man day shift was out and about chasing down witnesses or collecting paperwork around the city. The light came from a set of windows facing north and a double bank of fluorescent lights. The lights buzzed. They always did. Kennedy believed that the buzzing fluorescent-light bars were part of a subtle program of mind control and personality shaping developed somewhere down at One Police Plaza. He hadn't decided if the mind control was aimed at the prisoners they brought up or at the detectives themselves. The lieutenant had a private office, where he kept the portable radios and the plastic NYPD dashboard permits.

Kennedy had a large 7th Cavalry pennant, almost three by five, attached to the wall behind his desk. If Kennedy had a trademark within the NYPD it was this huge 7th Cavalry flag. It had been a gift from his first uniform partner, years back, when they had both been working out of an RMP way out in Queens. Kennedy's partner, an older black cop by the name of Weeks, had gotten trapped in a dead-end street in a rough industrial area. Street gangs were calling in Signal Thirteens, luring squad cars to this narrow street lined with tenements. As soon as a squad car got halfway down the street, gang members on the rooftops would start throwing Molotov cocktails and cinder blocks down on it. Sometimes they even closed off the escape route. Kennedy had been back at the station house doing paperwork on a B&E collar when Weeks's panicky call had come in. They sent every squad car in the precinct, but Kennedy had reached Floyd Bennett Field and called in a chopper. He had lied a bit—he had lied a lot—about the seriousness of the situation. But he got the chopper and they rounded up more than fifty black gang members in a raid that later passed into NYPD history as Kennedy's Last Stand. Weeks had come in with the flag the next day.

Stradazzi sat down on a broken tube chair and hopped it across the linoleum to Kennedy's desk. Dragging out a pack of Colts, he offered one to Kennedy, lit his own, pushed back off the desk edge with one foot, and nodded at the flag. "Is that story true? About the chopper raid?"

"More or less. It's not true that we strafed them."

"Only napalm, huh?"

Kennedy smiled and let it go. "So . . . let's hear it."

Stradazzi drew on the Colt for a full thirty seconds, obviously pleased with himself.

"Long version or short version? Yeah, okay. You ever hear of a small-time coke dealer, street name Mantecado?"

"Ice cream? Yeah, a little bit. So. . . ?"

"So I'm up against three *muchachas* doing my weird Ramon come-on come-on baby number, which they are ignoring as usual. One chick, she's very upset. *Muy trastornada*. The other girls are telling her to shut up. They say to be smart, not to make a scene. I get the idea that the first chick, she wants to do something. I don't get the idea that the stiff is, like, her brother or her boy-friend. You know, maybe she knows him from the neighborhood, something like that. Anyway, *las muchachas* more or less do the number on her and she pulls herself together. I can't hang around too much, you know. Tip myself. Spent too much time on Ramon to blow Ramon. Anyway, I like Ramon. So— Okay, okay! I'll rush it. What's the matter with your back?"

Kennedy had leaned back in his oak swivel chair, forgetting about the scratches Dudley had left on him. When he did feel them, he yelped and jerked forward again.

"Nothing. Got a couple of scratches."

As soon as he said it, he knew it was a mistake. Stradazzi positively glowed with prurient fire.

"Ah-hah! Marked you up a bit, huh? Eddie, you gotta watch out for those black broads. Get those legs around you and then they sink a few—"

"Wasn't a black broad. It was some Italian broad. Said her name was—"

"Stradazzi? Very funny, Kennedy. Anyway, the three of them are all togged out in really grubby clothes, clothes no self-respecting *hechizita* is going to walk around in, even in that shithole. The biggest one—they called her Nadine—she's carrying an apple basket with one of those claw things in it, and a pair of shears. Look like . . ."

"Garden tools?"

"Yeah, yeah, garden tools. And all of them have their knees all muddied up and worn. Definitely old clothes—clothes like you'd only wear to work in the yard. So—"

"The Homesteaders' Association. They've got a bunch of vegetable plots, all fenced in, right? Over on Tenth around Avenue C? You follow them there?"

"Well, I been all over them, right? So I don't want to get too close. And I wasn't sure if there was anything to it. Thing was, they left almost right away, and if there wasn't anything to it, you know, other than the usual brainless shit you get from young Spanish pussy, well, I'd have fucked the operation. So I marked them down and stayed with the people. Heard some of this and some of that. But mostly they were just complaining about how the neighborhood just isn't the same since they were children and you could only go to the Mission Evangelica y Bautista and say your *oraciónes* for *el pobrecito* across the street there. But I did get—"

"You got diddly. You get this Nadine's address?"

"No, but I did get—"

"You go over there later? To the gardens?"

"Not in my Ramon rig, I told you. Will you hold off for a second? I got the kid's momma!"

"What kid's momma? The broad's? How'd you get her momma if you don't know where the *fuck* Nadine *lives*?"

Stradazzi pushed the tube chair back so far Kennedy was certain he was going straight over and grinned at Kennedy, a huge, self-satisfied, and oddly engaging grin.

"Jesus, Kennedy, Detective Kennedy, sir, you have some kind of bad mood going on there. You recall, sir, I did mention a coke dealer name of Mantecado? Yesss . . . Well, Detective Kennedy, sir, I report that said small-time coke dealer owes one of our vice guys a big favor and the vice guy owes me, so he puts the blocks to Mantecado about which you don't want to know, and the

greaser coughs up that one of his shooters-in-training is missing, a
pendejo, a putz kid, by the name of Porfirio Magdalena Ruiz,
a.k.a. Salto Mortal—which means 'somersault,' Detective, sir, in
Spanish, sir—and guess who was into the Eighth just this very
morning to report on the disappearance of her son, whose name
happens to be Porfirio Ruiz? Shall I go on, sir?"

Stradazzi paused and raised his right eyebrow.

Kennedy had to grin back.

"You little bastard! You've been shagging me since I got in.
Where's the mother? Christ, you didn't go off half-cocked here
and pick up the mother, did you?"

Stradazzi looked hurt. "Mapp, Gideon, Massiah, Escobedo,
Miranda, Mallory, Elstad . . ." He pulled up an eyebrow and sent
Kennedy a wry look. "I know the rules, Kennedy. I pulled the
Missing Persons report. It seems that Mrs. Ruiz has a school
picture of her boy, whom she also refers to as Salto—because he
could do one from a standing position, go right over in the air and
land on his feet again."

Kennedy put out a hand. Stradazzi reached into his jacket
pocket and passed a 2 × 3 color photo across the littered desk to
Kennedy. The boy in the picture was clean and young, with a
strong well-made face, dark-brown eyes set well apart, a broad,
slightly flat nose, rich blue-black hair, an impish smile, and a good
clear intelligence shining out of the photo. A school kid, perhaps
closing in on seventeen. There was no resemblance other than a
superficial one between this bright teenager and the bloody distorted ruin Kennedy had stood watch over this morning. Kennedy
had intended, as a matter of routine, to check out the Missing
Persons entries for last night and this morning. He hadn't done it
yet partly because most desk officers won't even take an MP
sheet until twenty-four hours have passed.

"It could be him. How long's her kid been missing?"

"Since around three Sunday afternoon. He works Sundays as a
stocker at Los Hermanos Supermarket. That's why I went after
Mantecado."

"I was wondering about that." Kennedy found it hard to pull
his eyes off the photo. Kids who looked like that shouldn't end up
as a gutter cutlet for brown rats.

"Los Hermanos Supermarket is on the SNU shit list for coke
and smack dealings. Bag boys been handing it out at the cash

registers. Mantecado is always around there, by the door or across the street. When I heard that a Mrs. Ruiz had been in about her son, and that he worked at Los Hermanos, I hit on Street Narcotics for a name."

Kennedy got up and came around the desk. He was going to have to see Mrs. Ruiz fairly soon, and he wasn't looking forward to the interview.

"Marco, that's a neat story and I think you're leaving out a whole bunch of shit you think I shouldn't know about. Has somebody federal got his little fingers into Los Hermanos? I'm going to have to know sooner or later, if this Mantecado shit is connected."

Stradazzi shrugged, letting the chair come forward.

"I got a link. It's your problem now. Also you should know, the word is this Nadine broad, she's one of Mantecado's best customers. And she fucks who he tells her. You follow?"

Kennedy followed just fine. That was the trouble with Alphabet City, with any crime-prone location in New York. You couldn't take three steps to the right without tripping over a Narcotics stakeout or a DEA/FBI/NYPD Task Force operation, or Ward's latest Street Narcotics Apprehension Program. And whenever drugs came into the picture, all the fountains got muddied up. Maybe you had to bust a guy and you get a polite fuck-off from your Detective Supervisor—no no no can't touch *that* little shit. He's crucial to somebody else's investigation. Federal, state, local, Joint Force, U.N. police, aces within eights, games within games, thousands of games and all the players invisible, moving their markers on a cut-glass game board. You had to shine your light just so, if you wanted to see the rules.

"So you just lucked out with Mantecado?"

Stradazzi stood up and walked to the door, turning to face Kennedy just as he reached it.

"Sir, I'm not saying that there aren't some things going on here about Los Hermanos. But I don't think your case is going to be affected by it, whatever it is. I'd have been told to piss off otherwise."

Kennedy fought back a number of conflicting emotions. He had spent a few years in Narcotics himself. He got his Gold Third Grade from Narcotics work. It was a messy world, a brutal world, and it marked everyone who moved in it, cop or runner, dealer or snitch, major league with a snake-line straight into Cartagena or just a small-time banker in the back of the poolroom. Drugs had made the South Bronx what it was, and Eddie Kennedy had gotten all of the South Bronx he could handle three years ago. He wanted nothing more to do with it, and nothing more to do with narcotics on any side of the law.

Stradazzi shifted from one foot to the other. Something had come into the sunny room that neither man liked.

"Marco, I'm going to talk to Mrs. Ruiz, and I'll want to bounce this Nadine kid, see what she has to say. I think you did good work this morning, and I'll get Stokovich to put in a commendation, the full five one-sixty-twos."

"I'd appreciate that, sir. They told me about you. But?"

Kennedy said nothing for about ten seconds. "No, there's no 'but.' You did good work. I appreciate it, and I'll see to it that you get something out of it. See you downstairs in a minute?"

Stradazzi relaxed again, pulled his mouth around in that sardonic way. "Okay . . . thanks, Kennedy. *Hasta!*"

Kennedy listened to the ACU cop racketing down the stairs. There was always that shock, whenever you ran into the high-voltage underground cable: the hidden agenda. Cops from other cities, maybe they had the same trouble. But no place in the world was like New York. So many agencies playing so many games, guarding their cases, stealing witnesses—the constant sniper fire of jurisdictional warfare. Cop solidarity was a myth for the moviegoing suckers. Time was, when you were back in uniform, you could have trusted your partner. But Kennedy had no partner. Homicide cops worked alone. Now and then you ran into something like this, like a wind in a sealed room or a darker shadow in a dark alley. A hint here, a breath there. A report killed. A case closed suddenly. You hardly ever found out the whole story. If you did, it never made you feel good.

Kennedy's shots were ready at the shop on 23rd Street. He riffled through them in the detective's car. It was a new one, a Chrysler with tan vinyl seats, power windows, even an air conditioner. Stokovich had left the permit and the keys on his desk, along with a note asking Kennedy to call him at home at the end of the day. Stokovich lived up in Westchester County, in a tract house north of Yonkers. A very nice place, so Kennedy had heard. He'd never been asked up, but then he had never invited Stokovich up to his place in the Catskills.

The shots were excellent, sharp clear color photos of the scene and the body itself. He took out the Missing Persons file on Porfirio Magdalena Ruiz. There was no discernible similarity between the dead boy in the street and the school shot of Ruiz. But Kennedy knew it was the same kid, and he could never have told you why.

Mrs. Ruiz's file showed an address in the Riis houses, one of the projects on Avenue D. Apartment 556. She worked at something called a binder, in a factory over on the West Side. She would be at work right now. Kennedy checked his watch. It was 1151 hours. Nine minutes to noon. He had a date with Charlie Marcuse at the M.E.'s office over on East 33rd at noon. He closed the file and pulled out into the traffic on 23rd Street. He used the siren now and then on the way up. Well, that's what it was for, wasn't it?

Marcuse smelled of ammonia and brandy. Kennedy put a hip up on an empty stainless-steel gurney and watched old Charlie Marcuse, M.E. extraordinaire and a forensic pathologist for thirty-one years, struggling with his surgical gloves. There were four stainless tables in this part of the center. Each table had a little wooden pedestal at one end, a perforated steel sheet running its length, and a set of double sinks and taps at the other end. A large scale was suspended above each of the perforated steel tables. A white enamel basin hung from each scale. A twin set of fluorescent light banks and an adjustable high-intensity light on an articulated arm provided illumination for each table. The walls were solid ceramic tile, moss-green in color, and the floor was covered with Armstrong Cushion Floor or something like that. Couldn't have the M.E.'s getting shin splints.

"No other customers today, Charlie?"

Marcuse snugged the gloves down over the sleeves of his lab coat, sniffed at Kennedy through his gold-wires, and nodded at the attendant, Mervyn Polk. The man walked off toward the storage facilities down the hall. Kennedy had been there many times. A long room with a wall of stainless-steel lockers, temperature controls above each heavy door. The lockers themselves were large enough to hold a full-size gurney, and each gurney held one corpse. A shelf underneath each gurney held whatever personal effects the victim might have had.

"Eddie, we will never lack for customers here. Dying is the one thing you can count on everyone to do sooner or later. Say, Eddie, did you ever consider that the last thing a man wants to do—"

"Is the last thing he does? Gee, Charlie, I don't think I have. That's a wonderful thought. I'm going to have to get somebody to sew that into my pajamas."

"Fact is, we do have someone else due. Mondays are odd days, Eddie. You'd think people would get up to most of their shenanigans on Friday or Saturday night. But now and then you get a Monday—people are down, depressed, maybe the wife's been a special pain this morning."

"That what you have? A domestic?"

Marcuse stretched his arms up into the air, flexing his knotted fingers, reaching up to the ceiling. "Aaah . . . wooof! Not as limber as I used to be. What? Oh, yes. Yes, a sad one this—young wife, got a small baby boy, so I hear. Next door neighbors hear a fuss on Saturday night. But this is a good neighborhood, and in good neighborhoods the good neighbors mind their own business. Just ask Kitty Genovese, right? Anyway, the husband calls in, he's a wreck, just got home, found his young wife nude, beaten to death. Terrible ruckus. Everybody up in arms. Black menace in the streets. Who could have done this? Alarums and excursions, that sort of thing."

"Where is this? Up in the East Sixties?"

"Yes. You heard about this?"

"No. Just sounds like the East Sixties."

"Yes. That it do. Well, anyway, the gendarmerie arrive, encounter distraught hubby wringing hands upon the stoop. First Officer is guarding the scene. First Officer reports that hubby claims to have found wife in the bathroom, nude, in predictable physical disarray. Beaten to death, other ugly imputations. Detective examines wife and detects petechial hemorrhages in both lids."

"Suffocation?"

"The very one. Also, she's been dead rather longer than hubby would have us believe."

Kennedy shrugged. "Nearest and dearest."

Marcuse smiled at the old homicide axiom. "Yes . . . Well, here's the man of the hour now."

The attendant pushed a gurney in. The body on it was covered by a plain white sheet. Kennedy noted the arrangement of the limbs.

"Rigor all gone, Charlie?"

Marcuse nodded, drawing back the sheet. "Yes. As supple as a willow now. Passed very quickly."

Kennedy looked on as Marcuse flipped on the overhead and adjusted his microphone. The silent attendant flicked on the fluorescent bank. The body was clothed, still bloody, still a ruin. Kennedy opened his evidence cases and laid out the eleven Instamatic crime-scene shots for Marcuse to refer to if he had need.

"Charlie . . . you think the rapid passage of rigor is significant here? Anything suggestive of a drug or storage?"

Marcuse shook his head, dislodging a strand of silky gray hair. In the glare of the overhead, Kennedy could see that there was a yellow undertone to the pathologist's hair. Charlie was aging rapidly these days. Kennedy would miss the old bastard, and who the hell would replace him? Some slick from State with a Fiberglas suit and the personality of a wolverine. Likely.

"No, for God's sake, Eddie, it's almost ninety degrees out there. We're lucky he's not rancid. Got your things together?"

The attendant had delivered a series of wooden probes, plastic jars, vials, slides. There were a number of tissue and fluid samples to be taken. It was Kennedy's job to witness the process and to provide the evidential chain required by Criminal Procedure Law. Marcuse had anticipated many of Kennedy's requirements. It was one of the joys of working with the man. He thought like a detective, and he wasn't shy about making his own suggestions. Few defense counsels tried to challenge forensic evidence developed in an autopsy performed by Charles Marcuse.

Marcuse shot Kennedy a look from over the top of his glasses. "Mr. Kennedy. I give you the choice today. What will it be?"

Kennedy thought for a few seconds. "The one with that violin solo? The one that crashes about for a while and then the violin takes off on its own?"

Marcuse sighed and frowned at Kennedy. "The 'one that crashes about for a while'! Do I take it that you're referring to 'Scheherazade'?"

"Yes, that one."

"Liked it, did you?"

Kennedy grinned at him over the corpse. "Yeah! Neat beat, and okay lyrics. I give it a seven."

Marcuse and Von Karajan got under way at around the same time. The music helped. But not much.

As Mervyn and Marcuse shifted the body onto the autopsy table, Kennedy made certain that Officer Harris had been in to sign the PI form required by the Criminal Procedure Law. The PI, or Police Identification form, was a legal-size document detailing the circumstances under which the First Officer had discovered the body, his shield and precinct number, the location of the body, whatever he might have been able to discover regarding the event, and his official identification of the body now on the table as the same body he had discovered under the street mural in Alphabet City. Bodies had been mixed up before this, to the discomfort of all concerned except the defendant. It was upon details such as this that the evidential case rested, and since New York was averaging 1,800 to 1,900 murders a year, the NYPD and the Medical Examiner's office were fanatically scrupulous about documentation. Kennedy kept a copy of Harris's PI form in his case file, along with all the other paperwork done so far on this case. As Marcuse and Mervyn Polk finished the transfer, Kennedy put the file aside and walked over to a point just a little behind and to the left of the Assistant Medical Examiner. Technically the medico-legal pathological examination was the responsibility of the doctor alone, but it was up to Kennedy to request, and to witness, any particular procedures or samplings that he might consider pertinent to the case. Kennedy had a number of these in mind, beginning with the victim's shoes.

Marcuse adjusted the overhead microphone. A certain heaviness descended upon him, bowing his shoulders slightly and slowing his movements.

"Well, I am Charles Marcuse, forensic pathologist for the City of New York, office of the Medical Examiner. We will conduct a post-mortem examination on the body of an unidentified male . . ." Here he raised an eyebrow at Kennedy. Kennedy shook his head. Although he was fairly sure that the boy was "Salto" Ruiz, he had not yet obtained a positive ID from a family member. He had considered asking a sergeant from the 8th to go over to Mrs. Ruiz's flat in the Riis Project, but there was something in the schoolboy photo that made him want to handle the thing personally. He was going over there as soon as the autopsy was completed. Privately, Kennedy had no doubt the body was "Salto" Ruiz.

Marcuse gave the time and the date, and the location of the autopsy. Dropping into the formal jargon of the forensic pathologist, he commenced a description of the body before him.

"We have an unidentified male Caucasian, approximately fourteen to nineteen years of age, height five feet seven inches. Weight one hundred thirty-three pounds. The body is clothed in worn black running shoes, without socks, a pair of tan army-surplus-style pants secured at the cuffs by two yellow elastic bands. Subject shows an abrasion in the right knee area, visible through a rent in the fabric. Pants are secured by a military belt. Subject is also seen to be wearing a purple T-shirt. No other jewelry or tags are visible so far. Subject bears case tag number 115/67/85 and the attending investigator is Detective Edward Xavier Kennedy of the Midtown Central Detective Area Task Force, shield number four-two-four-seven. Assisting with me is Attendant Mervyn Polk. We will begin by removing the subject's clothing."

Marcuse and Mervyn spent a few minutes removing the outer clothing from the body. This was done as methodically as possible, without slicing or ripping any of it. Kennedy asked Mervyn to take some scrapings from the soles of the running shoes. While he was doing this, Kennedy saw that a few granules of a dark-brown material were trapped in the folds of the pants where they were held by the elastic bands. Mervyn used a pair of tweezers to secure one of the grains, which he then dropped into a white paper envelope. He delivered as many of these particles to Kennedy as he could secure. Kennedy marked the paper envelopes, in order, with the code prefix K116. Kennedy's Task Force had been assigned to investigate 115 murders so far this year. Kennedy used a simple numerical order to keep track of them, starting with number one at the first of January. He set the envelopes aside and went back to the table.

Mervyn took each article of clothing as it was removed and laid it out on a parallel table in the same position that it had occupied on the body. The shoes went at the foot, then the yellow elastics. The pants came off with difficulty, since some of the fecal matter had dried to the interior. Mervyn used a sterile stainless trowel to obtain as much of the fecal matter as possible. It was placed in a plastic container, sealed, and handed to Kennedy to mark.

The boy's underwear was still fairly damp. Mervyn took swabs and additional samples from the underwear and then set them apart to air-dry, in order to prevent any rot or additional damage to the fibers. The T-shirt came off easily except at the area of the collarbone, where much of the blood had dried to the material. The shirt was placed above the pants, and photographs were taken of each article and each step in the process. Marcuse kept up a casual but accurate description as they went along.

When the body was fully stripped, Mervyn took X-rays of it from several aspects. Marcuse and Mervyn then swabbed the body down as gently as possible, removing as much of the matted blood and foreign matter as they could without damaging the skin or the tissues exposed. Samples were obtained by swabs or by scrapings of the clotted blood, the gunpowder residue, and the stippling now visible around the bullet entry wound in the right temple, and from the edges of the long incision in the neck.

Kennedy stepped in closer to watch the swabs taken from the bullet wound. "Close, but not a contact wound?"

Marcuse shook his head. "No. You see the burns and the stippling. But there's no muzzle print, and in hard-tissue area like this you'd expect to see the characteristic star-shaped wound. But it was no more than a few inches away, and I'd say it was a large-caliber wound."

"At least a thirty-eight?" Kennedy thought so himself.

"At least."

The gentle cleaning continued. Bits of grit and small clots of blood were deposited in the sinks or, when Kennedy or Marcuse thought they might be worth keeping, in a growing collection of vials and containers on a side table. Marcuse was working around the rear of the head now.

"Aahh! Eddie, look at this."

Kennedy had already seen it. "Exit wound?"

After the blood and debris had been swabbed and sponged away, a large ragged opening could be seen in the rear portion of the boy's skull, just behind and below his left ear. Blood, skin, shards of skull bone, and oddments of flesh were visible, as well as pulpy segments of pinkish-gray brain matter. Marcuse took a track probe out of his tray and prodded the opening and the skin in the area.

"No fragments that I can see. We'll look more carefully later. Let's get this done."

Marcuse went over the body in silence, closely examining every aspect of the limbs, the chest, and the head. After a period of no more than five minutes, he straightened up and summarized for the tape.

"We have a normal adolescent male body with no congenital malformations visible. Eyes and conjunctiva appear normal, although ruptures and occlusion are evident in the right orb. Ears and nose appear normal, with some evidence of hemorrhage in the canals. Natural teeth are in fair condition. There is a well-healed scar two centimeters long on the right side at the front, and a vertical incision made with a single cut appears in the right portion of the neck, extending from the right ear to within three centimeters of the right clavicle, exposing sections of the right common carotid. There are no hesitation cuts visible in this region. Nine other recent incisions or penetrating wounds are visible on the digits. There is considerable post-mortem lividity present over the face and upper thoracic region. We find a large-diameter entrance wound with evidence of gunpowder residue and stippling in the region of the right temple, probably resulting from a large-caliber bullet. There is an apparent exit wound in the posterior left-hand region of the skull below and slightly to the posterior of the ear. Extensive tissue and skull fragmentation is evident and particles of the dura are visible. We observe a tattoo in a teardrop shape just beneath the left eye.

"On the left upper limb there is a well-healed linear scar one centimeter long in the left ante-cubital fossa and evidence of a recent needle mark in this same left ante-cubital fossa."

Marcuse droned on in this steady, almost rhythmic manner, detailing the external characteristics of the body. When he returned to synopsize the face and head regions, he referred again to the two injuries evident. He also found minor surface abrasions on the chest, both elbows, the left knee, and in the hollow of the Achilles' tendon.

Kennedy noted the knee abrasions, and placed a red line under the observation that there was a recent needle mark in the boy's left arm.

Marcuse completed his summary of the external aspects of the body before him by directing Mervyn to take clippings and scrapings from the finger- and toenails of the corpse. Kennedy, bearing in mind the possibility of Marielito drug connections, asked Marcuse to secure combings of pubic hair, additional blood samples for toxicologic examinations, as well as an anal swab. Some Marielito gangs made it a point to sodomize their victims. It was a trademark in the South Bronx. Bodies had been found propped up in that position, nude, and violently raped at or near the moment of their deaths. Kennedy wanted to know if this boy had been sexually assaulted.

The side-table collection was growing. Kennedy spent a few moments taping and marking various samples. Marcuse reached for his scalpel and Kennedy went for a glass of water. Marcuse laughed.

"Still time for snackies, Eddie. No? Too bad."

Kennedy came back with a glass of water, stepped a little away from the table, and took a breath. This part was never easy.

Kennedy took out the school photo and held it close to the face of the corpse. The dead boy was "Salto" Ruiz.

Marcuse made what is called a coronal mastoid incision in the boy's scalp, cutting a deep track, in one practiced motion, from a point just above the left ear all the way around to the right ear. The scalp on the forward portion of the skull was visibly loosened by this stroke. The pathologist then peeled the anterior portion of the scalp off and forward over the brow, exposing the pink marble of the skull. This was examined for fractures or other signs of violence. He then cut and pushed the thick scalp back from this region, shoving it forward until it completely covered the face, and down at the back until it folded around the ears. The crest of the skull itself was now fully exposed.

The M.E. used a small electric saw to cut into the bone, moving from right to left until he reached the midpoint of the forehead. He cut down toward the brow here for about an inch, then moved left again, came back up a half-inch, and completed his cut at the right temple.

He made three more angular cuts into the skull until he was able to remove an entire section. It came away with some difficulty, making a sucking liquid noise that was, for Kennedy, about the worst moment of the afternoon. He was in the habit of looking at his watch at this moment. He did today, and was shocked to see that it was only 1307 hours. Just a little after one o'clock in the afternoon. It was turning into a very long day.

"What's the zigzag for, Charlie?"

Kennedy knew what the peculiar skull cut was for, but feeding straight lines to Charlie Marcuse was one way to get through a day like this.

Marcuse looked over his glasses at Mervyn, who returned the look without smiling.

"Twist-caps, Eddie. It was Mervyn's idea. If it works out we're going to suggest the idea to the brewers. What do you think?"

The cut assisted in the exact replacement of the skull cap after the autopsy, and it was Marcuse's way of making sure that the right skull pieces got back together. Worse things had happened in the M.E.'s office.

The M.E. set the calvarium aside. The brain was mottled and red under the lights.

"Hemorrhaged. Not surprising. Lot of trauma here."

A series of color photos were taken at this point. Then Marcuse used a scalpel to slice away the connections and arteries that held the brain in the cavity. In less than forty seconds he held the brain in his hands.

"Extensive injuries. Bullet track. Bloody ruin, this is. Mervyn, get me two sections. Other than the trauma, it looks to be a normal brain. You can see the bullet track clearly. Eddie, look at this."

Marcuse held the bloody object, rather like a gray sponge full of maroon-colored liquid, up into the hot yellow light. It was clear from the ruptures and the ragged bits of tissue that it had suffered a massive injury. Something large had literally plowed through the brain, severing arteries and destroying cells. Marcuse placed it gently in the scales.

"Any fragments? Any sign of a slug in there?" Kennedy had gotten past the usual moment of illness. Once the body was open, it somehow was less than a body. You could get some emotional distance from it then.

Marcuse suggested an X-ray. "If there are fragments we'll find them. Mervyn, take care of this. Let's get a look at this skull."

The M.E. used a track probe to outline the bullet path, placing it in the entrance wound very carefully. It passed easily through the hole. Marcuse moved it gently and slowly through the various internal structures of the skull, calling out each sign of injury as it was revealed. The probe passed completely through the skull and came out of the exit wound. Photos were taken of the track probe in place.

"This what killed him, Charlie?"

Marcuse frowned in the harsh light.

"It didn't cure his migraines, that's for sure. But it's hard to say whether he was alive, half-alive, half-dead, or bleeding like a butchered hog when this brute went through his skull. If you ask me . . ."

Marcuse pondered it for a while. Kennedy said nothing.

"Just speculation right now. But I'd say he was at or near death when he was shot. Head-shot victims will bleed ferociously until the heart and lungs shut down. But although the brain is a wreck, there's not quite as much blood in here as I'd imagine. He'd lost a lot of blood before they did this to him."

"Enough to make him unconscious?" Kennedy had no idea why he asked that question. It was an emotional one, and for Kennedy a revelation of weakness. Marcuse glanced quickly up at the detective, and then down again at the empty skull.

"He never heard the shot, Eddie. I can tell you that."

There was a softness in his tone that healed Eddie as much as it cut him.

More photos were taken, of the brain, the skull cavity, with and without the track probe. Marcuse also explored the neck wound, and additional shots were taken of this large incision as the doctor peeled away various levels of subcutaneous tissue to lay bare the severed common carotid artery.

The next stage involved a Y-shaped incision across the chest area, known officially as a thoraco-abdominal incision. Most M.E.'s just call it the chest cut. Marcuse put his left hand on the center of the boy's chest, fingers spread to hold the skin and flesh in place. Using a large sterile scalpel, he began his cut on the boy's left shoulder, right at the bone point. Marcuse brought the blade around in a shallow curve, digging deep, cutting fast through the fine brown skin of the hairless chest, cutting through pectoral muscles and fatty tissue, finishing the cut in the same motion at the bone point of the right shoulder. Then he cut a vertical incision, deep and fast, starting at the breastbone where it was bisected by the first cut, running all the way to the crest of the pubic bone. The Y-shaped cut gaped open. There was no blood.

The skin and flesh had to be sliced away from the underlying cartilage and the covering of the rib cage. Marcuse peeled it back in a matter of a minute, revealing the thoracic and abdominal region from the breastbone all the way to the bladder.

There it is, thought Kennedy, the whole game laid out for you; Kennedy wondered why people say "I *have* a body," instead of, "I *am* a body." Nobody has one unless he took it from someone else. You *are* bodies, all of you. Meat is what we all are. It was a thought Kennedy did his best to forget and he frequently managed it for weeks at a time.

Marcuse snapped his way through the breastbone using a pair of cutters. The *crunch-pop crunch-pop crunch-pop* sound and the underlying squelch of gristle and bone giving way was nothing compared to the scent, vivid and miasmic and dense, a literal reek of old meat, aging blood, the very breath of mortality, rising into your nostrils and down your throat; the taste and smell of wet copper and damp stone. Kennedy found a stump of his Colt cigarillo and fired it up again. The bone had to be cut away from the pale, almost transparent membrane, giving way finally at the throat, the scalpel blade flickering deftly in the wrack.

Marcuse took the entire breast-plate away, peeling it back over the boy's shoulder, exposing the organs beneath it. Kennedy recognized the lungs and the liver, and the whorls and loops of the intestines. The heart, as expected, was hidden under the lungs.

"Looks pale but normal. We'll get that pericardial sac open, get you some heart blood for the toxicologists. Now let's see . . ."

With a marvelous economy Marcuse extracted the blood, then removed the lungs and the heart. They were weighed; Marcuse looked them over and pronounced them normal, and sent them over to Mervyn to take samples. He drew several syringes of fluid out of the various cavities, which were also measured and sampled. The remaining chest skin was pushed upward. Marcuse poked about in the throat for a while, emerging with those organs as well.

Bit by bit, sample by scrape, ounce by snip, the boy who

used to be was transformed into the forensic jigsaw that lies at the core of every killing. Kennedy had seen nearly ninety autopsies, but this gradual disintegration was always the moment when he finally declared the victim truly and thoroughly obliterated. There was a transference in the moment, something Kennedy hardly ever sensed on any level other than the limbic one; from this point on, the dead had no voice and hardly existed in the coherent form. They were nothing but volts and synapses in other people's bodies, as transitory as the glitter of light on a blade. Kennedy took them on at that moment, carried them somewhere inside him, brought their tales to the light as best he could. It was a primal thing with him, although he hardly sensed it, but it was the force that drove him.

By the time Rimsky-Korsakoff had brought his traveler to the Rock Surmounted by a Bronze Warrior, Marcuse was well into his final protocol. He summarized his findings again, citing the means by which the body had come to him, and the officers attendant at the autopsy. He went through the stages once more, briefly encapsulating his findings.

"Internal examination: No hernias were present in the diaphragm. Domes normal. Pleural cavities showed no fluid, air, or blood. Pericardium fluid contents normal, no pericarditis in evidence. Mediastinum contents normal as well. Teeth were his own, in poor repair. Nose—nares patent, blood present. Pharynx showed clotted blood. Tongue slightly abraded due to mastication under duress. Hyoid bone fracture of recent origin. Thymus weighed twelve grams. Sectioned normal. Thyroid weighed twenty grams and was also normal. Larynx and vocal cords normal. Mucosa and contents showed blood in small quantities. Trachea and bronchi mucosa normal. Contents normal, although some blood present here. Pulmonary pleura normal, and pulmonary vessels also normal. Right lung weighed four hundred and fifty grams, showed moderate congestion but no gross pneumonitis or tumor was noted. Left lung weighed four hundred and twenty-five grams, and also showed moderate congestion but no pneumonitis or tumor. Heart weighed three hundred and twenty grams, and was normal in size. Auricles normal in size and contents. Ventricals were also normal in size and contents. Tricuspid valve size and cusps normal. Pulmonary valve . . ."

As Marcuse went through the litany, Kennedy and Mervyn were labeling and securing the samples taken. Toxicology would get much of this, for blood typing, signs of sexual assault, and for tests of possible drug usage. The drug connection was getting stronger with every hard fact that emerged from Kennedy's investigation. Stradazzi's fairy tale about Mantecado called for some serious spadework. Kennedy's job was to find out who killed Porfirio Magdalena Ruiz and bring him before a judge to answer for it. If that involved kicking around in some goddam narco trap-line, that's what he would do.

". . . Aorta and large vessels of normal caliber and elasticity. Major branches in chest and abdomen are patent. Blood in heart and vessels is below normal quantity, and there are several post-mortem clots. Esophagus presents normal caliber, inflamed, mucosa bloody. Stomach shows minor incipient ulceration, erosion of stomach lining, and blood in mucosa. Meal last eaten appears to have been ground beef, lettuce and other vegetable material, potato, some liquid . . ."

"Special sauce lettuce cheese pickles onion on a sesame seed bun. Damn kid ate at McDonald's, Charlie. Put *that* down as the probable cause!"

Marcuse ignored this. ". . . Intestine normal, lumen patent, and appendix also normal. Mucosa and wall of the large and small intestine is normal. Liver shows signs of hepatitis with extensive periportal infiltration—lymphocytes and plasma cells to Pathology for verification of this. There was no acute necrosis. . . ."

Hepatitis. The kid had hepatitis. Drugs again. "Charlie, I want the toxicology report as soon as possible. The kid was a user, and I need to know how much of what." Marcuse nodded and went on.

". . . Gall bladder size and contents hepatic. Bile ducts patent. Spleen weighed two hundred and three grams and section normal. Pancreas normal. Mesenteric lymph nodes enlarged. Adrenals total weight eight grams normal on section. Urinary bladder contained only traces of urine—samples to Toxicology. Mucosa and wall normal. Ureters patent, right and left kidneys weighed one hundred thirty and one hundred twenty-six grams, sectioned normally. Prostate normal. Urethra inflamed . . ."

"Why was his urethra inflamed, Charlie?"

"Damned if I know, Eddie. Could be he was jerking off on a

regular basis. Too regular. Irritated the glans or some such. Not relevant, I'd say. We continue with the testes, which are normal and descended. Epididymes normal. There is a large entrance wound in the right temple with severe stippling and gunpowder residue. No starring. Meninges normal. Evidence of extensive subarachnoid hemorrhage. Skull is point-five centimeters in average thickness. Entrance hole in right temporal region measures one-point-four by one-point-two centimeters. There is a fracture and displacement of the right splenoid and temporal bone in the middle fossa. There is a large uneven exit hole in the left occipital bone measuring two by one-point-eight centimeters, and the plane of the bullet was about fifteen percent off the horizontal, downward from front to back. Ears were normal. No abnormalities were noted in the remainder of the osseous system. The brain weighed thirteen hundred and seventy-five grams. The bullet entered the right frontal lobe, passing downward and to the left, exiting from the brain at the junction of the pons and the medulla to the left of the midline and inferior to the cerebellum. Track diameter was irregular due to projectile tumbling, averaging two-point-three centimeters. Moderate hemorrhaging around the bullet track was noted. Bloodstained fluid was present in the ventricles, and hemorrhages were noted in the pons and the cerebellum. Medulla was normal on section. Pituitary body was normal. And the pineal . . ." Marcuse sighed and stretched again. A joint popped audibly. Kennedy waited a few feet away, listening to Marcuse but looking at a section of green tile.

". . . was undersized but normal. Blood work remains to be done. X-ray findings showed no bullet fragments in track."

Kennedy turned around. "It tumbled but it didn't break up at all. No fragments at all?"

"Nothing that showed up. It happens sometimes. Bullets are freakish. So is bone. I'd say it wasn't suggestive. If I track you correctly, you're positing a Teflon slug, something of that nature? Can't rule it out, of course. But on the evidence I'd say not. Get some lead wipings back from forensic labs—you'll see."

Kennedy was inclined to agree. Glazer or Teflon slugs were rare. Since they were designed to penetrate police body armor, even the new Kevlar vests, any sign that killers in town were getting access to Teflon slugs would have to go right to Nicastro this afternoon.

Marcuse was wrapping it up. "To summarize thus far: We can say that the deceased has been shot in the head at close range, the bullet entering the temporal aspect of the forehead close to the right eye and passing downward and to the left through skull and brain to exit from the skull in the left occipital region. There is also an incision-type wound measuring thirteen centimeters extending from a point just beneath the right ear in a line downward to the right collarbone, exposing and severing a portion of the right common carotid. There are no hesitation marks in this area. The cut was made cleanly and without hesitation by a narrow-bladed object with a very sharp edge. There are also various severe incisions in the digits and palm of both hands, suggestive of defense cuts. A recent needle mark was found in the left antecubital fossa. Blood work follows."

He paused here. Mervyn was already cleaning up the wreckage and sponging down the body. A newly pressed sheet waited on the side table. The M.E. thought for a moment, although Kennedy was sure he had already come to a decision in the first few minutes after he'd reached the crime scene down in Alphabet City.

"I, Charles Marcuse, have examined this body, and I have opened and examined the above-noted cavities and organs as recorded, and in my opinion the cause of death was severe and extensive injury to the right common carotid caused by the application of a narrow-bladed and sharp-edged tool, causing extreme loss of blood and consequent central-nervous-system shock and heart failure due to loss of blood pressure. Deceased was at or near the point of death when the projectile was fired into his brain, and since the prognosis for recovery from the initial wound after no more than two minutes would be negative, we feel that this second wound can only be described as contributory. And so, cause of death: knife wound to the carotid. Charles Marcuse, Assistant Medical Examiner for the City of New York at . . . thirteen forty-four hours this date in and for the City of New York . . . et cetera, et cetera, as they say. Mervyn, if you will. Edward, walk this way . . ."

Marcuse dropped a shoulder and lumbered off, quite intentionally dragging one foot, muttering to himself in a creditable and deliberate imitation of Boris Karloff. Kennedy followed him into the scrub room, still chewing on the plastic tip of the Colt cigarillo and thinking to himself . . .

Good afternoon, Mrs. Ruiz, I'm Detective Kennedy and I have some information about . . . No, no. Pick her up at work and . . . No. Wait until she's home?

He heard the flutter and snap as Mervyn threw the white sheet out over the corpse. It cracked at a corner, and then settled slowly over the ruins of Porfirio Magdalena Ruiz, billowing and rolling as it came down, like a fog from a chilly sea.

Charlie was pouring two 10cc shots of Martell into a pair of graduated cylinders as Kennedy came into the scrub room. He handed one to Kennedy and raised the other to the light.

"Here's to us!" said Marcuse.

Kennedy answered, "Who's like us?"

"Devil a one!" said Charlie, and waited again.

Kennedy smiled, lifted his cylinder.

"And they're all dead!"

They drained the vials and stood in silence, as good friends do.

CHAPTER 4

SALTO MORTAL

The traffic on Second Avenue was backed up all the way from the entrance to the Midtown Tunnel. Kennedy sat in the detective's car with the air-conditioning on high, waiting for a bus driver to stop arguing with a Sikh cabbie, waiting for him to stop slamming the roof of the cab with his fist, waiting for the Sikh to stop honking his horn, and getting none of it.

He called in for a patch to the Task Force desk. Farrell was in, and he took the call with a mouthful of chili dog and a snarl.

"Task Force, whaddya want?"

"Christ, Oliver—nice manners!"

"That you, Kennedy? Where you been?"

"At the M.E.'s. Why? Anybody asking?"

"Yeah. Got this guy Stradazzi, says Mrs. Ruiz been calling all morning, says she hears somebody was dead over on Avenue C, her neighbors are saying it was her kid. She's having a major shitfit, been calling the desk all day. Stradazzi says should he tell her? Wants you to give him a shout. Also Bruno says you should call him at sixteen hundred hours sharp—he's at home. You get anything on this one?"

"Yeah, I did. You want to know, I'll tell you, we can read all about it in the *Post* tomorrow. You have anything big on your desk right now?"

Farrell, sensing the dark shadow of imminent work rising out of the handset, let a few seconds pass.

"Oliver, it's nothing that'll cut into your day job. I want you to get the Patrol Supervisor to let me have some of his Third Platoon guys for a canvass tonight. Say around nineteen hundred hours?"

"Sure, Eddie. You be wanting some help with it from the squad? I'm up against it, but Frank's here doing the dog—yes, you are, you weird fucker—yes, he is, Eddie. Don't listen to that mope. And Wolf's court call didn't come in by thirteen hundred hours, so he's loose. I'll ask him, you want?"

"Wolf" was Wolfgar Maksins, a heavy-boned farm boy with bluish skin, and coarse hair the color of dead wheat cut into a spiky brush, shaved almost bald at the temples and tapering to a small pointed tuft at the back of his neck. There wasn't a female cop in the Lower Manhattan area who hadn't spent a few idle seconds wondering what Wolfgar would be like in bed. Wolf was doing his best to see that as many of them as humanly possible got to find out firsthand. He was a provisional sergeant, having passed the last test easily. Nobody called him Provisional Sergeant, however. It wasn't healthy. Wolfgar was a "provisional" sergeant because every man and woman in the NYPD who had passed the last sergeants' exam was currently hanging by his or her thumbs waiting for the society of black policemen known as The Guardians to settle their suit with the administration over the number of black officers who had failed to pass the test. It was a sore point with every ranker in the NYPD, a point of race and therefore saturated with legal nitroglycerine. Lines were being drawn in the force, and Wolfgar Maksins, along with Deke Fratelli, another member of Kennedy's squad who had also been promoted on the basis of the last test, was standing right on top of it. He could use some distracting.

"Yeah, ask Maksins if he'll give me a hand. I'll pick him up. Tell him I'll be there in about a half-hour. And clear that with the desk, okay Farrell?"

"One-oh-four, K."

A traffic officer, known as a brownie in New York, was breaking up the argument in front of Kennedy's car. She was a short overweight black woman with a carrying voice, and it took her about thirty seconds to send the bus driver back to his vehicle, bent almost double, like a sapling in a gale, by the force of the woman's personality. Kennedy found that he was still chewing on the stump of his Colt cigar. The brownie waved him through the intersection, holding the cross-street traffic back by leaning on the grillwork of the lead car. He brought the side window down and threw the cigar out into the gutter, squinting through the dust and fumes, noting with sardonic amusement as it bounced onto the sidewalk under a blue and red sign that read LITTERING IS FILTHY AND DISGUSTING SO DON'T DO IT!

He got all the way to 23rd Street before he ran into another major traffic jam. A pushcart peddler was repeatedly crashing his battered metal wagon into the rear of a tractor trailer. The tractor trailer had a sign on the back that read LORD ONE DAY AT A TIME and another one that read I BRAKE FOR HALLUCINATIONS! The pushcart man was missing his left ear. His face was distorted and white with rage. He must have been screaming quite loudly but no one could hear him through the noise of a hundred car horns blatting and wailing and fifty voices bellowing. Black fumes pumped out of the tractor trailer's stack and settled over the tangle of cabs and trucks and junkers and limos and wacked-out pushcart ped-dlers, muting the glare and softening the outlines so that in the hot midafternoon sun the whole demented collection acquired a soft amber glow like a seventeenth-century horizon. Kennedy found a swing channel on the radio and listened to Tommy Dorsey, feeling at home, feeling connected to everything, part of the town, until a large black dog with red eyes and a bad case of mange leaped up on the hood of his car and howled through the glass at him, yellow slaver hanging from its jaws, bad teeth glitter-ing, covering the hood with spit and grit. It stayed there until Kennedy hit the siren. The dog went straight up into the air about ten feet, yelping, fell away to the side, claws marking the paint job, and disappeared.

Kennedy was in a pretty good mood for quite a long time afterward. It was, after all, one of the great gridlock-gonzo inter-ludes of the season, and he'd been there to see it. His good mood lasted all the way to the squad room and held up for a good fifty-seven seconds after he got there.

Sergeant Oliver Farrell had not wasted the forty-five minutes it took Detective Kennedy to reach the squad room. He was ready with a number of persuasive reasons why he personally was unable to provide any material aid to Kennedy in his investiga-tion. Kennedy poured himself a cup of nearly-coffee, borrowed a package of Vantage Lights from Sergeant Benjamin Kolchinski's cache in the bottom drawer of his desk, wrote out a note for Kolchinski, left a dollar bill clipped to the note, broke open the pack, and was well into the typing of his Investigation Summary for Stokovich by the time Farrell had reached the end of his excuses, none of which Kennedy had heard. Farrell was nearing the magic number twenty, and he intended to bail out of the NYPD with his pension intact and his record of blameless if undistinguished service unsullied by any voluntary expenditure of effort. Farrell was a drone. Drink and the faintest tincture of timidity had shaped his face and his career, leaving both slightly puffed-up, tentative, and inconclusive. The infamous Knapp juggernaut had rolled perilously close to him during the black years of '72 and '73, stealing what little heart he might have had for the job and impressing his soul with an obsessive need to remain nearly invisible. This end he had achieved, being a man without mark or blemish, without opinion, and as sensitive to the shifting zephyrs of squad-room power politics as a fern in a glade. He was, oddly, not despised by the other men, who covered for him as best they could, but he was not respected, and respect in the society of men is breath and blood, something without which no man can flourish. Farrell was translucent by now, a difficult man to keep your mind on. By the end of his career he would be transparent or dead. It was an ugly thing to watch, and he was fortunate that the other men had enough character and grace to be gentle with him.

Maksins had already assembled much of the paperwork required by the day's efforts in the Ruiz investigation. Kennedy was nominally responsible for all the evidence, and for maintaining the Activity Log that Stokovich insisted upon. Stokovich wanted no prima donnas on the squad, and he was a bear for records, summaries, notes, duty rosters, assignment sheets. He wanted any man or woman under his command to be able to maintain notes and progress reports clearly enough that any other detective could be assigned at any stage of the investigation without disorientation or the need for lengthy briefings. Clarity such as that depended upon extensive records and detailed fieldwork. It also generated even more paperwork than the usual police action, pounds and reams and quires of it, along with cartons and boxes of hard evidence, tagged and annotated, cross-referenced and dated, signed for, vacuum-sealed, and nailed into reality like a deerskin on a plank. It was a good system. Stokovich's squad had one of the best efficiency ratings in the department, it was respected by the DA's office, and it solved a hell of a lot of its cases. Maksins and Kennedy pulled the case into shape over the next hour, wrapping the process up with a Response Report, a chronological record of the precise times, locations, dates, durations, and shield numbers of every official who had had any impact at all on the homicide case so far. Kennedy was good at this kind of thing. He had a reporter's instinct for the telltale item, a talent for separating crucial facts from the aggregate and laying them out accurately. Maksins put together an Index for the Homicide Investigation and typed out a series of three-by-five cards with specific information about the case.

Kennedy looked up from his battered Remington, sensing a body standing over him. Farrell was there, moving from one foot to another, looking pained and avid and bored, each emotion canceling the other, adding up to zero.

Kennedy drew on the Vantage. "Yes, Oliver?"

"Ah, it's sixteen hundred hours, Eddie. You're supposed to call the lieutenant?"

The phone rang eleven times before anyone picked it up. A woman's voice, deep and slightly accented: "So, yes?"

Kennedy knew the voice. Stokovich's wife called often and the lieutenant always took the call. Years ago, when Bruno Stokovich had been a patrolman, he'd refused a call from his mother. He had found her when he got home around four in the morning. She had been dead for several hours, lying in the hall with a broken hip, bleeding inside. Stokovich could always be reached by his family, no matter what was happening on the job. "They'll still be dead in the morning," he would say, picking up the call, softening visibly as he did so.

"Mrs. Stokovich, it's Detective Kennedy. Is the lieutenant around?"

"Yess, Edward. How *are* you? It goes well?"

"Yes, ma'am."

"And you are still with . . . Trudy?"

"Ah, no, ma'am. Trudy and I aren't seeing each other anymore."

"Sso! Too bad! You treated her bad, yes?"

"Yes, ma'am." Where the hell was Bruno?

He was on the line. "Thanks, Geli. Kennedy, you there?"

"Sir, you wanted me to call?"

"Yeah. How's it goin' with the thing this morning?"

He spoke elliptically. Mrs. Stokovich knew nothing about his work. He kept her apart from it. It was a common thing in the NYPD.

"Got an ID. Marcuse did the autopsy. Cause of death is a knife wound. Gunshot, large caliber. Needle marks too."

"Junkie?"

Kennedy thought it over. Stokovich breathed into the phone, wheezing faintly. He's been playing with his boys, Kennedy thought. He could see him up there in the suburbs, pounding down a slope of fresh-cut lawn, shirt off, calling out to his kid: "Pass, pass, this way, kid." Something about this scene made Kennedy tight and sad. He ignored it.

"Yes, I'd say. Kid had hepatitis too. But I'd say he was recent. Toxicology will be in tomorrow. Something else too . . . I think he had coffee grains in his cuffs."

Stokovich snorted. "Coffee? Like in 'coffee to fuck up the sniffers'? Like in coke or heroin trafficking?"

"Well, he may have been a stock boy at Los Hermanos so the coffee may mean nothing, but—"

"Los Hermanos? How'd we get *there*?"

There it was again. The secret reaction, the inside track. The lieutenant had frozen over.

"Well, sir, we have a probable ID—MP filed this morning. Lady named Ruiz says her son's been missing since yesterday and he was a stock boy there. Picture fits too."

"Who've you got on it?"

"Maksins is helping out. I'm taking him over to see the mother in a minute."

"Maksins? Where's Robinson? And Farrell?"

"Robinson got a line on the Gypsies. He's out with Fratelli now. Farrell is here. You want him?"

"Farrell? Fuck, no. Look, you doing a canvass on this?"

"Yes, sir, I have one lined up for nineteen hundred hours. We'll grid the block and do some stop-and-frisk. Farrell set it up with the Eighth."

"You're on overtime now, right?"

This stopped Kennedy for a second.

"Yes—yeah, I am. I mean, I will be . . ."

"Look Eddie, forget the canvass. After you've—"

"Forget the canvass! Lieutenant, why the—"

"Hey, Kennedy! I said fuck the canvass. A canvass is definitely contraindicated now and . . ."

Contraindicated! Where in the name of God had Bruno rooted out a word like *contraindicated*?

". . . and I do not want a canvass done this tour. That's the name of *that* game, Eddie! I don't want a bunch of hairbags from the Eighth stepping all over the territory and fucking things up!"

"What things, Lieutenant?" Not a wise question, but this case had its hook in Kennedy. He could feel it with his tongue.

"What? Well, you know, just generally jerking it over. You been on since oh-six-hundred hours. I say you get a statement from the kid's mother and then you go home. You get anywhere with the Adeline Muro case?"

Kennedy supressed a snarl. How the hell could he get anywhere with the Adeline Muro rape-homicide when Stokovich had hammered him into this recent thing and kept him at it all day?

"Not a lot, sir. You put me on to this one. I put a citywide out on her husband's cousin, the kid they were calling Mokie? But so far zip. I figure we'll have to go on the street for him. I'd like to shake The Ratboy on this one. He owes us. But I haven't gotten on to him yet."

"Excuses, Eddie. I'm hearing excuses. That's not like you, buddy. You running down or what? You just haul ass over to mama's and get something definite going about your little stiffie this morning. *Com-pren-day, amigo?*"

Yeah, thought Kennedy. I *comprende* just fine.

"Yes, sir. I'll do that. See you tomorrow. Sir."

A street crew was playing a game of slam-dunk on Avenue D when Kennedy and Maksins pulled into the block off Houston Street. A runner who'd been sitting on the steps of the Scorpio Tavern at Houston and C kept ahead of them all the way into Alphabet City, jinking and zagging off the right fender of the Chrysler, his wiry black body pumping away at the pedals of a Blue Max BMX bicycle, the slanting sun catching lights in his afro. Every now and then he'd turn around and flash a mouth full of large white teeth in their direction. Maksins smiled back at him. Nothing bothered Maksins.

Maksins had only one problem, and there wasn't one damned thing he could do about that: his dubious sergeant's rank. It left him in a kind of no man's land inside the NYPD. How do you act like a sergeant, providing leadership, *using* your rank, when some judge at State might take the whole thing away from you without notice? Then where are you? The whole concept of a sergeant who wasn't a sergeant even though he'd earned his rank made Wolfgar Maksins' teeth hurt. It also made him hate the blacks just a little bit more than usual. Kennedy could feel him smiling at the small black child riding dangerously close to the detective's car. He could see the way the smile tugged at Wolfgar's cheeks but failed to get into his eyes. Maybe it was just as well Kennedy was at the wheel.

The Jacob Riis Houses stood in a windblown lot pegged with spindly elms, set off from the potholed street and the shattered sidewalks by a low wire fence. The project was a large one, a massive mud-colored brick pile about seventeen stories high. Most of the lower floors had bars or chicken wire over the windows. The doorway and the lobby were covered with pitted white tile, to make it easier to clean off the spray paint. The double-glass doors had three locks, all broken. One of the heavy glass panels had been kicked in again. It was now covered with plywood.

About a hundred people of all ages, blacks and Hispanics mostly, were strolling or loitering on the block. Few of them gave any sign at all that they recognized the squad car, and no one missed their arrival. A few young black males emerged from a low burned-out building in the middle of the block opposite the project. They took up positions along the graffiti-coated walls, folding their heavy arms, talking softly among themselves, closing up their faces, and missing nothing.

Kennedy parked the car right in front of the walkway and let Central know where they were. He reached under the dash to flick the carburetor shut-off, triggered the alarm system, and felt for his ankle gun out of habit. It was there, a smooth little Smith & Wesson Bodyguard Airweight with a shrouded hammer. A friend of Kennedy's, a retired detective by the name of Eddie Condon, now running a bar called Metropolitan Improvement next to the Headquarters building, had once snagged his ankle gun on a sock during a hostage incident. The snag had almost killed him. Kennedy had bought the Airweight the day after he heard this story.

Wolfgar Maksins extricated himself from the passenger seat, keeping an eye on the far side of the street. Somebody called out something and Maksins raised his right hand, middle finger upright, and hooked his balls with his left hand.

"Goddamit, Wolf, don't do that shit! I've had a long day."

Maksins completed the gesture and turned to face Kennedy, baring a row of even white teeth in a humorless grin and looking past Kennedy to the project door.

"Fuck the jigs, Eddie. Fuck them all."

"Thank you, Wolf. Thank you for your constructive attitude. Shall we?"

Maksins walked a little behind Kennedy, to his left. His suit jacket was unbuttoned. Nothing would have made Wolf Maksins happier than to have one of the citizens standing nearby flash a weapon and make an ugly face. Maksins was an International Practical Shooting Competitions champion, a machinelike executioner up at Rodman's Neck. His off-duty gun was a Browning. Kennedy had seen him put nine rounds into the ten ring at fifty yards in under six seconds. Tell the truth, Kennedy found Maksins just a little scary.

The lobby emptied out as the detectives walked in. Young girls in sprayed-on tank tops stared boldly at them and hit hard on their heels as they walked by, making their heavy breasts bounce under the fabric, calling them assholes in soft Cuban Spanish, calling them faggots in black Swain talk. The elevator, miraculously, was working. Kennedy didn't like elevators. Cops had died in elevators. Gang kids in Harlem liked to ride on top of the cars. Now and then a couple of patrolmen would look up and find a sawed-off shotgun sticking down through the trapdoor, somebody laughing behind it, strung out on speed or blacktar heroin, giving the cops a few seconds to savor the moment before he fired. Once, in the Bronx, it had been a Molotov cocktail. In a way Kennedy was glad when the dented panel slid back and they saw the fresh pile of human shit steaming in the left rear corner. They took the stairs up to Mrs. Ruiz's apartment on the fifth floor.

The hallway smelled of spices, grass, urine, and stale overheated air. All the light bulbs were guarded by little mesh screens. The walls were marked up and scuffed. Gang codes were sprayed

over everything, even the doors. Yet there was music coming
from some of the places. Al Roker's voice was booming out of a TV
from behind one of the doors. Storm Field was talking down the
hall. Television was stitching the nation back together again this
afternoon. Kennedy stood in front of number 556 for ten seconds,
resisting a wave of fatigue.

Maksins watched him for a moment; his brush-cut spikes scraped
a light bulb overhead, and his pale-blue eyes were empty. He
looks like somebody, thought Kennedy. Who?

His arms and legs were leaden. All he wanted was sleep.
Rutger Hauer's name came to Kennedy as he rang the bell.

Esmerelda Ruiz couldn't have been older than thirty. She
had the oval face and black coral eyes of a South American Indian,
long shining black hair and a narrow waist above well-thought-out
hips and strong muscular legs. Her breasts were heavy under the
frilly purple party dress. It took Kennedy a few seconds to realize
that Mrs. Ruiz had dressed for them, for company. Her eyes were
flat and dry, her lips tightly held, little cut-lines and creases
marking the flesh. A pair of votive candles was burning on a table
behind her, in front of an icon of the Virgin of Guadaloupe. White
feathers were scattered around the candles. She stood in the
doorway while the hot air poured out around her hips, fluttered
her skirt, and rolled over Kennedy's wrists and hands. Music was
coming from somewhere in a back room, and there was the sound
of soft, desolate crying, the catch-and-gasp crying of a small child
who hopes that pity will be felt and the punishment softened.
Bare pieces of furniture stood here and there in the appearance of
order. The floor had been swept. An aged man sat in an emerald-
green crushed-velvet wingback with his hands crossed over his
sunken lap. His baggy black trousers had caught on the velvet
when he had sat down, exposing a pair of twiglike calves coated in
black hair. He had no socks on, but his heavy black shoes were
gleaming and his head was up, showing emaciated features cut out
of a rough block of teak by a blunt instrument in a skilled hand.
He wore a guayabera shirt of pale green. In his hand he held a
portrait, framed in cheap laquered wood, of Porfirio Magdalena
Ruiz. Esmerelda Ruiz did not cry then, although from time to
time her deep-set eyes would shine more clearly in the afternoon
light, and it would appear to Kennedy that the ridges and creases

around her mouth would soften and waver, as if something insubstantial but palpable had been drawn across her skin by an invisible hand.

Perhaps because there was nothing in the hot little room that looked strong enough to take his weight, Maksins moved quietly across it to the window and put a hip against the ledge. His face was closed and set, expecting lies. The old man paid him no attention at all, but there was something other than grief in the room: a guardedness, a reserve.

Kennedy put his badge away and set his face into sympathetic lines. Leaning forward, he held the photo that Stradazzi had given him. Mrs. Ruiz did not watch his hand until the snapshot flipped upright about a yard from her face. Then only her eyes moved, as if to move anything else would tear something delicate.

"Ma'am, you were into the station asking after your boy? Porfirio? That right?"

Her head came forward and back, once, in slow time.

"And this is a picture of that boy? Your boy?"

"Si." Her voice was soft and high.

"Ma'am, have you got someone in the building who can come and take care of things for you for a while? I think I'm going to have to ask you to come uptown for a bit. I think you're going to have to be pretty strong about this, ma'am. We think your boy may have gotten into some very bad trouble."

"Salto is dead, yes?"

Maksins sighed from the window and Kennedy gave him a hard look, softening as he turned back to Mrs. Ruiz. What the hell could he do?

"It looks as if that may be, ma'am. I hope it isn't your boy, but we do have someone who looks very much like him. Is there someone around who can take care of things?"

The old man in the wingback spoke up in a clear unwavering voice. "She will not go with you. I will do that. There is no need for her to see this. 'Stá bien, niña?"

"Bien, papá. Señor, this boy you have, it is ver' bad, the way he looks? It is bad?"

Kennedy didn't look over at Wolf. Before he could answer her, Maksins stepped away from the window.

"Ma'am, you have any idea where your boy has been in the

past couple of days? When was the last time you saw him? Who was he with?"

"I tell them this at the station, señor."

Kennedy interrupted. "Yes, ma'am. But we need to go over it again. We understand he was a stock boy at the grocery? Los Hermanos? Was he working there Sunday?"

"Yes, señor. He was suppose' to be helping them with a truck. But he was goin' to church first."

"So the last you saw him, he was going to the church? Which one was that, ma'am?"

"Mission Evangelica y Bautista. On East Eighth Street?"

"We know the one, ma'am. Did he go alone? Did he usually meet anyone? Did someone go with him?"

There was a long silent moment here. Her control was solid and deep. There would be no scene in front of the *policía*. But the softness left her face and there was a colder light coming from her. She looked down at her hands. Kennedy got the feeling that she was fighting an emotion other than grief. He guessed it was shame.

"Ma'am, did he go to the mission? Was he telling you the truth? Is that where he went?"

"No. He was with that *puta*. The whore."

Puta was said in a breathy explosion. Her face closed up tighter.

"He went with a *puta*, ma'am? A girl? Do you know this girl's name?"

"*Si*. She is a *locita* from Salvador. *Papá—Aiuda me! La nombre, favor?*"

"Wangermann y Buentella. Nadine, *una caballera negra*."

Kennedy was taking this down. "You say her name is Wangermann y Buentella? Long black hair? You know where she lives, sir?" This was directed at the grandfather.

The man started to say something, but his daughter broke in, leaning forward out of the chair, looking down at the floor, throwing a rosary at her feet.

"*A cuestas, señor! A cuestas!*"

"*Si, señora. Lo siento.* But where does she live on her back? Do you know?"

"In the street, señor. And I have seen her at the Caamanos."

She got up then, and stood for a moment in the center of the room, passing through levels of grief and rage, twisting on the spike of it. The old man sat and watched her like an obsidian idol, with no kindness in his face. She walked over to him and took the framed picture out of his arthritic hands easily, although he tried to keep it.

She came back to Kennedy and dropped the picture at his feet.

Carefully, with deliberation, she put a foot on the picture, a small bare brown foot with a hard callused ridge on the edge, her toes spread out over her son's face.

"*Diablito, señor*. Drugs and *putas*. Does he have a small . . . *lágrima* . . . you know what I mean?"

"A tear? Yes, ma'am. On his cheek. A tattoo."

"*Una lágrima. Si.* So I don' give him another one, okay?"

She put her weight forward onto the glass, cracking it and crushing the picture beneath.

Formal identifications at the Medical Examiner's office on the East Side are usually done in a special room. Few people want to stand in the same room with what may be left of a father or a lover. Arturo Rimbaldo waited in silence before the glass wall in the elevator room, a short frail packet of dry wood inside his starched guayabera shirt, waiting without expectancy, saying nothing to Kennedy while the attendant downstairs prepared the corpse of Porfirio Ruiz. An elevator motor whined. The body rose into view.

Kennedy watched Esmerelda Ruiz's father as he studied the image behind the glass. Two full minutes passed in this way, the old man quietly studying the face of his grandson, thinking God-knew-what behind that absolutely immobile face. Kennedy looked over the man's head at the face on the other side. Marcuse had done a decent job of reshaping the basic features, but there was something slightly out of register about it, a wrongness to it. Kennedy finally realized that the wrongness came from the fact that although the face was the same, the act of shaping it with fingers could never make it the same as a face showing real emotion, even the open blank shock that Kennedy saw from time to time, the face that came to a victim when he realized he was dying, that it was over.

Rimbaldo finally turned to Kennedy and said, in careful diction, not wishing to be misunderstood by this alien cop, not wishing to be in his debt even for the price of a moment's toleration: "Where is Salto? *A donde?*"

Kennedy knew what he meant, what he wanted. But he tried to turn it aside. "That's not your grandson, sir?"

The eyes in the weathered brown face were yellow and sunken in the skull, taxidermic eyes, shining like plastic buttons stitched in place.

"Perhaps. Let me touch him."

What was the point? They walked down the hall to the elevator and rode downstairs and Kennedy showed him what was left of his Porfirio Magdalena Ruiz.

"Yes, señor," said the old man. "That is Salto. That's my daughter's boy." He stood that way for a long time, inches away from the trolley, his hands half-raised either to touch the body or to fend something off.

There was a form to sign. He waved away the yellow Bic that Kennedy handed him, reaching instead into a pocket of his oversize black suit pants to find an old Parker fountain pen in emerald-green lucite. The pen had a gold nib, as clean as a scalpel, and when the man put it to the form, rich black ink flowed seamlessly and thickly from the nib. The old man wrote the characters of his name in full, in a stylized hand, certain and steady and without hesitation. When Kennedy took the forms away he could see that the signature floated above the dotted line and that even where a downstroke had required the man to cross the green line, it was done quickly, in a cutting slash, the nib rising again to the name. No quarter, thought Kennedy. Like Santa Ana at the Alamo. Play the De Guello and give them no quarter. The old man must be a son of a bitch to live with. A man like Kennedy's own father. How he must have ridden the boy. What it was like to be a child in this man's house, it was too late to ask.

It was full dark by the time they got back to the Riis Houses to let the grandfather out at the curb. Reedy music was coming from a store across the street. Overhead the city glowed smoky orange. Cars were racing down the FDR on the far side of the project lot. Kids were playing in the street. Maksins and Kennedy watched him walk slowly up the path toward the gritty doorway.

"Hard-nosed little fucker, eh, Eddie?"

Kennedy looked across at Maksins.

"Yeah. He is. What time is it?"

Maksins held his watch up to the light coming from the store across the street. "Twenty hundred hours, my son. A little after. Monday night, Budweiser time."

"You don't want to chase down this little hooker? This Nadine number?"

Maksins smiled over at Kennedy. "Kennedy. You been on since six this morning! You look like forty miles of bad road. You want to fuck up those nifty new Florsheims of yours, climbing around in every wet basement and every pond-scum hotel in Alphabet City, in the goddam *dark* yet, well then, you just run along and *do* that! Me, I've got eight hours loose before the wife gets off the evening shift, and if I don't have a cold beer in this mitt before the little hand gets to the six, I'm going to hold you responsible. Besides, all your finks are still out looking to score. You won't get anything tonight. Give it a break, okay? The kid'll still be dead in the morning."

Kennedy was thinking about his apartment. Even Dudley would be out somewhere raising a little hell.

"Who's on tonight? Kolchinski?"

"Yeah, but he's on that Angel bust. They're supposed to bag a material witness sometime tonight. Leave the sheet on the peg. One of the night guys can drive around, try to get a line on this broad. Enough's enough, Eddie."

He's right, said Kennedy to himself. What's the problem here? You don't want to go home, get some sleep?

No. He didn't. He realized he was rubbing the place on his leg where the spike had gone in.

"Yeah, Wolfie. Okay. It's Miller time, hah?"

Wolfie laughed once, staring out the side window at four black males in do-rag head scarves, old clothes. Two of the boys were carrying cheap plaid lumberjack shirts. A third youth was flipping a ragged vest over his back.

"Check it out, Eddie. It's street-crew time. Check out the throwaways."

Kennedy leaned over to get a better look at the group. He could see the shirts in their hands. The shirts went on before a mugging and came off right after. It helped to screw up the pursuit. It changed the description. Throwaways always marked a

crew of muggers, usually heading out for the midtown area, looking for victims.

Maksins watched them turn the corner. "You want to fuck
them up a little, Eddie? Bet you the first drink they got their tools
on them."

"What are you, Citywide Street Crime? I thought you were
thirsty. Now you want to dance some niggers around?"

Maksins turned back to Kennedy and grinned.

"Yeah, Eddie. I do."

"Wolfie, you gonna bounce every nigger in town? Your attitude sucks, buddy."

Maksins turned away and looked down the street where the
crew had disappeared. He was thinking that the city was full of
street crews looking for trouble.

"You like to fuck them around, don't you, Wolfie?"

"Yeah, Eddie. It's what I do best. Come on. The little hand is
almost on the six and I don't see a beer in this car. I don't get a
beer soon, something terrible happens."

"You're a weird fucker, Wolfie."

"I'll drink to that."

CHAPTER 5

BLOODS

Krush and Jimmy Jee went over the turnstile at the 116th Street entrance to the downtown IND like a pair of Dobermans, squeezing by the doors of the last car just as the train started rolling. The aging black in the bulletproof cage never even looked up.

There was a Transit cop in the car, a Latin kid. He saw them come over the rail and it was his job to do something about that, but he was a "cream" in a car full of home boys and bloods from the black projects around Morningside Heights. He kept his mouth shut and settled for a hard look at Krush and Jimmy.

Jimmy was weighty, short and muscular, with bad skin the texture and color of quarry clay, but Krush was something else. He was lean and hard-looking; like so many of the street blacks up in Harlem he had that special glow, the light of a Burundi or a Bantu from East Africa. They had chiseled faces and long necks and a graceful syncopated way of going; they had a kind of amber halo about them, and skin with the tint of blue smoke. Krush knew he was good-looking, but good looks had been a problem in Rikers, getting him "maytagged" at least eight times before he got old enough and fast enough to cause some pain in the process, and he had hooked up with Jimmy on his last tour in the prison, partly because Jimmy was, at fifteen, too mean to bother, even for the roughest. Not that Jimmy hadn't been maytagged as well, once or twice. The trick was to make the trade-off of sex for blood too irritating. Since Krush's last stay at Rikers he and Jimmy had formed an "association." Jimmy had the moves and Krush had the judgment.

This far down the line it was still home country. There were no "poppy loves" or "vics" in the car, no white people at all, but by the time the train got down past 86th Street the magical transformation had begun. "Heads" and "poppy loves" and assorted victims were appearing here and there against the wall of black skin like little popcorn puffs in a skillet. Krush and Jimmy Jee could feel a heat in their chests, a sick joy with no bottom.

"Be gettin' busy, my man," said Jimmy, just to hear his voice. Krush smiled at a pair of white girls in matching Daniel Hechter sweatshirts.

"Word up, fool. We be fresh tonight." *Fresh* meant well-dressed, the only path to respect back in the housing project they lived in. *Fresh* was new jeans or a suit of clothes, maybe a gold tooth. Swatch watches, Gucci loafers, a sweater from Perry Ellis; neither of them looked any further than that. The way to get those things, Krush and Jimmy had decided two years back, was to get out on the streets of Manhattan and take the money. There was an expression on the streets at the time: "Manhattan make it and Brooklyn take it"—or Queens, or Harlem. The point was, as Krush said so often it had become a kind of incantation for Jimmy Jee: "You better take it, 'cause they sure ain't goin' to give you none!" They called their work "fiending the heads."

The pair wasn't fresh yet. Krush was wearing faded Levis, still muddy from this afternoon's stickball game, a gray sweatshirt with the hood up over his head, and a pair of Reeboks he'd taken from a kid who'd come into the projects from East Harlem to buy heroin from Krush's older brother. Jimmy Jee had a do-rag on, a kind of pirate head-scarf pulled tight around his city curls; a white T-shirt stretched over his chest; jeans, and white sneakers. Both kids were carrying about a dollar in change and a pair of "throwaways."

They got off the train at the 42nd Street station and walked up the filthy stairs to Eighth Avenue in a crush of Monday-night daters. Out on The Deuce there were ten thousand people milling about a mile-square area full of fry shops, porno parlors, head shops, electronic stores, clubs, bars, theaters, bookshops. Between Sixth and Eighth, 42nd Street is brighter than Vegas, a million candlepower of pinlights and strobes pulsing and fluttering through smog and smoke from a thousand cars and buses. It's a permanent honky-tonk fantasy. Krush and Jimmy Jee had to turn down three offers of cocaine and six bargain-rate blow jobs from assorted transvestites before they got twenty yards along the littered sidewalk. They strolled across the asphalt and potholes of Eighth Avenue to a pretzel vendor in front of the Port Authority Bus Terminal. He gave them a couple of charred pretzels and a can of Dr. Pepper just for good will. Krush and Jimmy never even had to push him. It was always that easy.

Around the time that Krush and Jimmy were chipping away at their pretzels, and Wolfie Maksins was putting away his third beer at Jackson Hole on Third at 36th, a business major from Buffalo, second year and a B average, by the name of Jamie Spiegel was closing the door to room 1445 at an aging midtown hotel on Broadway. Jamie was supposed to be on a train for Wilmington, Delaware, but he'd danced the schedule around enough to free up a week in Manhattan. He was twenty-one, slightly overweight, and he'd postponed this experience long enough. First a couple of hard-core flicks at something like the Pussycat, then a live sex show up at a place he'd read about in *Screw,* and then a few bucks dropped at one of those private-viewing video booths in the basement at the Show World Center. He was taking a roll of the hotel toilet paper. What the hell. So he was sick. Jamie bathed for an hour in hotel shampoo, splashed Blue Stratos all over his pale body, and bought himself a twelve-pack of ribbed condoms. After killing a six-pack of Kronenbourg that he'd smuggled past the concierge (hotel beer was three bucks a bottle!), he was ready for the sleazoid delights of 42nd Street. He sure as hell hoped it was ready for him. Jamie split up his money, shoving two hundred under a loose corner of the wall-to-wall in the hall closet. (A maid found this a week later when she came in to clean. She laughed when she saw it, since she'd loosened the corner herself. She thought of it as her trap-line, and it came up with something for the kitty at least once a month. Jamie had other problems by that time, anyway.) He put the remaining one hundred into two flat packets. One packet went into his Bass loafers, under the foam insole. The other went into the right-hand pocket of his Calvin Klein jeans, where it made a nice neat little outline as the thin denim fabric stretched over Jamie's soft thigh.

"Diamond season?" said Jimmy. Krush looked over his shoulder at the chubby Jew talking to a uniform cop up at the corner of Eighth and 46th. The Jew was Hasidic, an obvious victim down in this area. He had the black felt homburg, the temple curls. Krush looked for "pocket prints," signs that the man was carrying a fat wallet or a gun; many of the merchants from the diamond district on West 47th Street had carry permits. Diamonds got traded on a handshake and a family name, carted in Baggies across the street, like peanut butter sandwiches, between scruffy little third-floor shops and basement vaults; more money on the street in any afternoon than Amsterdam or Zurich. Diamond season.

"You be in crime two year and you don' know no DT when you be seein' him. He knock you so fast you be bleedin' in The Great Adventure before you say please mister postman!" Krush sometimes felt like giving up on Jimmy Jee. Man was a mope and no mistake. But strong. Jimmy still didn't get it.

"He be a vic, man!" Jimmy's voice always got shrill when he was angry, way up there in the high notes, like a bird. Krush thought of Jimmy as Birdman because of this voice. "You be jivin' me, man. That's my poppy love and he be goin this night!"

"Ain't no hymie poppy love be on The Deuce Monday night, fool! He be home in Mount Vernon with his fat lady and his VCR, watching his fucking hymie cartoons. Jewboy be on the rag ever' Monday, man. Ain't no Jewboy that, and that ain't no vic. That be a DT, so shut the fuck up!"

Krush watched Jimmy think this one through but he kept an eye on the chubby man in the dark suit. Something was telling him right here that the man was a detective, but he couldn't say just what. The mark strolled away up Eighth. Krush watched his ankles. Big heavy black shoes. Maybe at the curb. Just before the man stepped off to cross 47th, Krush caught a flash of buckle and belt under the man's right cuff. A DT all right. So The Man was on The Deuce tonight. Krush thought about the pretzel vendor they'd put the moves on; The Man loved those pretzel carts. All over town Krush had seen pretzel men by their pushcarts with their wires hanging out their dumb-ass cuffs and their fucking guns shoved into the steamer. Krush's older brother—now *there* was a master, good old Duke of Destruction himself—he once saw the man working his stupid pretzel-cart number outside a shooting gallery on 125th Street. The Duke had pulled in a crew and they'd taken the pushcart cop like the Russian cavalry. Con Ed truck on the corner tried to follow and two of the Duke's boys had spray-painted the windows. The Con Ed truck had gone through the front of a check-cashing parlor, spilling plainclothes cops like fleas off a rat. The Duke came home with a gold shield, an NYPD ID card, a Smith & Wesson Model 10 .38 Special, *and* the DT's drop gun, a Llama .32 with masking tape on the handles. The event had made The Duke from the Heights to Drew Hamilton Houses.

Krush liked to stop thinking about The Duke at this point. The rest of the story was sort of a downer. The Duke had hit the wrong clubhouse on a rip-off scam last February and Krush had found him in the airshaft behind their block on 118th Street at Manhattan. Somebody had given him a "necktie." His throat had been cut just wide enough and deep enough to allow his killer to reach up inside and pull the thick muscle of his tongue out through the wound. They left it hanging down over the bloody shirt. Krush had been looking for him for two days. He never told his mother just exactly how the boy had died. A uniform sergeant from the 31st had shown her the pictures a week later, trying to get some information about Krush. This man was marked down in Krush's book. Jimmy was poking him again.

"Word up, Mister K. Got us some fine white pussy up the street." Jimmy pulled Krush into the dark of a closed storefront. They had reached 55th, the northern limit of their hunting ground. If they hit nothing good this far north they'd cross to Broadway and go down toward The Deuce again. There were fewer people on the street up here. It was a dead area in between the action on 42nd and the café scene up above Columbus Circle on the West Side. Krush stood in the doorway for a moment, trying to figure out what Jimmy was talking about. There was movement inside a cigar store across the street. A woman in a scarlet cloth coat was paying for cigarettes at the counter. Even from this distance, close to sixty feet, Jimmy had seen the gold bangle on her wrist as it caught the light inside the store. Out on the street a car was idling at the curb. The woman was still talking to the store clerk. It looked like there was no one in the Buick.

"I be on it, man. That's gold. That's a stack. Check it out, man." Krush had some misgivings. Well, the job had its risks, right?

Eighth was fairly thick with cars, but the shops up here had their iron down, slatted flexible-steel grates that rolled down over the entire front of the store. They were secured by case-hardened padlocks. In the midtown area, entire city blocks could turn into a canyon of grated steel fronts. It had been years since New York had stayed open all night. Here and there a local store catered to people from the brownstones. Sometimes Krush and Jimmy simply waited in the dark across from a neighborhood deli—a parallel to jungle cats at a watering hole that had not escaped Krush's vivid imagination.

"Jimmy, man. That's a vic. Let's go." Jimmy nodded once. Krush got a look at his heavy face in the glow of the streetlights. He was a little wide around the eyes, and his throat was working. He could have been stoned, frightened, or thinking about rape. Thinking about spreading some fine white legs and getting some of that uptown honey on his fingers. Krush could feel his crotch warming up, and his belly got numb.

"Shit, man. Get paid and get pussy too." Jimmy was a pace in front, bracing to rush the woman as soon as she came out of the store, take her in a storm of boots and fists, knock her to the ground and rip that gold away. Krush had to jerk his shoulder once, twice.

The routine was a classic purse snatch, with some assault thrown in, the idea being to stay on the vic no longer than fifteen, maybe twenty seconds. Get paid and get laid but don't get made, that was the creed. But the idling Buick had given Krush an idea. If the doors were unlocked?

"Yo, Jimmy. Wait. We goin' now, get into the bitch's wheels. Be *inside* when she get out. Give her a *time*, man. Maybe even score her keys, cards. Shit! Have us a party up in some fucking penthouse way *up* there, man!"

Jimmy and Krush had never been in a white woman's home, at least not when the owner had been there. Even then, the kind of places they could take were mostly transitional brownstones in the West 70's or 80's, and once they'd gotten by the doorman in a building on 38th Street near the heliport. But they had fantasies about white money and white women, about apartments as big as the mess hall at Spofford, all covered in white furs and white marble, with white drapes that moved back as silent and smooth as a blade through table cream. And beyond the window there it *was:* the whole *n chee lah dah,* as Jimmy put it, maybe a look at Manhattan from Central Park West with that big square box of the park, a black hole cut right out of the core of the city. Krush used to lie down on the roof on the nights when his mother had men in and imagine the way the lights of the buildings all around Central Park would reflect off the waters of Harlem Lake and the reservoir at night. Everything would be black and those lights in the water would glitter. He'd be on the balcony and he'd have one of those big round glasses in his hand. Live like he was *meant* to live, like it was in *Ebony,* be a sleek black man in a white apartment.

He thought about this all the way across the street, watching the woman argue with the clerk. Was this a trap? Was this *too* good? He thought it could be, but sometimes you had to take chances. Jimmy ran ahead a step, too anxious. Krush moved up and they made the streetside of the burgundy Buick together. Jimmy turned to cover the street. Krush got a hand on the latch and tugged it. Something huge flew up at the window from the dark interior of the car. Eighty pounds of dog crashed against the glass. The car rocked, and even through the Detroit glass Krush and Jimmy could hear the yammering of the thing. It dropped away and launched itself at the window again, droplets scattering on the glass. Jimmy stumbled back into the street. Headlights caught him in a glare and now the sound of rubber was louder than that crazy motherfucking dog. Krush was still holding the door, not tugging it, not thinking anything right now. He was fascinated by that *thing* in the car. It was every man's nightmare out of the basements, out of every dark alley and every ruined building. Nothing to see of it but those goddam yellow eyes and the spit running, and those teeth coming out of all that pink wet mouth, teeth like whale ribs on a shore, like fucking dinosaur ribs. The car jerked again as the dog hit the window. Jimmy came back to Krush and literally ripped him away from the car as the whole street came alive with horns and cabbies yelling. Krush let Jimmy pull him away from the Buick, and as they stumbled back across the street Krush could see that white bitch in the store, the gold heavy on her wrist, shining in the light; he couldn't believe it—the white bitch was waving at him. Bye-bye, she was waving, and she had a smile on worse than her fucking dog. New York women, he thought. Strange bitches. Jimmy dragged him around the corner onto 55th, into the darkness of the cross street. Jimmy was half-crying, half-laughing, still racing away down the street with Krush loping along behind him, being hauled away like a blind man. Krush could think of only one thing.

"Man," he kept saying to himself, "gonna get *me* a pet too!"

Jamie sat in the audience at the Pussycat Theater on Seventh Avenue like a Saul struck by God on the road to Damascus, a man confronted by a revelation. There was nothing in Buffalo—there was nothing on the planet—that could get a business major ready for something like this. All around him, in witless raptures, sat other men, black guys, white guys. Jamie could see a Chinese guy a few seats away and it came to him as a kind of jolt that even Chinese guys liked to look at pussy. It gave Jamie a nice feeling. There's hope for the world, he thought, when men of all races can sit down together and ogle some pussy. And what pussy this was: twenty feet wide in living color and Dolby stereo, looking for all the world like the entrance to paradise complete with gates of wrought-gold and copper and an endless vision of soft pink clouds billowing away to a flush of deepest rose. Like a sunset, thought Jamie Spiegel; blond pussy is like a sunset in heaven. All around him the men in the room stared at the screen like prisoners freed, a wet sheen on every forehead, every bottom lip shining too. And the sound? "Like surf," said Jamie, half aloud, into the luminous, flickering dark, as he tugged at his zipper.

Jimmy and Krush ran into some home boys at Broadway and 53rd. There was Ronnie Holloway, a myopic albino who called himself Ahmad Khan on the street. Ahmad Khan? Krush hated that phony Africa Muslim shit. What the fuck was Africa to Krush? His own name, the name his mother called him by, the name his father gave him, was Dennis McEnery, and Krush had a pretty good idea that he wasn't born wherever the McEnerys came from. So it was a slave name, or the name some white man had given his grandmother when she came up to live in Harlem. Krush was his street name down here in The Deuce, and with some of his friends back on 116th Street. He was known by other names in other blocks. Now and then he took the IRT to the Melrose area

of the South Bronx along with some of the bloods from his way.
They'd take out a bodega, or fiend a few housewives shopping
along Third Avenue. On these runs Krush's name was Skate.
Jimmy Jee called himself Velvet. They took names from cartoon
shows, from dimly perceived and distorted versions of black success in America. Krush's brother called himself The Duke because
he thought The Duke of Earl was a black king of Louisiana in the
Civil War. The Civil War was the war where the black soldiers
fought all the cracker sheriffs down in Dixie after a cracker assas-
sin killed Mister Lincoln. Dixie was any place south of Baltimore.
The South, when they thought of it, was a place full of snaggle-
toothed skinny white trash who rode horses across endless fields of
okra and black-eyed peas. They lived in shacks and they all had
guns. They had licenses to hang niggers on the Fourth of July.
The Duke's only friend on the street had given up crime after The
Duke's death and was now making money collecting dollars from
home boys and their mommas to buy a huge black homeland
in Liberia, which Krush had been told was an island in the Pacific
where black men had built a free nation after the Second World
War.

Up in Morningside Heights the older blacks used to sit around
and call Krush Denny-boy and talk to him about what Harlem had
been like when they were kids. The stories were told in soft
voices, the talk going back and forth on slow summer nights when
it was too hot to stay indoors, too hot to sleep. The block would be
full of little kids playing seven-up and soccer in the road. Ladies
would hang out of windows, leaning on blankets, calling to each
other. Somebody would put a radio out on the ledge; they'd tune
it in to a bop station. The notes would go out from roof to roof and
cover the street with a cloak of music. Here and there on the
stoops Dennis could see the glow of cigarettes and pipes being
smoked in the dark. The bottoms of beer bottles would flash in the
streetlights. Older kids would dance under a lamp post. The
people would all come out, even the oldest ones. Everybody
would stroll from stoop to stoop, talking in low voices, telling
stories about who was seeing who, asking what happened to that
kid who used to play the piano at The Palm, and how was your
daddy's heart.

There was a kind of courtliness to it, a civility and grace that
Krush could hardly remember now. People on the street said

"Good evening" and spoke in clear voices. Nobody swore or cursed out in front of the older folks. Kids went and got things, and carried them back without spilling them. Daddies would call out across the street for their kids to leave off that fussing with those cans, you get back here now, you don't want a whipping. And when he went back he could smell pipe smoke from the dark corner of the stair where his uncle always sat, puffing away on a bowl, smoking Old Virginia that came in a red wrapper. The man seemed too old to live but he was still there whenever Krush went home, and the same pipe burned all the way down on the side where he held the match to it, his cheeks going in and out and the smoke coming up in blue clouds. Uncle Ray used to claim that there was a time you could sleep over in Morningside Park, nights it was too hot. The people, they'd just leave the doors open and they'd stroll over around midnight with a sheet or a blanket, up into the low green hills where the grass was still cool. People would spread their blankets and pass around a bottle of brandy or sherry. The married people, or the ones who were going together, they'd go off a little ways, into the darker places, and you could see the lights of their cigarettes and hear their low talk carrying in the quiet. Uncle Ray said sometimes there'd be two hundred people all sleeping around, babies and little children. Uncle Ray said it was summer camp. Krush heard this story often, and every time he heard it he'd listen to it and think, shit, I ain't never gonna get so old I sit around talking dumb shit like this. You go into Morningside Park with a sheet nowadays and the thieves and the faggots would run like hell. Think you be a ghost. Sleep in the park? Leave your door unlocked? Shit.

The little albino who called himself Ahmad Khan was bragging to Jimmy Jee about a hit the boys had just made. Ahmad was a front man for a jostle operation. He could still look like a kid if it was dark enough, although he was nineteen. His crew consisted of two other boys, The Scoop and an asthmatic by the name of Franklyn—called, on the street, Chokes. They had spotted a pair of poppy loves, an older white couple, obvious tourists from one of the hotels, coming out of that dago trap called Mamma Leone's, off Eighth. They were strolling along 48th Street, looking at the marquees for Broadway shows, not paying any attention to the crowds around them. Ahmad had cruised by once, checking them out for gold chains and getting an idea of the woman's grip on her handbag. It was a big leather satchel, still open, and Ahmad had seen a lizard-skin pocketbook inside. Rather than simply fiend the couple, a risky undertaking in the well-lit street, the crew had decided to lift that lizard-skin purse.

Ahmad was the blocker. His job was to get a little in front of the couple as they walked, timing this part just right. He wanted to be two paces ahead of them when they got to the traffic light at the corner. He was too small to be seen as a threat, even if this couple was alert enough to check him out. It was funny how the vics handled themselves on the street. There were more than 40,000 incidents of petty robbery, mugging, and jostling on the streets of New York last year. Yet all the vics figured it would happen to somebody else. They wandered along like people in a daze, never looking hard at the people around them, never thinking ahead. Krush thought they were soft and stupid. They were asking to be hit.

Ahmad had gotten into the blocking position without drawing any suspicion from the poppy loves. Chokes was already in place, across the street on the far side, coming back in Ahmad's direction. The light was red now. Scoop would have gotten close up behind the couple. The hit would take place when the light changed. Only tourists and poppy loves ever stopped to wait for the green. Everybody else in New York paid no attention at all to the color of traffic lights. When the light went green, Ahmad stepped off the curb about one pace in front of the vics. He watched Chokes getting closer. When Chokes was ten feet away, Ahmad faked a trip, catching his toe on a section of asphalt. The vics walked right into him. Ahmad fell flat on his face, striking the road with a flat palm to emphasize the impact. The vics, horrified, got all tangled up with each other, the woman gasping, the man reaching down to help the little black child up. Apologies were everywhere and the man dug into his pocket for a dollar at exactly the moment that Scoop lifted the lizard-skin pocketbook out of the open satchel like a man taking a French fry out of hot oil. Scoop held the thing no more than two seconds. It went into Choke's brown Bloomingdale's bag as he went past. Scoop stepped around the vics and Ahmad. Ahmad was smiling up at the couple, saying no harm had been done. It was his fault. Yeah okay well he could use the dollar and thank you sir. You have a nice day now. The vics walked off thinking they were lucky they hadn't been attacked by a gang of black panthers for assaulting a crippled child. Ahmad, Scoop, and Choke had an American Express Gold Card, seventy-nine dollars, a Connecticut driver's license, a bunch of photos of grandchildren, and, so Ahmad claimed at the top of his shrill street voice, a red rubber condom with ticklers on it.

The crew was going back home to Harlem to get some smoke from Carlos and then they were going over to Lenox to hang out and put the moves on some women. It was always a good idea to get off the street once you'd made a hit. The cops would get the 10-22 pretty soon, and there weren't a lot of crazed nigger albinos out on The Deuce. Cops would stop and frisk anybody who looked "hinky." Getting caught with a Gold Card was a ticket to Central Booking for the night, and then off to Manhattan Criminal, to be released on their own recognizance in the morning. Chokes always got asthma in the tank, so they were getting out now. Ahmad offered the card to Krush for fifty, but Krush had no intention of carrying a stolen card this early in the night. Still, the success of this home crew put a knot in his stomach. Seventy-nine dollars would buy Krush and Jimmy much food. It came into Krush's mind to fiend Ahmad and his crew right here, and he was halfway into a move when a blue-and-white with a pair of jakes pulled up to the curb and called to them. Krush went north; Jimmy went west along 53rd; Ahmad, Chokes, and Scoop went everywhere else. Krush heard later that the jakes had caught Ahmad in a stall at the Show World Center. The black chick in the ticket booth had fingered him to a beat cop when the two jakes in the radio car had put out a call to the whole Midtown South patrol area. Why the hell did the cops work so hard to snag one nigger thief?

By the time Jimmy and Krush hooked up again at their usual spot at the north doors of the Port Authority on 42nd, the fun was going out of the evening. They were getting hungry, they'd been jerked around by a white bitch, and that little yellow fucker had already gotten paid. It was late and somebody was going to give it up fast or bleed.

Jamie Spiegel was getting tired. He had been in and out of every porn shop he could find since the show had ended at the Pussycat. A live sex show up on Eighth had cost him $25. That had been one awful experience, Jamie decided. A bored black man and a skinny white chick had done some pretty athletic things on the stage under one of those ultraviolet lights. The hall was painted black and red, the chairs were sticky, and the place smelled like a basement. Some creature with a bony face and orange lipstick had come up close to Jamie in the dark and run a hand over his crotch, asking him for money, offering to blow him in the seat. The thing had been in a skirt, the thing had breasts—or something like them, since Jamie had been flashed briefly—and it had long hair, but there was too much hair on wrists that were just a little too thick. The voice was wrong too. Jamie had been at a loss for words until the thing had pulled the tank top off and shaken two perfect breasts in his face, reaching deeper into his lap. Jamie felt himself getting hard and was on the brink of saying what the hell when the stage lights came up for intermission and he'd seen the bulge in those transparent bikini panties under the leather skirt. Then he'd pushed the creature away and gotten the hell out. It was laughing at him when he reached the curtain under the red exit sign.

The air out on the street felt as if it had come straight in off the sea. Another one of those things, a white one this time, had caught his wrist outside and asked him when it could have some of that sweet dick. Its arms were scabbed all along the inner forearm, and the eyes, rimmed in dead black, were unfocused and yellow. Jamie wrenched his hand away and stepped back. It called him a faggot motherfucker and turned away to a Spanish-looking hardcase, who had then followed Jamie all the way from 46th Street to 42nd. Jamie had found a couple of beat cops under a marquee featuring a flick called *Hunt Them Down and Kill Them*. The cops told him to stay off the side streets. He knew he had TOURIST PERVO WIMP tattooed on his forehead. He could see the two baby cops thinking about who he was and what he was doing down here. They had their crisp blue hats pushed back on their heads. The one who was twirling his night stick had to be younger than Jamie. They grinned at him and walked away.

Jamie thought how nice it would be to have one of those guns on his belt. He'd go find that greaser and scare the shit out of him. Or the guy would take it away from him and shove it up Jamie's nose. He saw the Show World Center sign on Eighth and headed for the brightly lit store. A black girl who looked like a cheerleader took five bucks from him and gave him a stack of bronze tokens for the video booths.

Down in the basement there were rows and rows of cubicles, like metal lockers, only they were big enough to stand up in. Each booth had a red light over the door, like a signal, to tell you whether the booth was empty or not. A card told you what kind of video short was showing inside. Jamie found something called "Two On One Breakaway," dropped in a token, and stepped inside the metal cabinet. The door had a twist lock, and Jamie felt better when he got his back up against it. The film ran on a panel of aluminum set into the door, and Jamie stood blinking into the projector for thirty seconds, dazed, while two men in Hawaiian shirts shared a woman on his chest. When he realized he was leaning against the screen, he moved away and laughed and started to relax. He had to keep feeding the box tokens or it would shut the film off every five minutes. Where the hell did they find guys built like that? And how could the chick *do* that? It had to be hell on the back muscles. Oh, God! Not both of them at once! Yeah, she was going to give it the old college try. Jamie stood transfixed at the sheer madness of the exercise, when all hell broke loose outside the booth.

Somebody very heavy was running across the floor. Now everybody was yelling at once. Somebody crashed against the door of Jamie's cubicle. It clanged like a breadbox. Jamie jerked open the door and spilled out into the crowded hall. What was it? A raid? There were cops all over the place. Three of them—one beefy number in stripes and two fullback types—were kicking at a booth. Guys were standing around the room. Jamie saw one old man standing in an open door with his slacks rumpled around his feet. The cops got the booth door off. A porn flick played across their blue shirts for a second or two as they reached inside and dragged out a little albino kid.

Shit, he was just a kid. Jamie was going to say something to a cop near him. You didn't bust babies in Buffalo, cop or no. But this was New York. Then Jamie got a good look at the kid and he could see he was right out of control. He came out of the booth kicking and howling. The sergeant tried to put a lock on his thick little arm but the albino's head came around and he clamped down on the man's wrist. Blood came out around those strong white teeth. The cop bellowed and a night stick came out of the tangle. There was a hollow *thwock*, like a rim shot on a snare drum. The albino let go as the stick cracked him across the cheek.

"I got AIDS, you fuckers! You're a dead fucker! I got AIDS and you're a dead pig!" The cops pulled back in a wave and the kid scampered into the press. He got about five yards. He ran right into another night stick. A black policewoman dropped him with a stroke across his shins. He went down in a heap. The rest of the police were on him at once and he was in the bag. All the way up the stairs you could hear him screaming: "I got AIDS, you bastards! You bastards all be dyin', I got AIDS."

On Jamie's back the two guys in the Hawaiian shirts were coming around the clubhouse turn and the woman was tossing her hair. It's time to go home, thought Jamie.

Jimmy and Krush were through casting about in The Deuce, only half serious about making some kind of score. The streets were packed for the midnight shows lined up side by side all along 42nd from Sixth to Seventh. Huge blue limousines, windows as black as marble, were sliding around the corners. The crowds were flowing around Krush and Jimmy, unconsciously giving them a little room. Krush and Jimmy saw them all as a stream of Swatch watches, Vuarnet and Serengeti glasses, Calvin Klein jeans, Guess? jackets, satin and black leather, fourteen-karat gold chains in endless loops around slender necks, faggots with bulging purses, poppy loves and marks and vics staggering along the street dazzled by the lights, heavy with cash, cash, cash, and none of it for them. So *much* fucking gold around. Krush could tell you the price of any car on the street; he knew logos and brand names at fifty yards. He could smell a woman from up the block and could read her scent and know if it was Opium or Tuxedo or Charlie. It told him what she'd have on under the dress and which card she'd carry. Opium and Tuxedo meant black and lacy, and a Gold American Express. Charlie meant Calvin Klein jockey shorts with cutaway thighs and a Citibank Visa.

Here comes another limo, gray and as long as a subway car. Krush and Jimmy used to carry spray cans to mark up the Els back their way. One night they'd taken a dash along Central Park South, holding their spray cans, keeping the buttons down, strafing the people in front of the Essex and the New York Athletic Club, finishing up circling the limos in front of the Plaza like a pair of crazy Apaches whooping and yelling, dashing in and out with those cans spraying lime-green Day-Glo all over the doorman and all over five of those big burgundy Caddies out front. The jakes had chased them on foot all the way down Madison from 60th to 44th. Two of the jakes had been black Uncle Toms, and Krush and Jimmy would slow down and taunt them, come up to the curb and call to them: "Let's *go*, bro! Here we are, shines." At 44th they'd cut over to Third, then down Third to 38th, back to Madison, up, and along 42nd to the entrance to Grand Central at Vanderbilt. They could have run all that whole spring night, shoving the citizens off the sidewalk and kicking at the fruit stands, with the jakes on their tails and the sirens going *yip yip yip* all over the town. Times like that were the best times Krush ever had, times that made his skin burn and little blue thunderbolts jump from his finger tips.

Krush didn't know what was wrong with him tonight. He was dreaming around in the road like a junkie with his head in the sky. Get your mind on business, fool. Take Care of Business is the name of the game. He looked at Jimmy, walking a few steps to the left, dragging his fingers across a store window. A citizen pushed by Krush as he slowed down. Krush smelled Blue Stratos, caught a glimpse of a thick, soft, white neck and a tousle of blue-black curls, and in between the hair and the folded skin, Krush saw a heavy gold link chain.

"Yo, Jimmy! Get over here!" Jimmy came out of his fog and angled through the crowd to Krush. Krush inclined his head eastward along The Deuce. Jimmy picked the target out right away, a glint of gold over a thick neck, a suggestion of softness there, and weight above the hips. Good leather belt buried in flab, new jeans too tight. Bass Weejuns and little white socks. They were moving in seconds.

Jamie was walking quickly, concentrating on not turning around. The air had changed as soon as he got out of the Show World sleaze palace. Maybe he was just tired, but all this porn, it was really a downer. It was all such brainless garbage, badly shot and mindless plots set around the idea that just the sight of a ready cock was enough to turn women into idiots, begging for it, pleading for it, loving whatever the hell you did to them. That was so much garbage, Jamie could vouch for that. The women at school were harder to bring down than an air force jet, and just as likely to fill your ego full of holes if you ran some of that nonsense on them. And the booth films were worse. Pain, bondage, dimwits in leather diapers waving rubber tubing around. The whole damned block ought to be burned out, thought Jamie, and lost in this vision he almost walked right over a tall black kid slowing down in front of him. Jamie dodged but he made solid contact with the kid. He looked away fast as he slid by, just glimpsing a pair of wide eyes and a narrow Arabic nose, a mouth pulled down, something not quite right in the whole impression. Okay, he said to himself. Just keep going and don't make eye contact, you dork. Jamie could feel the boy checking him out. He pulled his shoulders up and tried to convey a mixture of indifference and menace. He failed.

Jimmy was walking faster now, staying on the vic's store-side, sending no physical signals to anyone but trying to weave his way through the people and get a few yards ahead of the kid with the blue curls. Krush had moved up to within six or seven feet and he was giving the vic a thorough going-over.

You look with your soul—The Duke had once explained it to him. Try to feel what's coming off the vic. Is he scared? Is he in shape? Is he a Bernie Goetz, a vic with a gun? Don't want no vic with no gun, do we? Will he take a choke? How? The check list was endless but Krush could run through it in fifteen seconds. . . .

Jimmy paid no attention to these considerations. He had learned to leave the "sizing" to Krush. He coasted on that talent. It wasn't his job. His job was to get in there and throw the choke, put it in solid and put the vic out. And if the vic gave him a problem, that was okay, too, because Jimmy liked to fight. He stayed in shape and he had always found something way down in there he could use.

Jimmy *liked* it, that was the thing. Hitting on some vic was like a night at the shoreline for Jimmy Jee. Fuck over some asshole vic! Pow pow *pow*! The little shitstorm always made him feel *good*. Like coming in your jeans. It was sweet to see them go down, maybe begging. Kick them again and see the face go slack and the pig eyes go all weepy. All *right* now, let's get busy. Jimmy's legs were trembling and his breath was coming in short and sharp.

* * *

Jamie felt nothing but a vague unease. It was an unease he had gotten used to. He had never been a fighter, although he wouldn't back off if there was no way out. But these streets down here . . . the black guys and those crazy Latino dudes, no fat on them, twitchy and jumpy and they looked right at you when you went by. Jamie tried but he just couldn't keep the eye-to-eye stuff going. All he could think about was, what if they want to take you up on it? What're you going to do then, chubby? Jamie had never felt like a chubby little Jewish kid before. He was feeling that way now. Too white, and too Jewish.

He stopped abruptly and stepped into a brightly lit store-front. The windows were packed with cheap watches and Lloyd stereo boom boxes. Oh, yeah, *there's* a treat. Buy one of those little hand zappers with the shock poles. Looks like an electric shaver. Let's see Victor Kiam shave with that sucker. I liked it so much I bought the company! Well, he had sixty dollars. Jamie looked up and saw a heavyset black dude watching him from the curb. As soon as their eyes met in the reflection from the plate glass, the man spun off and disappeared out of the light. Jamie had no idea who he was, but he didn't like it at all. Time to get off the street.

Krush cursed quietly to himself. Jimmy always did something stupid when they were sizing up a vic. There he was, getting in too close and the vic standing in front of glass. The whole street was like a hall of mirrors. You used the glass to keep a vic in sight without being on his case too lean. And you didn't cut off like you'd been goosed if he saw you. Jimmy got himself in the vic's glass and as soon as the kid looked up there was ole Jimmy Jee dancing off into the street so fucking cool. *Ain't nobody here, bro. Be cool.* Jimmy came to a stop five doors up, and now here came a couple of jakes. Krush could see two uniform cops—heavy white guys with serious meat on them—ambling along The Deuce, hats back, no ties, the older one carrying a shitload of breast bars above the tin. Krush knew all about breast bars. The jakes got them for combat, or for thumping bloods in the back of the RMPs. Look at them come, like they owned the whole block, swinging the stick and staring down every black on the street, grinning and talking away. The younger one had a chili dog and he was drip-ping the sauce onto his shirt, talking with his mouth full. The older one was giving Jimmy a hard look. Jimmy's throwaway was stuffed into his back pocket. The jakes knew what *that* was, for sure. *Just be cool, Jimmy.* Krush stood with his back to the sidewalk and strained to see up the block. The vic stepped out, between the cops and Krush, and went right out into the triangle formed by Broadway, Seventh, and 42nd, losing himself in the crowd across the intersection. *We losin' him!*

Jamie's hotel was farther up Broadway, and the way was well lit. He began to feel that he had been acting like an ass. There was no one on his trail. He patted the twenties in his front pocket, and he could feel the roll under his insole; he had cash and he was hungry. Room service was staggering: thirteen bucks for a thin burger and limp lettuce. A Brew 'n Burger came up on his right. It was bright and packed with people. Jamie decided to go in. He felt safer as soon as he went in through the greasy glass doors, and although the restaurant smelled like roasted rooster he found himself a window booth and sat back, sighing. Safe.

Krush and Jimmy watched the mark as he settled into the booth. They watched him as he slipped his jacket off. A gold chain showed in the light as he leaned forward to slip off the sleeves.

"*He* ain' no DT, man!" Jimmy had some doubts about Krush. He wasn't paying attention. Jimmy still didn't think that overweight Jew in the side curls had been a decoy cop, and he felt a thin line of contempt shine through his image of Krush. Boy be losin' his balls.

Krush had already decided that this was the vic. The kid was no detective. He was too scared. Real fear was something the street crews could sense. Fear was what drew them in. If the vic had just once come around with a hard look, made eye-to-eye talk, let the boys know there would be some bleedin', the chances were good that Krush and Jimmy would have passed him by. Not out of respect. It was a simple calculation. A true vic *knew* he was a victim. He was waiting for it, and when it came he knew in his guts that he'd lie down and lick the curbside if only the bad guys would leave him alone. They all fantasized about physical danger. They stood up and cheered for Rambo and Rocky. All Krush and Jimmy had going for them was the bone-deep soul-center knowledge of pain, of hurting, of muscle and weapons. They *knew* this element. No true vic ever did. Krush and Jimmy came across the street and went into the Brew 'n Burger and sat down at the counter with their backs to Jamie. Drive him out into the street. Then do it.

It took a minute but Jamie finally recognised the heavy black guy. He dropped some cash and ran, looking for a cop.

What could they do in the street? Out under the lights? Jamie jogged along toward his hotel, side-stepping the strollers and couples, feeling his weight on the roll in his shoe, worried, scanning the streets for a cop. He got to a call box at the corner of Broadway and 43rd and hit the red buzzer. Then he looked back and saw those two black guys from the restaurant. It was sure as hell the same two who had been near him at the electronic shop. Jamie ran off before the box operator could answer him. The sign on the call box made it clear. Nobody was coming if there was nobody answering. The tinny radio voice was lost in the street noise when it came, but Jamie was already halfway up the block. There had to be cops around! This town was a nightmare, something out of Dante. Jamie decided to lose those guys. He dodged around a cab, cut across the traffic on Broadway, and went down an alley between 44th and 45th. Out of the light, he put on some speed. There was a channel between a theater and a hotel, a row of Dumpsters. He raced up the channel. There was a line of yellow cabs outside a theater up ahead on 46th. Get a cab and get out. Take the goddam cab all the way to Buffalo. He looked back over his shoulder and there was no one there. He was almost out of the alley. Three people were climbing into a cab no more than thirty feet ahead. Where the hell are the cops? A woman was looking at him now, watching him run toward the cab. She looked frightened. Wait up, thought Jamie. Wait the fuck up! The woman was staring right at him. He didn't know that he was just a running silhouette in the alley. He raised a hand. Wait the—

Jimmy had the vic by the throat; one thickly muscled arm was all it took. He plucked the kid off his feet and jerked him into the dark. Krush stuck his head out for a look up and down the alley. Up at 46th a woman in a cab was looking their way, her mouth open. The cab accelerated in a dusty cloud and was gone. Down the lane there was nothing. When Krush looked back, there was something wrong with the picture. He tried to make it fit for a full

three seconds. Jimmy was supposed to be behind the kid, choking
him with a forearm, holding onto his left bicep with his right
hand, shoving the back of the vic's head with his left hand. Five
seconds of that and they always went down. So why were there
two black shapes a foot apart? For one chilled second Krush had a
tremor of doubt. Was this a DT? Was there a gun? Then he heard
Jimmy's voice.

"Say, bro. Got us a hymie cocksucker here, ain't we, dickhead?
Ain't we?"

What the hell was Jimmy doing? Krush stepped back into the
doorway. Jimmy had one hand on the vic's chest. The other hand
was holding a butterfly knife with bone handles. What the fuck?

"What you be doin', fool!" Krush knew Jimmy carried a tool
sometimes, a screwdriver or a sock full of sand. But the jakes
hated knives. If they caught you with one on The Deuce you were
in for a bad beating, resisting arrest in the cells at Midtown South.
Jimmy had been strange all night, and now Krush could see why.

Jimmy was shivering. He looked away for a second, over at
Krush. "You be losin' yo' balls, man. I say we fuck with this
dickhead a little. He been a real pain in the ass all evening." He
did his trick with the butterfly knife. Thumb off the top horn, flip
the handle arm closed, a wrist flick, snap snap, a circle of steel
flashing, and it was open again. He was going to kill the vic. Krush
knew that.

"My man. . . ." Krush started forward.

"Dickhead!" Jimmy screamed. The knife went in and out; the
vic made a sound like a small stringed instrument. Jimmy brought
a fist around and struck him into the ground. Jimmy Jee went
down on a knee, tugging at the gold chain. Krush was a pace
away. Murder. Endless maytag nights in B block.

Jimmy ripped the pocket away. A deck of bills fluttered out
onto the ground. The vic was wheezing and shaking. Krush got a
brief picture of the last three seconds of his brother's life, maybe
how it had been for him, with the red blood pumping out of The
Duke, his heart thumping and hammering. Murder and the fucking maytag nights. Cuban neckties. Who the fuck was Jimmy, do
this shit to Krush? Who the fuck was the vic, make all this
trouble? And Jimmy? Could he keep his fucking mouth shut?
Could he? Could he?

The vic was trembling all over. A black pool was bubbling out of his shirt front. Krush could see the boy's left hand where it lay stretched out on the ground. The tips of his fingers seemed to glow. Was everything going to pour out of this boy? Would they find him in a lake of black syrup, the way Krush had found his brother?

"Shit, Krush! Krush! Dennis, yo! Wake the fuck up! Are the jakes coming?"

Jimmy had called him Dennis. Where was everything going? He was supposed to be able to do this stuff. He was chilled-out. He could kill! He always knew he could kill. It was supposed to feel good. It came to Krush that his mother would come to court and she'd hear his street name. They'd read her his record and she'd have to look at pictures of the vic lying in his blood. Dennis McEnery, a.k.a. Krush. Jimmy got the vic's pants down. He tugged the jeans over the boy's fat thighs and the underwear came down with it. Oh, sweet Jesus.

"Jewboys got a stack on them. Wearing belts and shit. Where's the stack, Jewboy?" Jimmy's hands were flying over the pale white body, dipping into the pools of blood. Jimmy wrenched a shoe off. A second deck of bills appeared. Jimmy scooped them up and went off at a dead run. Krush stood in the alley, listening to a perfect hollow silence. Murder One. Murder One.

Ten blocks south and seven streets east, Eddie Kennedy, drunk and happy, was climbing into a cab outside the bar. He sang a Ry Cooder song to himself all the way up First Avenue, leaning against the door of the cab, half asleep. Tired enough to sleep well, to sleep the whole night and wake up fine. Go to work, run down this Nadine kid. One thing you could count on was work. There was always some shit going on somewhere in town. Always something for a cop to do. Monday down. Four to go.

The 23rd Street subway platform was almost empty. Krush and Jimmy Jee paid the freight to the lady in the cage and walked all the way down to the far end of the platform, on the watch for Transit cops. There was no talk. They were both pretty winded from the run down from 46th Street. Down at the end of the line Jimmy Jee counted out the cash and a credit card. He kept the heavy gold chain with the little tube-thing on it. Krush took his share in silence. The partnership was over. Would this stupid nigger know how to shut up? Would he talk?

It took a long time for the northbound IND to come along. Jimmy Jee was standing when they both heard it. He was dancing with nerves and excitement, hopping from one foot to the other. Krush could see him working it out in his mind, see him making himself the star. Jimmy Jee would tell every home boy on the block. He was too stupid to shut up about it. Jimmy Jee wanted respect.

The lead car of the train shot out of the tunnel and the air was full of thunder and the shriek of iron wheels braking.

CHAPTER 6

THREE HUNDRED TWENTY-TWO HOURS

At oh-one-hundred-seventeen hours, under a sky as lowdown and greasy-gray as the belly of a sixty-three Dodge, Detective Edward Kennedy developed liquidly out of the curbside door of a Checker taxi and overtipped the bored Chicano driver. He was still humming his Ry Cooder song as the taxi pulled away into the darkness beyond the street lamps. Pissed, thought Kennedy. I am seriously pissed.

Kennedy felt himself called by nature and he gave the problem some slow and ponderous consideration. Okay, first, let's try turning around on the sidewalk so we can find the door to the apartment building. Start with a three-quarter turn to the left. Come on, Eddie. You can do it.

Kennedy raised his right foot and brought it across the scuffed toe of his burgundy Eagle, settling it delicately into a position on the sidewalk approximately four inches past and slightly to the rear of his left foot.

The stance was rapidly degenerating into a slow fall when he heard a voice out of the night air.

"Mr. Kennedy?"

Hell. This was worth a look, even if he was about to fall over. He worked out a decent head-swivel by breaking it down into manageable units, starting with a lateral tug along the horizontal plane of his jaw, which brought his head around some. Next a slight extension of the shoulder to get some leverage on his upper body, followed by a thirty-degree torque at the midsection. This failed to resolve the problem entirely, but it did give him some small satisfaction. He was also rewarded by the intriguing sight of a single pale-yellow eye floating in the air a few inches above a dusty branch of the undernourished elm tree outside Roderigo's Café Reggio.

"You all right, Mr. Kennedy?"

Now wait a minute! What the fuck is this? Kennedy was not a superstitious man, but he'd seen some things in his career that had left him feeling a little uncertain about ghosts and demons, that sort of shit. Now and then, in the Bronx, for instance, he'd seen some voodoo working. Sacrifice killings. Funny blue fires in those empty buildings near the old courthouse, up at Third and 159th Street. Evil *lived*! That was true. But not outside the affairs of men. Or women. Especially women, now that you mention it. Like Trudy. Nice tits, though. *Great* tits, now that we're on the subject. But weird. Very weird.

"You want me to come down, Eddie?"

Christ! He'd forgotten about the vision! See! That's how weird Trudy was. You could be facing the most incredible unbelievable and outrageous magical mysterious phenomenon like this oddly familiar single yellow eye sailing around in the atmosphere and talking directly at him like it had just done again for the third time and *pow* along comes a bizarre piece of work like Trudy the dietician, and *poof* there goes your contemplation of the fucking infinite! A sense of compelling urgency overcame Kennedy. Who knew how long the . . . the . . . manifestation! How long the manifestation would continue. Kennedy was blowing his chance to boldly go where no man had gone before. He might have only seconds to open a path into a new dimension. Talk to it, you asshole! Say something . . . dazzling. Profound.

"So . . . how's it goin'?"

The yellow eye shifted slightly, snapped out of existence for a second, and then reappeared. Suddenly a set of sharp white fangs materialized just below the eye.

"*Rrrroowrr?*"

Despite the heat of the night, Kennedy experienced a pronounced chilling sensation along his spine. The thing had some serious dentistry going on there. There was something in this for Kennedy. We got one yellow eye. We got us some teeth. There's something here just a little familiar.

"Eddie? You look like shit!"

Abuse. Fucking abuse. This ghost, or demon or devil or whatever—it had a nasty mouth on it. With serious fangs. What did it need a set of manglers like those for? And if it *was* really a demon or the devil or what, then was it all that smart of a guy such as Eddie Kennedy to open up some kind of meaningful dia—

"Eddie? Mr. Kennedy, you wait there! I'm coming down before you get into trouble. And who you talking to, anyway?"

Ah-hah! Puzzle piled on puzzle here. The voice that Evil was using was a voice Kennedy knew. The voice belonged to Jackson, the doorman of Kennedy's building. Was this significant? Was Evil trying to establish direct contact with Kennedy by taking control of his doorman's soul? No! Was it possible that all the doormen in Manhattan were in reality the . . . the minions! Yeah! The minions of Evil! It was not only possible, it was a dead certainty. The scope of the thing was staggering! Kennedy patted his belt, looking for his portable. Put a call in to Central right now. Signal Thirteen! A Citywide! Officer Needs Assistance. Evil has taken possession of all the doormen! Send the ESU guys! Get Koch up! Find Cuomo! Here's your ticket to First Grade, Kennedy. The thing is not to show fear. Evil had a set of teeth on it like the headwaiter at Fiorella's. Keep Evil talking until the ESU bus gets here.

"So . . . you believe this fucking water shortage? You think it'll ever rain in the right place? Hah?"

The eye went away, came back. The fangs came back and went away. Kennedy sensed something subtle taking place around him. The ground was moving. Yes! The sidewalk was definitely rocking. A little to the left, then back to the right. A stiletto-tipped thrust of cold hard panic caught him in the center of his belly. He looked up at Evil.

"Look, ahh, be cool here, okay? You don't want to do something we're gonna have to run you in for, right? How's that gonna look on your résumé?"

A sound came from behind him: keys rattling and heavy footsteps. Kennedy, sensing more trickery, refused to fall for it. The steps got closer.

"Eddie, what are you doing?"

Two things happened simultaneously. Evil popped right out of existence. Gone! And reappeared on the sidewalk right next to

Kennedy in the body of Calvin Jackson. Kennedy turned carefully, controlling his fear. It sure looked like Jackson. Five nine,
about 165 pounds. Skin a deep blue-black color, and the same
broad fan of lines at the corners of his eyes. The uniform was
wrong, though.

"Calvin? What're you wearing?"

Jackson looked down at himself. "I'm wearing my robe and
my pajamas, Eddie. You know what time it is?"

Kennedy straightened his right arm out in front of him,
extended his wrist. His watch was gone.

Jackson's face cracked open along a complicated network of
seams and fissures, showing Kennedy a set of strong white teeth
set off nicely by a pair of gold incisors.

"Eddie, you are pissed! Let's get you to bed."

"Calvin . . . Evil stole my goddam watch!"

In a room still smelling faintly of burned duck-down, Kennedy lay on a bed that had finally stopped rolling up and to the
left. Eighteen bars of pale-blue light striped the lower portion of
the bed and laddered up the far wall to within a few inches of the
bullet-marked Budweiser mirror. Items of his clothing lay in places
around the floor. His tweed jacket was in a pile on the bottom of
the bedroom closet, where Dudley had taken it while Kennedy sat
on the bathroom floor. In the farthest distance a siren was sound-
ing. Dudley's ears swiveled, pointed, and he opened his eye for a
moment. It closed again by millimeters, the way cats' eyes will
when they are at ease and weary. Dudley listened to Kennedy's
breathing. It was regular and slow. There was no sign of quickness
or a break in the pattern. In another forty seconds Dudley was
fully asleep.

Downstairs at Roderigo's the Rottweiler settled in behind the
bar. Bats flitted in the darkness above the streetlights. A massive
gray cloud moved across the midtown area and out over Central
Park. Dusty winds stirred the surface of the lakes and ponds.
Wrappers and ashes, cellophane and dry grasses skittered and
fluttered down the walkways. In the room below Kennedy's a
woman moved in her sleep. Outside an all-night deli at Second
and East 74th Street the grill of an empty cab ticked as it cooled.
A chain of lights on the 59th Street Bridge was reflected on the

greasy swells of the East River, deliquescent scintillations, breaking and forming.

A digital clock radio with ruby-colored numerals emitted a
low continual buzz. A colon between the numerals pulsed every
second. After fifty-nine pulses, one of the ruby numbers would
add a section or drop a bar to form a new number. A yard of cord
hanging from the blinds moved a little in the breeze. The clock
showed military time.

It flashed 0319 and then it changed to 0320. Fifty-nine pulses
later it changed silently to 0321.

At 0322, Kennedy opened his eyes. He was lying on his left
side, away from the window, holding a pillow up against his belly.
His mouth was very dry. His left cheek felt numb, and the
circulation was clamped off in his left arm. He rolled over onto his
back and saw a small child standing in the bars of pale light at the
foot of his bed. He could see in the blue light that the child was
black. He was naked, and there was a purple liquid running freely
down the insides of both legs. His legs were very skinny, and the
knees were scored and scabbed. The top of his skull was gone.
The cut was Marcuse's cut, a squared incision down into the
forehead and back up again. But the calvarium was gone. There
was a long Y-shaped incision covering the boy's torso. He was
holding something in his right hand, holding it out to Kennedy as
he stood barefoot on a fold of the duck-down comforter no more
than a foot away from Kennedy's legs. The thing in his hands was
a brain. It looked like a gray sponge full of purple syrup. The
syrup was dripping slowly from the brain, and wherever the drops
hit on the rumpled down comforter there was a flash of red light,
like a spark or candle flame.

Kennedy's heart and his belly muscles and his lungs reached
absolute zero in one breath. He could feel the skin on his face
icing up. His eyes seemed to burn. He tried to speak but his
muscles had become sluggish and dull.

The child closed his hand and more purple drops came from
the brain in his hand, striking the bedding in pinpoint explosions
of red and violet flame. When Kennedy looked carefully into each
explosion, he could see streets, faces, gestures, landscapes. They'd
flare up and out of the coverlet, waver, dance, a tiny moving
image, traffic lights, crowded blocks, theater signs, storefronts,
mouths open, birds flying.

Kennedy went down very deep, came up with the faintest tremor of movement in his chest. He worked on it, felt it grow. It swelled up through his shoulders, opened his throat, flowed down into his arms. He spread both hands out beside him on the bed, gathered himself, and pushed himself back and up, kicking at the covers, backing up and away.

The room was, of course, quite empty.

CHAPTER 7

TUESDAY

Morning came to Kennedy in the usual manner, ricochet radiance striking his pillow early. He got up slowly, like an athlete feeling bruises, limping slightly as he crossed the room, rubbing his face, touching the tender places in his memory where the dream had left its marks. Dudley threaded himself in and out of Kennedy's legs, half in an attempt to get breakfast on the road and half of it nothing more than an amiable greeting from one survivor to another. Kennedy stood at the bathroom sink with his hands on either side and looked carefully at the image in the mirror.

Whatever was happening to him wasn't easily detected. He stood for a while, leaning on the sink, staring at his reflection in the pitted mirror. His short arms were covered with red hair; his hands where they lay on the porcelain surface were broad, strong. One knuckle rode high on the tendons, a souvenir from a Bronx dealer who had ducked his head forward just as Kennedy had thrown a sucker punch at him. The hand healed eventually, but the knuckle didn't.

What was working on the detective now was the unfamiliar sensation that he was outside the core of things. All the years he'd been on the force, he'd never given more than a passing thought to what he was doing. Part of this came from the job itself, composed as it was of second-by-second decisions, snap judgments, action taken on the balls of your feet, at a dead run, many times at the highest pitch of nerves. Like most good cops, Kennedy had lived so long on adrenaline and a kind of careless adolescent joy in the game, trading on his wits, his street sense, his inborn skywalker's balance, that he never noticed the erosion of his contemplative side. Few cops care to indulge in self-examination, partly because it's a hindrance to the work; it clouds the instinct, slows the reactions in a subtle way that frequently proves fatal. And partly because most policemen who have been effective in the field have done things they'd rather not think about, things they'd rather not see dragged out into the daylight for the civil-liberties guys to poke around in. And there were other kinds of memories, the ones that came up on you from your blind side, stuff you told yourself you could cover up very nicely with a couple of coats of Jack Daniel's. So how was it that all the things he had trained himself never to think about seemed to be thinking about him?

After a shave and a shower he felt distinctly revived. He sat at the small round table where he ate his breakfast, idly breaking off sections of sugar donut and feeding them to Dudley, watching the sunlight move over the cat's fur. Dudley's single eye opened and closed as he ate. A trace of white sugar powder had stuck to his rough black nose.

"Hey, hammerhead. Clean your face off."

Dudley looked up from his donut pieces. Part of his tongue was sticking out of his mouth. The overall effect made Kennedy feel a little better about life.

Reaching over the table to brush away the sugar, he stroked the cat under the whiskers, running the side of his hand back toward the animal's neck. Dudley pushed his large delta-shaped head up into Kennedy's hand. A low chirruping sound came from his chest.

"You're supposed to purr, hammerhead. Not chirp. Birds chirp. Cats don't chirp. It's embarrassing to have a roommate who chirps."

Dudley settled onto the tabletop, enjoying the sound of Kennedy's voice, watching his face as the man talked.

"Duds, old chap. How was your night? Bad night? You go out, get laid? You get to that blue-point over at Lon Ky's yet? You stayed in, huh? You're a lying son of a bitch, you know. I think I saw you in that tree outside Roderigo's last night. Am I right? Were you up there freaking out your buddy? Hah?"

Perhaps there was something in Kennedy's voice, a subhar-

monic, an unfamiliar demisemiquaver. With his tongue still caught
between his teeth, the cat stared solemnly at the man, one forepaw extended, claws flexed.

"No comment, hah? You have a good night, later on? You
sleep right through? Nothing . . . disturb you? You didn't hear
anything?"

The tone made the cat restless. "*Rrroowr.*"

"Yeah? That's what you always say."

Stokovich called a general conference for the task force at
0845 hours. The skeleton crew stayed around for the start of it,
nodding over their coffee, propped up against the filing cabinets,
collars loose, ties pulled off. A huge black-bearded man with blood
on his knuckles lay on the holding-cell floor, greasy black jeans
pulled taut over a belly like a spinnaker, arms out wide, chin up,
mouth open, wheezing, putting out fumes Kennedy could smell
across the room. Kolchinski, Wolf Maksins, and Detective Frank
Robinson were all leaning against the bars of the cage. Maksins
was trying to lob roasted peanuts into the man's open mouth.
Kolchinski and Robinson were providing him with moral support
and forward fire data.

The general conference was standard procedure. At least
once a week, under Stokovich about three times a week, all the
shifts in Kennedy's Detective Area Task Force gathered together
in the squad room to go over the progress each detective, or each
unit, had made on various investigations. Stokovich ran the meeting and made whatever alterations in duty assignments he felt
were necessary as the cases progressed. This morning, with members of the graveyard shift still around, there were eleven men in
the room. There were no women detectives in this Task Force.
Stokovich had a problem with female detectives. He hated them.
He'd work with them on certain cases, he believed that he was
always polite and respectful to them, he believed that he would
never do anything to impede the career of a woman detective, no
matter what kind of an incompetent bitch she truly was, and he
did his level best to keep them out of his squad. He felt this even
more strongly about black female detectives.

Like Wolfgar Maksins, like others in the squad, Lieutenant
Stokovich was quite capable of polite contempt for black cops. It
was typical of them, however, that they would have gone cheerfully

into a fire fight to rescue Detective Frank Robinson, who was as thoroughly black as it is possible to get. If you had called them on this, most of them would have looked at you with that dead-eyed glare that cops reserve for anyone who isn't a cop. How could an outsider understand that Frank Robinson wasn't a black—he was a cop.

This magical eradication of racial identity was a common thing, wrought by the daily fires of New York life and squad-room friendship. In every masculine community there are three trials by which each male member will be judged and disposition carried out on his soul, and at none of these trials will a single word be spoken in open court. In male cop societies the first trial is a test of heart. Does this newcomer have a spine? Can he defend his place and his dignity? Has he made his mark on the street? Does he have the balls to go in first? The second trial is mind. Is he stupid enough to go in first every time? Or will he learn how to use his balls? And the third test is a trial of loyalty. Can this man be loyal, and if so, to whom is his loyalty given? If it's given to the Commissioner, the borough bosses, and the administration, then he fails. If it's placed on the anvil, between the Book and the Street, if he can step back from it and leave it there, at the mercy of the caprices of cop fate, knowing that there is no way to do a cop's job in the way the city truly calls for it to be done without placing his reputation and his career and sometimes his freedom at risk—if he can leave his loyalty on that anvil, then he passes. These decisions are made about every man and woman who comes to work as a cop, and the only way to achieve the respect and affection of other detectives is to be found worthy. There is no other way. No legislation, no departmental memorandum, no fiat from the fourteenth floor, and no quota hiring system can ever accomplish it. Frank Robinson had passed. Oliver Farrell had failed. Robinson would always be a man among men. Farrell had been born insubstantial and would die invisible and there would never be one goddam thing he could do about it. Nobody in the squad room ever talked openly about this part of the job, but nobody ever missed the effect of it either.

"Christ, Maksins, I think Eddie's dead!"

Wolf came over from the cage to get a better look. He and Frank Robinson were standing on either side of Kennedy's desk, looking down on him with counterfeit compassion.

"You want us to call a priest, Eddie? You may have died during the night."

Maksins was holding something behind his back. When Kennedy looked up from his papers, the huge blond brought his heavy hand out. He was holding a crucifix. He pushed this across the desk at Kennedy.

"Stand back, Van Helsing! This will hold him off!"

Robinson laughed. "No, get a sunlamp! Jesus, Eddie. What'd you *do* last night? Last time I saw eyes like that, man was three days in Maspeth Creek." The smile went away as he got a longer look at Kennedy. "Got the flu, Eddie?"

Kennedy was pleased to see Stokovich coming out of his office wearing his executive face.

"No, no, Frank. Got a little wrecked with Wolfie last night. Slept lousy. Give me a break, hah?"

Robinson wanted to dig a little, but Stokovich was already talking. Leaning up against the bulletin board, he got right into it, in his fashion, letting the men catch up however they could.

"Okay, okay, listen up. I've got that little shit Sorvino on the phone this morning. Some of you guys are letting your case-summary copies disappear between here and the DA's office. I told the DA that we'd have all case briefings in his hands every afternoon. That's *every* afternoon, Kolchinski. I read your summary on that Hell's Angels asshole and it's a nice piece of work. I don't see much from the canvass. You give the second platoon a bounce again, I think you'll get something from the street this afternoon. There's a regular club meeting in Jersey, so maybe the neighbors will have more to say without those shmucks in the area. You get anything from Daphne over there?"

"Not a lot, sir," Kolchinski said. "He had the flag up when we took him, the whole nine yards of liquid sky straight up the arm. He tapped it in when we came through the door and he's been on the nod ever since. I'd like Maksins here to give me a hand when we question him. Guy's a monster and I don't want to dance with him again. It took three men to take him out of the Scorpio this morning. But he'll roll over. He's gonna be sick soon."

Kennedy looked across the room at Kolchinski. Ben was a heavy-featured Pole with a hairless skull. He could bench-press four hundred pounds. It was not usual for him to ask for anyone's help with a suspect. Stokovich shook his head.

"Not Maksins. I got plans for you, Wolfie. You have a court call today?"

"No, sir. They've gone into chambers to jack their way around the Fourth."

Stokovich looked down at a clipboard. "You've got Seaforth hearing that? 'Go Forth and Sin No More.' Good luck with that dildo. He rolls over on the Fourth like he had a coin slot in his back. So you've got some time?"

Maksins didn't talk much. When he did, it was in a voice that didn't go with the narrow-hipped body: a tenor voice that hit each consonant hard, like a xylophone player learning the scale. English was a second language to him.

"Yes, sir. I have the time. I was going to go over to Fourteenth Street, look-see if our fist-fucker is back in business and kick some fluffs over on Christopher Street."

Maksins was trying to locate a young Cuban male prostitute who had been seen in the company of an older gay male at a hellfire club. The older man had later been discovered dead in his Barrow Street town house. The M.E.'s report suggested that the cause of death was a human fist inserted into the man's rectum. A black leather glove with chromed nailheads had been found at the scene. The body was trussed and suspended by its ankles. There were also some satanic nuances. Satanism was making converts in the demimondaine latitudes of Manhattan gays. It was ironic that a womanizer like Wolfgar Maksins had been assigned to the case. Ironic but also appropriate. He was a good-looking man, and he found it easy to get information from the secretive and cellular gay community. He had learned to use this lever. He wasn't above some low-level flirtation if it would free up a conversation. Now and then this flirtation would be taken too literally. This was always a mistake.

Stokovich turned away before Maksins had finished speaking—pushing the room, demanding more and better and sooner. Kennedy watched him from his desk and felt again a sense of diminishment, a lack in himself. Where the hell did Stokovich get the energy?

"Okay. Who's next? Robinson? You've got a lecture at the Academy, don't you? You get that Friction Ridge handbook I sent you? Yeah? Good. You were supposed to run down those Armenians. Anything? No? Well, why don't you try our buddies down on Mulberry? These Gypsies hit three old moustache petes and a widow on Hester Street. They're jerking off all over the San Gennaro society too, so get Deke here to go on the street for you. Okay, Deke?"

Fratelli smiled his pirate's smile, and touched the side of his sharply hooked nose with a forefinger. He was dressed in his Armani best again today, a double-breasted black suit in raw silk, patent-leather loafers, a charcoal-gray shirt, and a thin scarlet tie. Fratelli had been born on Mott Street. He had a cousin in an honored society. Fratelli would finish his career in Intelligence, handing the news both ways, helping the NYPD work with the Sidernese factions. Deke Fratelli was another new-minted sergeant whose rank was in limbo pending the outcome of the Guardians' suit. Unlike Maksins, Fratelli took it lightly. He understood that a race was like a family, and your family was supposed to use whatever it took to help you along in life. It worked for him; it worked for the Irish too. Why the hell shouldn't the blacks put a branch into the spokes if it could get a few more black men into management? Deke believed that his rank would hold. He had scored in the top seven percent citywide.

"Don't have to, boss. I was going to tell Frank anyway, story is that the Gypsies are in a room at the Holland right now. I've got two guys from Midtown South sitting on them. Soon as we wrap here, me and Frank'll bop over and bag 'em."

Stokovich looked at Fratelli for a second. "Shit, Deke, do I want to know how you did that?"

"Maybe we owe a favor—a guy needs a break on street parking or something."

"I don't want to know. You scare me, Fratelli. Eddie, what's the story on the Ruiz kid?"

Kennedy had the sheet under his hand. "I took the grandfather up to the M.E.'s and got a positive. Kearny sent the package over this morning. Can you ask Patrol if the ACU guys and the RMPs could look for a primary crime-scene location. Probably indoors. There'll be a lot of blood. It'll be someplace like one of those DAMP projects, or a warehouse. Whoever did it, I figure they had something going with the kid. I've got a sheet from Toxicology says the kid was whacked out on speed when he died. Looks like a drug hit—maybe the kid was getting fast with the bank. He was sharp enough to think of it. Pendleton sent up the tape. I'm going to play it for some of the Anti-Crime guys, see if we can get a matchup. Computer has nothing on the kid. Teletype's got nothing. No prints available either. We're looking for a Salvadoran chick named Nadine, a hooker who works for that asshole Mantecado. Kid was with her. It all ties into Los Hermanos. I'd like to talk to whatever narco guys we have on that store. And on the Muro thing, we haven't tagged that Olvera guy. He wasn't in the church on Myrtle, so we'll have to get back out there sooner or later. Mokie Muro's supposed to be in the Bronx, I hear?"

Stokovich nodded. "Yeah, you're right. I can't get any help from Quantico, but everything we have says that Mokie and this Tinto guy are the ones we want. That's yours, Eddie."

A kind of pressure wave went through the room. It was gone in a second, as Stokovich went down his case lists, and the talk went around as the Task Force traded information, offered suggestions, and the work assignments got handed out in a way that only seemed casual. Stokovich knew how to run men, from the rear, with an easy hand and no negotiations allowed. As the meeting broke up, Farrell came over to Kennedy and asked him where the Green Book was. When Farrell asked Kennedy for the book, Kennedy knew what was coming.

Hell. He had known yesterday.

In Stokovich's office, on the wall facing his desk, Stokovich kept a pair of eight-by-ten color photos of the twin suns of his professional life: Richard J. Nicastro, the hardcase Chief of Detectives, and Benjamin Ward, the Commissioner. When Kennedy came into the office, Stokovich was leaning back in his padded swivel chair with his feet up on his blotter, writing in a small black leather notebook with a gold lieutenant's shield embossed on the cover. Stokovich wrote in blue marker, in a controlled hand, quickly and concisely.

Kennedy stood in the center of the room, watching the bank of Motorola handsets charging in their racks as the big white GE clock ticked through three minutes. Kennedy was working hard on holding in his temper. Being able to keep other people waiting was Stokovich's reward for ten years of having had it done to him. One of the prices you paid for the badge was being treated like a child.

Stokovich finished with a flourish, snapped the book shut, and took his feet off the desk.

"Eddie, I'm gonna pull you off the Ruiz thing. You know why?"

Kennedy shrugged. "I know it's got the spooks all over it. Do I get to find out what the hell is going on?"

"What do you care? You don't have enough other work, we'll find you some. I got homicides up the ying-yang in the Green Book." Stokovich had good antennae. Kennedy was off, and he'd been off ever since he came in yesterday.

Kennedy walked over and sat down in the oak chair in front of the commander's desk. Stokovich offered him a stick of Dentyne.

"It just pisses me off a little, Bruno. I have this ACU guy, Stradazzi—I get the feeling he knows more about the Ruiz case than I do. He's got spook written all over him, but I talk to a friend in Personnel and I get a simple Italian patrolman with no marks—no marks at all, you know—which is interesting. Everybody's got some shit on their records, even before you get out of the Academy. But not Stradazzi. Hey, that's okay by me, Bruno. What gets me is you. You know goddam well that Stradazzi is with State, or he's one of your FBI trainees, or he's from Justice, or the DEA. Christ, maybe he's from Alcohol, Tobacco and Firearms. So he's a liaison guy. Why not say so? Am I in or out around here? What's the big secret?"

"Eddie . . . you know I can't tell you every fucking bit of stuff goes on in the squad. I'll tell you this. You got a sheet from one of the Field Associates."

It seemed to Kennedy that the floor of Stokovich's office had dropped about three feet. His stomach did a slow roll. "A Field Associate! Those shits rat on Patrol, not on detectives! What the fuck are you telling me!"

Stokovich raised a hand, palm out, and spoke soothingly, softly, as if to a child.

"Eddie, take it easy. I put it wrong. What I mean is, you pissed off somebody yesterday, and whoever you pissed off is one of Internal Affairs' little stoolies. So whoever it is filed a formal complaint against you and you're going to have to talk to a couple of dorks from Internal Affairs. Just routine."

Kennedy stood up. "Routine! You tell me I have to take a call from a pair of college-boy suits from IAD! No fucking way, sir, all due respect, sir. I have a couple of questions, sir. Have you filed a PD468-123 on me, sir?"

"No, Eddie, it's not that—"

"Are you instituting a command discipline here, and if you are, on what schedule? Schedule A? Did I miss a meal somewhere? Maybe I don't have my locker secured or properly tagged? No? Shit, don't tell me I engaged in unnecessary conversation? God, not *that*! Or, holy shit, sir, you don't mean to tell me that I have failed to maintain a neat and clean personal appearance? I mean, I know my eyes are a little red, but red eyes aren't a uniform violation, are they? If they are, you better file on that dork Bozeman because every time he goes for a walk they have to warn off the seven-twenty-sevens from La Guardia!"

In spite of himself, Stokovich had to laugh.

"Or, wait, is it Schedule B? That's it, a fucking Schedule B? Let's see . . . Nope, here's my gun! And . . . Yep, here's my shield! And my ID. You want to check them out, sir? Or is it Schedule C? Am I going to hear from the departmental advocate?"

"Eddie, will you sit down and shut the fuck up!"

"Has the Zone Commander filed a PD468-121? Charges and specifications, all seven copies, sir? If so, sir, then I formally request a goddam lawyer, sir!"

"Sit down, Kennedy, or I *will* slap your ass with a command discipline! You're only two months shy of getting your last CD cleared off your sheet, so don't be an asshole about this. Sit, will you? Eddie? Come on!"

Kennedy stayed where he was for a full minute. Out in the squad room there was absolute silence. It pressed against the wall. He managed to cap his anger long enough to sit down. Stokovich, for all his ambition, had always been a fair man. Kennedy could not believe that his commander was about to let one of the notorious Field Associates start a precedent by filing on a gold shield.

Field Associate! What a name! Spy, snitch, stoolie, fink, rat, weasel—they were closer to the mark. Kennedy had heard—hell, the whole Department had heard—about this latest scheme from the Commissioner's office. Nobody knew just how many Field Associates there were. Department gossip put it at maybe four or five snitches in each precinct, for a total of close to four hundred of them in all five boroughs. The rumor had it that they were recruited by Internal Affairs while they were still in the Academy. Staff instructors in the classes kept an eye out for trainees who had the right qualities—Christ only knows what *those* were—and one day the kid got a visit from a member of IAD. The deal was simple: Complete your training; go to your assignment; take up your patrol duties like any ordinary police officer. Ride in the RMPs, or walk a post with a Portable. Make your friends. Keep your nose clean. And report to us regularly about the men and women you work with. Let us know if they're doing anything they shouldn't be doing. Take down their names and badge numbers and get back to us, in secret, with your shit list. Oh yeah, and don't for heaven's sake worry about your buddies finding out what you're up to, because your name will never come into it. The guy you're ratting on will never know where the accusation came from. Just give us the names, and we'll do the rest.

"The rest" had become pretty well known in the NYPD. Each precinct had someone called the Integrity Control Officer. Usually a lieutenant or better, the Integrity Control Officer had only one precinct responsibility, and that was to insure that everybody in the precinct, every civilian and every Member of Service, stayed straight. They were a direct result of the Knapp Commission scandals of the early seventies. Kennedy had once looked up the "Duties and Responsibilities of the Integrity Control Officer" in the Patrol Guide. They were worth remembering.

The Integrity Control Officer . . .

• Develops an Integrity Control Program . . . responsive to Precinct conditions.

• Observes precinct conditions and visits Corruption Prone locations at irregular hours.

• Assists the Precinct Commander in developing sources of information among members of the command regarding integrity matters.

• Gathers information from all sources regarding criminals residing, frequenting, operating, or employed within the precinct and determines if unnecessary contact exists between such persons and Members of the Service.

- Instructs uniformed members during roll call training on the proper methods of identifying, reporting, and combatting corruption.

- Maintains rapport with uniformed Members of the Service . . . to seek symptoms of corruption.

- Conducts investigations . . . in response to official communications received from Patrol Borough Field Internal Affairs units.

- Compiles, maintains, and updates CONFIDENTIAL PERFORMANCE PROFILE of subordinate members, verifies the PROFILE annually with the CENTRAL PERSONNEL INDEX of the Personnel Bureau, and forwards all necessary PROFILE information to member's Commanding Officer when member is transferred.

- Conducts CONFIDENTIAL PERFORMANCE PROFILE check when new members are assigned to Command.

- Inspects Time Cards, Overtime Records, Property.

- Maintains . . . CORRUPTION PRONE LOCATION FILE.

- Develops liaison with Patrol Borough Field Internal Affairs Unit to exchange information for self-initiated anticorruption programs.

Kennedy had read all this with mixed emotions. The Serpico case had triggered the worst political and ethical crisis ever encountered by a North American police department, and a depressing number of the resulting allegations raised by the Percy Whitman Knapp Commission had proven to be true. Although there were a number of cases in which members of the NYPD had been skimming profits from narcotics investigations, or stealing heroin from evidence vaults and reselling it to the syndicate, most of the men and women in the NYPD had felt, with some justice, that they had all been inferentially ruined by the Knapp hearings. Kennedy knew many good cops who had been driven out of the service by the scandals, or who had turned into drones and toadies like Oliver Farrell, just to stay out of trouble. Many of the so-called corrupt practices of the NYPD were simple procedural faults. But in the hysterical aftermath of the Knapp Commission, when the New York press discovered that papers could be sold at staggering rates by crucifying some confused and frightened patrolman for everything from public swearing to alleged brutality, the survivors of that holocaust, including current Commissioner Benjamin Ward, had decided to purge the force of thousands of experienced officers. They were considered tainted by the fact that they were in uniform and had served during the sixties and seventies.

Ward and the brass at One Police Plaza got their chance on June 30, 1975, when New York's Deputy Mayor James A. Cavanagh ordered the dismissal of nineteen thousand civil servants by midnight. The city of New York came within inches of bankruptcy in the next year, until the Municipal Assistance Corporation, chaired by investment banker Felix G. Rohatyn, managed to put together a workable funding arrangement for the city. But by the time the fires had stopped burning in everybody's bank accounts, seven thousand New York City police officers had been fired or forced into early retirement. No one believed that every one of these seven thousand men and women had been let go because of the Knapp Commission traumas, but some of those dropped were rumored to have been on departmental hit lists.

In a way, the NYPD has been shaped by these two disasters. The Knapp Commission assaulted the pride of the department, and the Big Mac crisis of 1975 drove out most of its experienced, streetwise officers. In 1983 fewer than half the uniform patrol officers had more than three years of experience on the street. And it showed.

Many of the outrageous patrol-side incidents making headlines in 1985 could be traced back to a serious shortage of skilled and seasoned officers, or to the changes in experienced officers whose pride and spirit had been cracked fatally during the 1970's. Kennedy, like every other member of the force, knew that when you have a year in which more than a hundred revolvers are lost, an accident a day is reported in the squad cars, there is routine drug and alcohol abuse in the patrol function, and hiring quotas allow substandard recruits into the system to please various ethnic voting blocs, then you are asking for just what the city was getting: trouble in the NYPD. And when the administration of the NYPD had such serious doubts about its own officers that it sent permanent moles out into the precincts to spy on fellow members, then you had a managerial class that had virtually lost its entire police force. The NYPD practice of running full-time grab-bag entrapment and intelligence operations against its own people had outraged police departments all over Canada and the United States. As far as Kennedy was concerned, the surprising fact wasn't that so many officers had no pride and no interest in the job; it was that so many of them still cared.

He didn't know, and he was sure Stokovich didn't know, whether the mole who had filed on Kennedy was reporting to the Precinct Integrity Control Officer, or direct to some operative at Internal Affairs. The usual reaction to negative reports from Integrity Control officers, or from Field Associates, was to set up a sting operation against the accused man. The stings were sometimes obvious, sometimes less so. Kennedy's first partner had run afoul of an IAD sting, one of the classics: the mysterious magical bank drop. Even a membership in the Honor Legion hadn't stopped the IAD slicks from going after him.

The man had been on a routine post patrol when an apparent purse snatching had taken place about halfway up the block. A black male had raced past a woman, snagging her purse as he went by, the typical tactic. The woman screamed, and Kennedy's partner had gone after the purse snatcher on foot. The black male raced around a far corner and ducked out of sight. By the time the police officer had reached the corner, the man was gone. But a brown business envelope was lying in the alley. When he picked it up he could see that the envelope held three ten-dollar bills. There were no other identifying marks, and no other paper inside. Just thirty dollars in a brown envelope. Of course when he got back out on the street, the woman was gone as well. Maybe in Bent Forks, Nebraska, or Climax, Pennsylvania, or another small town, the policeman would have taken it right to the only bank and handed it over to Maudie behind the counter. In New York City, after spending the next half-hour trying to find the woman, he called in a report. When a buddy in an RMP suggested they keep a ten each and hand in the last one at the desk, he agreed. The IAD guys came out of the woodwork and busted him for corruption.

There were a hundred similar scams, each one run against an unsuspecting officer after he had been fingered by an anonymous accuser as "corruption-prone." They left money lying around, or they offered him a free meal at a local greasy spoon. They tried to sell him a carton of cigarettes that had "fallen off a truck" or a shirt at a discount. They tried to get him to accept a free drink at a local bar, or they arranged for him to be offered a "civil servant discount" at a grocery. And every time the officer went for it, the slicks would rise up out of the ground as if it had been sown with dragon's teeth, and another cop's career hit the wall. Was it fighting corruption or was it entrapment? Was the cop a criminal or a victim? And what cop could ever be bought so cheaply? It was a farce!

Detective Kennedy was entitled to his anger; he knew that you can't do the job without being in technical violation of at least ten obscure regulations in one of the Big Three bibles: the Patrol Guide, 620 pages; the Detective's Guide, over 500 pages; or the Administrative Guide, pushing a flat 1,000 pages this year. It was widely believed by the membership that the guides had been written the same way the Internal Revenue guide had been written, so deliberately prolix and confusing, salted with hidden contradictions and procedural cul-de-sacs, that on any day every working cop was in violation of *something*. It made a kind of sense to Kennedy, because as long as they had you on paper violations, they had your career in the palms of their hands. They could break you anytime. You lived and worked on their suffrance. Even Oliver Farrell, who had managed to pare the job down to a few safe moves, had run afoul of a couple of regulations last year. And no detective in the NYPD could forget that Detective Eddie Egan, the cop who had broken the French Connection, was rewarded for his services by being hounded out of the NYPD on precisely this kind of paperwork violation. And when he had hit the street, Eddie Egan owed a month in back rent and had exactly $89.79 in the bank.

"I am calm, Bruno. But no way am I hanging around to talk to the slicks on this one. I'm a goddam Gold Shield Second Grade and I'm fucking well not going to do it! They can have the shield if they want it. Just let them come ahead and take it off me themselves."

Stokovich exhaled slowly, settling into the chair. For a long while the two men sat in the small hot room and looked at each other. Kennedy watched the light change on the side of Stokovich's cheek. He had cut himself, shaving probably, below the ear. Kennedy felt a sweet calmness slide over him. He had taken his position. Whatever came out of it, he could live with it.

"Eddie . . . I didn't think you'd get this pissed off about some Department bullshit. You and me, we've had more shit flying around our file folders than most of the guys in the Task Force."

"Yeah, Bruno, that's true. And you've also got forty-eight departmental citations and awards. I have nineteen, including the Combat Cross with the celery. You're in the Honor Legion. So's Wolf Maksins. Deke Fratelli was up for the Medal of Honor the year before last, and I think he should have gotten it. Kolchinski has three Merit Medals, a Combat Cross, and there isn't a man out in the squad room who doesn't have bars up the ying-yang for police duty. Look at that plaque. The whole Task Force got a third Unit Citation in 1983. You're a lieutenant in the goddam NYPD and you and I we do not *take* shit from IAD and we sure as shit take no shit from moles and snitches and I for one want to have this snitch standing right up here in front of me. So should you, Bruno."

"Jesus, Eddie . . . okay, okay. I see your point. Maybe you're right. Maybe we should raise the shit over this one. It's not an IAD complaint, exactly. It's a complaint through the Equal Rights office, under 'Prohibited Conduct.' One 'A,' it says. 'Racial slurs' and 'prejudice toward any racial group.' Relax! Relax, Eddie! I know it's bullshit. But the IAD guys *have* to investigate it. Can you think of anybody you pissed off yesterday?"

"Yeah. Bergman. Sergeant Bergman. He was desk officer at the Eighth yesterday, gave me a hard time about getting Marco Stradazzi brought in. Said I bypassed the chain. Also, maybe I was a little hard on a PW name of Stokes."

"Stokes? Don't tell me, a short black broad, nice body, eyes like she spends her weekends cutting the balls off boy scouts from Westport?"

"Yeah! That's her. How come you know her?"

"She's a steward for The Guardians. She's always on the prod around the white guys. Ask Robinson about her. She's a good cop, but she sees Klansmen under her bed. Frank had her once, on a canvass a couple months back. Remember the case? Nineteen-year-old retarded kid was into all those sexual assaults by the Con Ed plant on Fourteenth? Stokes was on the third platoon, four to midnight. Robinson wanted a few people to go through the shit on the roof of the Franklin Delano Roosevelt School, on Avenue D near Fourteenth? The sergeant told Stokes and a couple of other officers to climb up onto the roof and poke around. Stokes told the sergeant no, she wouldn't."

"What do you mean, she wouldn't? She's a cop."

"She's a black female cop. That's different. She said the sergeant was only sending her up onto the roof because it was too shitty a detail for his favorite guys. He was sending her because she was a woman and a black, and that was racial prejudice. She said she'd go to the EEO if she had to. She knew her fucking rights!"

"Was the sergeant handing her a shit detail? You know, busting her balls? She's an abrasive bitch."

"Well, Robinson says no. The suspect was tossing clothing and evidence onto the roof. But the roof was covered with pigeon shit, old garbage. Nobody wanted to go up. Robinson says she was standing nearby, looking bored. Says the sergeant hardly looked at her, just told her to get up there and look around. Robinson doesn't think he was ragging her ass. Anyway, she didn't have to do it."

"Sergeant backed down?"

"Yeah. More trouble if he chases her up there. She'd go straight to headquarters. He'd have to prove that he wasn't a racist son of a bitch, which he is, anyway. I tell you, Eddie, it's a different force today."

"Bruno . . . you think she's the mole?"

Stokovich shook his head. "Nah . . . she's right up front with it. A mole, he'd be a party guy, everybody's bud. See him at all the rackets—he'd know your favorite scotch. Stokes is a ball-breaker but she's no mole."

"So where do we go from here? The mole could have been any one of twenty different officers who came and went at the crime scene yesterday. What do you want to do?"

Stokovich thought it over for a minute.

"Look, Eddie . . . this Ruiz case is right smack into a narco operation. Give me the Ruiz case, I can muscle it through without having to go official. I'll take it from here. You've got solid leads, and I know the narcotics man in the sector. And I can work with Stradazzi. Guy's not with anybody outside, but he's got a rabbi downtown. He's being cut in on some Intelligence operations. You can do this . . ."

Stokovich flipped a carbon copy of an EMS report onto Kennedy's lap.

"EMS scraped this turkey off the rails at the Twenty-third Street IND around midnight last night. He had a stack, and a gold chain with a mezuzah on it. Mezuzah was reported stolen from a kid named Jamie Spiegel, got himself stabbed over on West Forty-sixth Street about an hour before. Spiegel is in Bellevue. You look into this. I'd like to know how the John Doe on the tracks got himself from A to B. I think he got some help. You take this, it gets you out of the building for a while. I stall the EEO and the slicks. Time works its magical spell. The papers get lost. IAD and the EEO guys get bored, find some other shmuck to hassle. When in doubt, ask for it in triplicate. How about it?"

It looked good to Kennedy.

"What about Mokie Muro? And that Olvera guy? Days are going by here, Bruno. We gotta *do* something about those bastards. This Muro thing, it's working on me. All of us. I think those shits are up in the Bronx."

Stokovich was nodding. "Yeah, and don't we have a citywide out on them? We got every cop in the city jumping out of his skin on *that* one."

"Yeah, well, you got me doing this jumper."

Stokovich shrugged and popped another stick of gum.

"So? Do both. What's the matter? You a cop or what? Take the city's money—"

"Do the city's work. Who can I have?"

Stokovich locked his hands behind his head and pulled hard. "*Rrrrooowff!* Jesus Christ I'm getting stiff. You *ever* going to go to work, Kennedy? Take Wolfie. He needs a run. But keep a leash on him. He bites somebody, it's your ass!"

Maksins was leaning against the bars of the holding tank, watching the biker, listening to him talk in his sleep. He had his suit jacket thrown over a shoulder, a custom-cut white shirt, pleated navy-blue slacks, a thin lizard-skin belt with a gold buckle. The butt of a large revolver was hanging out of a molded-leather Jackass rig on Maksins' left side.

When Maksins saw Kennedy heading across the room, he came over to his desk. The room had cleared out. Most of the men didn't like to hang around when somebody was locking horns with the lieutenant. The fact that Maksins was still in the room meant that Stokovich had probably told him beforehand that he and Kennedy would be working together this shift. Maksins tugged at the crease of his navy-blue slacks and sat down on the edge of Kennedy's desk, pulling out his revolver. He put it down on top of a case file. Kennedy picked it up and turned it in the light.

It was a heavy blued piece with a vented rib running along the top of the barrel. The hand grips were oversized, shaped in zebrawood, crazily striped. The weapon must have weighed close to four pounds.

"You got it, hah?"

Maksins took the piece back, popped the cylinder out and spun it twice with a flick of his thumb. "Yes, I did. Had a time getting it by Tactics. Stokovich had some moaning and groaning to do about the thing. But I made it. Dan Wesson Model Fifteen. Four interchangeable barrels. Quick shift front sights. Had to send away for a special Jackass harness. You like it?"

Kennedy wasn't a weapons fan. His duty gun was a Chief with a .38 Special load. Now and then he wore his Airweight in an ankle holster. It depended on the clothes he was wearing. Chief, Airweight, it didn't matter. He was lousy with both.

"It's a cannon, Wolfie. You fire this inside the city limits, you'll blow out windows all the way up Fifth. Nice looking, though."

Maksins put it away and actually sat there scuffing the toe of his loafer over the linoleum, his head down, stalling.

Finally: "You know, Eddie, I had the shines on my case pretty bad, year before I came down here."

Kennedy knew the story. He let Wolf tell it.

"You know, Knapp may have fucked up Patrol. I know the guys major in doing the dog now, as far as narco busts or numbers. Integrity officer sees you even talking to a policy runner or a bookie, even a pusher, before you know it you're bagged for 'seen-in-corruption-prone-location-with-known-perpetrators.' So now you can't talk to any of your best street sources—the bankers, the guy who runs the bar, the local pimps. The guys who are most likely to help you with the serious cases because they've got a vested interest in seeing the block stay quiet. You know what I'm talking about? Yeah, well, after Knapp you have these snitches all over. They see you talking to a bad guy—pow. Right away, they make you for association. Knapp sent the bosses into a tizzy. You can't even make a simple drug collar now unless you've got a supervisor at your back. You know the TOP changes that went through all the departments? Temporary Operating Procedures? When I was in Narcotics, we couldn't even do a stop-and frisk, turn a guy's pockets, until we had a boss there with us. Not to protect the perp. To make sure that we weren't just stripping the guy and taking his money. This is in Harlem, right? All because a few guys in Preventative and Enforcement Patrol got into shaking down the dealers and the pushers and levying the fine right on the spot. I mean, that's really all that Bob Leuci and his squad was doing. Best way to get the assholes off the street was to take away their capital. The courts wouldn't do it. So the narco squads did it on their own. I did it. I kicked their asses off the street and I took away their money. The PEP guys did it too. So, did the silks on the Knapp commission ever ask about the rate of drug busts? Did they ever ask if there were fewer black kids dying in puke because of a hot shot or toxic smack? No, they didn't. The Knapp lawyers only wanted to nail cops. I was working in Harlem and I know that the PEP guys did real work—they scared the piss out of pushers and dealers. What did Knapp or Goodman ever do besides bust good cops?"

Kennedy had never heard such a speech from Maksins. "Hey, Wolfie, if you're trying to hand me Bob Leuci as a good cop, what about his partners? He wore a wire against his own."

"Yeah. He did. They had him by the balls. You read his book?"

"Yeah, I read it. What about it?"

"Read it again, Eddie. Leuci, he's learned something. I think the guy wishes he'd never so much as waved at one of those three-piece suits from Justice. I say the guy's trying to send his squad a message. He figured he could get it across in his own book. He did, too."

Kennedy got up and put on his coat. "Wolfie, you are a very strange person. I did not hear you say what you just said about Harlem. I think you should be very careful about saying things like that around here."

Maksins looked over toward Stokovich's office door.

"Him? He sees it just the same way, Eddie."

"No, he doesn't, Wolfie. He can't."

Maksins and Kennedy followed a nurse with wispy blue hair and an orthopedic brace on her left leg down a long hall reeking of Lysol to Jamie Spiegel's ward in Bellevue Hospital. There were four beds in the room. A plump woman wearing a pastel-striped dress got up when the detectives came into the room. She went right at them, stopping them in the middle of the ward, wearing a blend of hostility and supplication, smelling of floral perfume and medicinal hand cream. She held a white vinyl purse as big as a pullman pillow over her breasts. Her cheeks had been dusted with something like white flour and her mascara had run down into the creases under her eyes. She was distracted enough to have allowed it to dry there.

"That," she declared, gesturing over her shoulder in the direction of a slope of starched sheeting from which ran several clear plastic tubes—"that is my son. I want you to know that I am dis-*gus*-ted, *ab*-so-*lute*-ly dis-*gus*-ted at the way you have allowed the *worst* elements of the city to as-*sault* an innocent young child in the very *lobby* of his hotel! I fully *in*-tend to—"

Kennedy flipped out his shield. "Ma'am, I'm Detective Kennedy and this is Sergeant Maksins. Are you the mother of Jamie Spiegel? If so, ma'am, we are very sorry for what has happened, and we'd like to hear the story from your son. Can you step outside and have a word with Sergeant Maksins while I talk to your boy?"

Kennedy could feel Maksins cringing from a yard away, but the woman went with him, her voice rising and falling in a harsh snappish cadence, like a lapdog with a grievance.

The boy on the bed appeared to be sleeping as Kennedy stepped closer. He looked a little shrunken, as if he had pulled away from the flesh that covered him. He had skin like milky water, and he smelled of cigarette smoke. A hesitancy in his breathing made Kennedy think the boy was only pretending to sleep.

"Mr. Spiegel? I'm Detective Kennedy. Can I talk to you for a moment?"

The boy opened his eyes and looked about the room. "Is she gone? My mother?"

Kennedy grinned at the kid. "Yeah, she's gone. What the hell happened to you?"

The kid looked younger than the twenty-one years set down on his chart. He stared down the coverlet at a spot on his midriff where a tube ran out from under a gauze band. A tousle of curly hair angled out from the back of his head. He sighed and looked up at Kennedy.

"I sure screwed up this time. Do you have to tell my mother what I was doing when I got stabbed? I mean, what a putz!"

"What were you doing?"

"I . . . ahh, I was . . ."

Kennedy got it immediately. "You were catching the skin flicks along Forty-second Street? Kid, if I can keep it from your mom, I will. But you're twenty-one and I think getting stabbed is kind of a drastic punishment for taking in a few porn shops. Want to tell me about it?"

Jamie did. He talked easily and with self-deprecating humor about his night on The Deuce. Kennedy kept his face straight and wrote steadily in another brand-new steno pad. Now and then he'd ask the boy to go over a detail, or to explain precisely where he had been when a particular move was made. Spiegel seemed to fear that he was somehow liable for damages, or open to charges, for having caused such a fuss along 46th Street. He was in some pain, and the wound, although draining well, had been deep. He didn't seem to know much about the kind of weapon. He did say that he heard a snicking sound just before he was stabbed. Kennedy suggested a switch-blade, although he knew from the ESU report that a butterfly knife had been found on the body of their prime suspect in the case. Spiegel said no, it had been a more complicated sound, a series of sounds really, like a ratchet or a chain. When the knife went in, Jamie had tried to believe that it was just a punch. He hadn't really felt the cut. But then the man had knocked him down, and as he fell he knew he'd been cut.

"The guy, the one who stabbed me? You be careful with him,

eh? He likes to hurt people. The other one, he was out of it. I
don't think he really wanted to hurt me, you know? But that one,
the guy with the marks all over his face? He liked it. He was into
it, you know?" When he realized the ambiguity of the phrase,
Spiegel laughed and then winced. Kennedy liked him.

The boy had a fairly clear memory of the evening. Although
he'd been frightened, he had managed to notice quite a bit. He
gave Kennedy a good description of both muggers. He described
the one who stabbed him as a racist. The man had called him a
Jewboy. The name had had an odd effect on the mugger. The
more he had used it, the closer he had come to stabbing Spiegel.

"It was funny, you know? Like he wanted to do it to me all
along? Like he was mad at me for something? I don't know what. I
was the one being killed."

Were any names used? The boy thought about it for almost
four minutes. Kennedy waited in silence.

"Yes. The crazy one? The one who stabbed me? He called me
a bunch of names. Dickhead, Jewboy. And when I was . . . after I
had fallen down? He said, 'Hey crush-crush,' and then something
about a guy named Jake? And another name. But he said it.
Crush-crush . . . and this guy Jake."

"Jake probably meant a cop. They call cops 'jakes' on the
street. Can you think of that other name?"

He tried, lying on the bed in a patched green hospital gown,
tubes in his stomach, tubes up his nose. He tried very hard.
Kennedy had a brief flash of the boy lying nude on a flat perforated-
steel table with Charlie Marcuse leaning over him, bringing a
scalpel down under a beam of sulphurous light, the edge glittering
and Charlie's rubber fingers settling into the puffy blue skin
under the boy's throat. A pump labored in the background.

"No, Mr. Kennedy. I can't get the name. I didn't feel so good
at that point. I'm sorry."

Kennedy snapped the pad shut. "Forget that, kid. I'm the
one who's sorry. Get some sleep."

Wolf had Mrs. Spiegel backed up against the wall outside the
room. He was leaning over her, one hand on the wall, the other in
his lizard-skin belt. It took Kennedy a second or two to realize
that Maksins was flirting with the woman. She was staring up at
him, brightness in her eyes, holding her breath, her hands clutch-
ing the huge white bag. Maksins pushed himself off the wall and

extended his hand. Mrs. Spiegel took it. Kennedy thought she would lick it, but she folded it into one of her hands and disappeared in a puff of rouge and white powder. Maksins had unexpected talents.

They fought traffic all the way across 34th Street to Ninth Avenue and worked their way around toward Midtown Central. Maksins listened to the Patrol Division Communications cross-talk while Kennedy bulled his tan Chrysler around cabs and trucks and through the masses of jaywalkers at every major intersection. The sun was high above, shining down into the streets between the walls and storefronts of lower midtown. There was a two-hour period this late in the season when daylight came right down to the ground level. The cross-talk was full of "south eddie" and "north charlie" and an angry ACU car telling Communications "no further no further" and somebody else wanted "any housing for a missing person?" You could tell the white Bronx voices and the black Brooklyn voices and the upstate twang of an older male down at Communications. *"Nine Eddie, you're ten ninety-eight stand by. One Adam, K. One Adam report of two male blacks breaking into an auto at Beaver and Broadway. Nothing further. One Adam, K? South Boy, you're out on a sixty-one. Ten four."*

"What d'you listen to that stuff for? If there's a city-wide, we'll hear the beep. Wolfie?"

"I don't know, Eddie. Makes me feel like a cop, I guess. Mrs. Spiegel says the kid'll be laid up for a couple of weeks. You get anything out of him?"

"Enough."

At Midtown Central the desk officer referred them to a harried plainclothes cop by the name of "Peruggio, Anthony B., up the stairs and to your left. Sir. Have a nice day. Sir." They found Peruggio arguing with a Crime Unit man in a dirty Knicks jacket. They wandered around the cluttered squad room for a while, turning over report sheets and flirting with the black PW on the typewriter at the far end of the room. Finally Peruggio told the Anti-Crime Unit man to do something anatomically improbable and headed in their direction with a face on him that could shatter glass.

"You here about that jumper last night? I got the sheet in the office. Which one's Kennedy? You Kennedy? Look, I always wanted to tell you, you did a nice job on that chicken hawk up in the Bronx. You're the one, aren't you? Eighty-sixed the fucker? I ain't got the wrong Kennedy, have I?"

Kennedy concentrated on keeping his reaction small, not letting anything show. This happened from time to time.

"Yeah. I'm that Kennedy. You have the EMS report? I hope somebody took shots."

Peruggio pushed through a litter of papers, photos, tapes, letters, envelopes, type balls, empty cigarette packs, finally coming up with a large manila envelope which he threw across the desk. It opened when it hit, spilling a fan of glossy 8 × 10's out onto the floor. Wolf scooped them up in one low motion and dropped them in front of Kennedy.

"Oh, fuck," said Kennedy.

In four of the twelve shots there were two bloody heaps of clothing and tissue, about six feet apart, shadowed and hard in the white glare of a powerful flash. It took you a moment or two to sort out the body parts and the bits and make some kind of coherent guess as to just what it was you were looking at. When you did, you got it like a gestalt, all in one corruscating and searing jolt.

"Leave it to the uptown trains, huh? Barreled right into him, spread him out like a bialy widda shmeer, huh? One of the guys from Emergency Services hooped into his boots over it. You see this little pulpy bit over here? Halfway to the wall? No, down from that. Guy's liver, would you believe it? Fucking liver pops right out. Not a mark on it, either. Coulda picked it up, hosed it down, and fried it right up. With onions, huh, Kennedy? So what the fuck you want with this dipshit, anyway? You're homicide now, ain't you?"

Maksins waited for Kennedy to answer this one. He pulled the shots together and sat down in a hard metal chair, easing his Dan Wesson out and turning it in his huge hands, his pale-blue eyes on Kennedy.

Peruggio lit a stogie as Kennedy laid it out for him. The jumper's effects had included an item, a gold mezuzah on a link chain, that had been taken from a stabbing victim up on West 46th last night. They had interviewed the boy at Bellevue and he had given them reason to believe that there were two men working in concert and that one of the men was still at large.

Peruggio sucked wetly on the stogie. He had a blond gunfighter's moustache, stained with tobacco juice. He looked like a short-timer; he had a big belly and heavily veined hands, and he carried his piece in an ankle holster. Whatever he hadn't seen in the NYPD he had read about later. A jumper was yesterday's news.

"You got a jumper here—he's dead. You got a maybe accessory to felony assault. You got a kid with a scar who when the case comes to trial a year from now, he's bored with the whole thing, he don't wanna come to Noo Yawk anymore. You got the kid's *meshugana* or whatever. Why you wanna go jerking around looking for somebody else?"

"We think your jumper was pushed."

Peruggio snorted into his cigar. "So what? How the hell will you make that stick? Even if you find this kid, what makes you think he'll roll over? You got zip witnesses. I know, because we turned that place upside down and as usual everybody was suddenly struck blind and deaf. Maybe the kid confesses, you get him after his shyster talks to him, and suddenly he was coerced into an ill-advised admission of guilt by two brutal cops. Give it up, Kennedy!"

Kennedy got a little tactless. "Look, ahh, Tony, you on the Mayor's Committee or something? Why do you want this thing shitcanned? You want to call this suicide?"

"Hey! I don't give a fuck if you call it chicken cacciatore! I'm just saying why call it a murder when you can call it a suicide and we all go for a drink, huh? You don't have enough murders in this city, you gotta go make one up?"

Maksins and Kennedy sighed and stood up. There had been some pressure coming down from Administration to lower the murder stats in New York this year. I Love New York, the Murder Capital of the World. Some of the bosses had made it clear that an iffy call between murder and suicide could be called suicide. Enough calls like that, *et voila!* The murder rate in New York has dropped. Everybody wins! It looked like Peruggio was slightly slanted.

"Well, thanks for your input, Sergeant. We'll just run the usual checks on it. If you don't mind, hah?" Kennedy put his hand out. Peruggio puffed on the cigar for a while, staring at Kennedy. He tossed a file folder onto his desk and pulled some papers out of a drawer. "Okay, hotshot. There you go. And top o' the marnin' to yez!"

Maksins got up and collected the papers again. As they were leaving Peruggio's office, he was calling upstairs. That didn't matter to either of them.

They had a link between the Spiegel knifing and a John Doe killed an hour later. The victim had given them a description that seemed to fit what was left of the John Doe. And best of all, he had given them a name. They went to the computer room of the precinct. The female attendant was busy running a clipboardful of names for the station Crime Units. A couple of black patrolmen were standing in the hall when Kennedy and Maksins came up. They tipped their hats back, smiled, scuffed a little. Gold shields get that kind of treatment in the NYPD. One of the patrolmen offered to get the men a couple of coffees. Maksins and Kennedy said yes, thanks, that would be great. The attendant raised her hand, held up five fingers. Five minutes? Kennedy nodded. They waited in the hall with the patrolman eyeing both of them, obviously hungry for his own gold.

Well, that's how you get it, thought Kennedy. A gold shield is different from anything else in the NYPD. Technically, a gold-shield detective is a simple patrolman. He's not a sergeant. He's not even headed in that direction. The gold-shield designation is a separate fork in the promotion lines within the NYPD. He's chosen from the uniform ranks, tested in something like plain-clothes Anti-Crime work, or in small-time narcotics undercover assignments. If he shows wit, nerve, some ambition, and a major helping of style, he loses his "tin" and gets a "gold." He gets that chiseled gold badge, and he becomes part of the mythical elite of the NYPD. But he's technically a patrolman on special duty. He gets paid according to three grades: third, second, and first grade, with first being the highest. The pay is called grade money. A second-grade gold shield ranks with a sergeant, although he has slightly more unofficial status than a detective sergeant. First grade brings more money. Most of the active gold shields in the NYPD are third grade. Kennedy was a second-grade gold. By the time a man or woman gets to first grade, he or she is close to retirement. Few ranks in the NYPD have the special aura of freedom and power that a gold detective's shield can deliver. But unlike sergeants, lieutenants, and so on, a gold shield—because he is always a patrolman operating on special duty with grade money—can be broken back to uniform with terrible speed. It's called "flopped back to the bag" and it can happen to a gold shield with the kind of random, unpredictable, and devastating effect of a cardiac stroke. One day you make some boss unhappy, or you screw up magnificently by losing a prisoner or blowing a publicized case. The gold is gone. You are in uniform, on a portable beat, saluting a boy-child linebacker from an upstate high school.

The attendant waved to them from the CATCH room. CATCH stands for Computer-Assisted Terminal Criminal Hunt, and it delivers NYSIIS, or Criminal Identification Numbers. They are actually two separate systems, but they work together in a very effective way. CATCH uses a hard-copy microfilm file to deliver full-size photographs of every man and woman ever formally photographed during an in-state booking process. The computer terminal connected to the CATCH system carries disk memory codes indicating which microfilm file a suspect's photo has been stored under. The names are cross-referenced and updated regularly. It takes the attendant about five minutes to search all possible variations of a name, including street names or aliases, legally altered names, nicknames, typical abbreviations, and a range of similar-sounding or phonetically linked names. The search area can be narrowed by entering the investigating officer's opinions about the race of the suspect, his age, any prior convictions, even a possible address or a known associate. The system takes up a large room in several city precincts, and it can be used by any officer or detective with a good reason. A printer delivers hard-copy data along with a facsimile photograph of the wanted person. The only way a suspect can have his photo deleted from the CATCH system is to apply through a lawyer and have the records purged. This rarely happens. Kennedy was going to the CATCH system first, before doing any other investigating, because he had one solid clue that, with some luck and a good operator on the CATCH machine, might shorten the whole case. In his steno pad, under a long column of scratched notes, he had printed the words:

CRUTCH
CROSS
CRUSH

DOUBLED?
CROTCH
CHRIS?

The Spiegel boy had been pretty specific about the names.
Kennedy had gone back to the names three times, each time
asking the question as if it had never been asked before. He got
the same name, or a variable of it that was too close to argue
about, and Kennedy believed it was a solid lead. The shadowy
alternate name, the one Spiegel had been unable to recall, might
have been the man's birth name. Unless the kid had been quite
confused, Kennedy was sure that the name he had heard was a
street name. Muggers, street people, pushers, even undercover
cops—they all had a string of operating names, a different name
for a different circle or a different block. Kennedy talked it over
with the woman in the cotton-candy red hairdo. She thought it
over for a while, drumming on the keypad in front of her. Finally,
she typed CRUTCH onto the green monitor. She typed the search
code, hit ENTER, and sat back. In thirty seconds, three NYSIIS
number codes appeared.

Each NYSIIS number indicated a film wheel and frame number. One was an actual name, but it belonged to a criminal who
had been sent to Attica only six months before. The second man
was a cripple, which was how he got the nickname. He was
definitely out. The third name was a young black male with a
string of felonies. Possible. Kennedy made a note of all the NYSIIS
files, and the attendant took down the coordinates of his microfilm mug shot.

CROSS delivered up seventeen possible suspects. The street
name was popular, although most of the people who used it were
either white southerners or female. They asked for a hard-copy
printout of eight of the CROSS items.

CRUSH gave the detectives sixteen possible names. Three of
them used the street name in a different spelling: one CRRUSH,
one KRUSH, and one KRUSH-GROOVE. Kennedy rejected the KRUSH-
GROOVE on an instinct. This felt right. The kid was here somewhere.
He could smell the kid.

They went down the list of CRUSHes first. There were nine
black CRUSHes. One was listed DOA Lenox Hill three months
ago. One was in Attica, according to the best information. Ken-

nedy made a note of his name and address anyway. It had happened before. A guy gets out of Attica on a parole or a work-release, and he's back in the neighborhood without anybody telling the local precinct, let alone CATCH or FINEST computer terminals.

Two were wanted for armed robbery by the FBI. Kennedy wrote them out, but rated them at the bottom. New York was a hot town for any FBI targets. There were more FBI men in New York than in Washington. It wasn't likely that an FBI armed robbery suspect would be mugging kids on The Deuce.

The fifth had been paralyzed in a shooting incident at the Caamanos Bar in Alphabet City. Coincidence, but irrelevant.

The sixth CRUSH was a stripper in Long Island City. Out, but let's take her name anyway.

Seven was DOA Yonkers a year ago. Out. Not a lucky street name, either.

Eight was a definite possible—a string of felony assaults, some "criminal sale of controlled substance," all five degrees for this kid, D felony, C felony, B felony, an A-11 felony, and an A-1 felony. Kid was a slow learner. Kennedy made a note.

Nine was a minister in something called the Unification Church of Schaefer City. Possible.

KRUSH gave them a boy with a series of felony assaults; a couple of hits for fraudulent accosting, probably for a three-card monte scam; criminal possession of stolen property, under second degree; a couple of weapons charges. The sheet was nasty but not big-time nasty. The kid was the right age, sixteen years old. His name was Dennis McEnery, and he'd been in and out of Spofford like a bread van. The profile was right. He showed an address on West 114th Street, near Morningside Park. He was cross-referenced to an Apollo McEnery, same address, the subject of an outstanding homicide investigation. Apollo McEnery had had a series of street names, including Greek, Creed, Sundown, and The Duke. He had been found behind a building in his home area on February 17, 1984. Dennis McEnery was sometimes known as Skate. He had been sent to Rikers Island last year. The file listed his caseworker as well.

Kennedy straightened up from the table. Maksins was riffling through a pile of computer paper and writing down notes on the edges.

"Wolf . . . how'd you like to give the Spiegel kid a call? Ask him, does the name Dennis McEnery mean anything to him? Let him take his time."

Maksins went out to make the call. Kennedy and the operator went back to the terminal. They skipped CROTCH for no particular reason other than that it was a dumb name, and went through seventy-six CHRISes before Maksins came back from the phone. He had a very lupine leer in place, which was only natural.

"Spiegel says it was Dennis! The John Doe called his partner Dennis. Or Dennis called his partner that. Who *is* the John Doe?"

Kennedy didn't agree there could be any doubt. "The kid was certain about the build, the body type, the skin, everything. No way the John Doe is Dennis McEnery. I figure our guy here, Krush, he's the shover, not the shovee."

Maksins shrugged. "I still don't see how you figure this. How'd they link the mezuzah, the cash, all the goods, to the stabbing up on Forty-sixth? That's Midtown Central and the jumper is in the Eleventh. They post it on the teletype. I can't believe Central Street Crime was that fast on the night shifts. Usually, you don't get teletype CSCU until the next day, if you're lucky."

Kennedy thought so too. "I don't know, Wolfie. I didn't catch this case anyway. Stokovich had it on his desk. You know how he prowls around downstairs, picking up the gossip. I think he came across it accidentally. Peruggio did get the effects out on to FATN and I guess somebody up at Midtown was listening, because they called him right up and got a positive on the goods. Stokovich is the man who called it a possible homicide. He jerked me off the Ruiz case and gave me this one."

Maksins was still working this through when Kennedy had signed the record sheet for the CATCH operator. They went down to the main floor and signed out at the desk. It occurred to Kennedy that they might put out an FATN for a Dennis McEnery, with a bullet for the desk officers at the 26th and the 28th precincts. Calls like that were only put out on the air in a hot-pursuit case. Too many outsiders had access to monitoring equipment. Maksins said he'd take care of that, and Kennedy went outside to get some air. The precinct house smelled of the same thing that all precinct houses smell of: dust and dead air, sweat and coffee and shoe leather and sixty years of somebody else's problems.

The car had been parked in the shade, but for the past hour it had been out in the sun, so when Kennedy cracked it open the dashboard and the vinyl bench seat shimmered in the overcooked air. He reached inside and took out the radio. It burned his fingers. So did the door handle when he leaned back into it.

"One-oh-four to Central, K?"

"One-oh-four, K."

"Central, get me the Task Force, Lieutenant Stokovich."

There was some cross-talk on the patrol channel. Kennedy listened to it idly, the way a man will follow the action of a game, hearing it but not letting any of it reach him. The block was crowded with blue-and-white patrol cars. Over everything in the bright street, over the hot chrome and the dusty paint and the tiers of dull-paned windows looking down into the street and above the ragged roof lines, Manhattan sounded throughout, a susurrus, like the sound of a crowd in a distant stadium or the slow sliding retraction of tide on a gravel beach. It carried you up and rolled you over and drove you down day after day, a murmurous roaring, a whispering vibrato rumor of strange half-heard calls, a familiar name, a soft suggestion, a hiss or a cry almost heard, almost remembered. In New York they learn not to hear it, because once it gets your attention you can never be free of it. If you said any of this to Kennedy he wouldn't have known what you were talking about.

. . . *South boy south charlie shots fired shots fired that's at B'way and Twenty-eighth see the woman no no eighty-five me at base that's a ten fifty-four we've got a man down send a bus yes yes hold it up there no further no further are you out there north ida see the portable see the portable radio check central radio check north portable yes portable I read you five by five central k north boy north boy k north boy central yes north boy we have a barricaded EDP at the Holland House room two twenty-five slow it down slow it down all units we've got a bus on the scene no further no further emergency services is on the scene . . .*

Kennedy caught the Holland House reference and sent up a small prayer that it wasn't Fratelli or Robinson who was involved. EDP meant emotionally disturbed person, and a barricaded EDP was a bad situation. If he picked up a Signal Thirteen, Kennedy was going to go right over.

A uniform patrolwoman stepped in front of him. "Sir? Are

you Detective Kennedy? There's a Lieutenant Stokovich on the landline inside? He's asking for you?"

Going back into the precinct house was like stepping into a stone chapel, shadowed and cool after the heat on the street. Kennedy took a phone from the operator behind the duty desk.

"Kennedy?"

"Yes, it's me, Bruno. I just wanted to let you know we've got a positive on that John Doe jumper. We saw the Spiegel kid and he gave us a lead, turns into an address on West a Hundred-fourteenth Street. Kid named Dennis McEnery. Wolfie's putting it out on FINEST. You want us to let the guys at the Two-seven pick him up?"

"No, Eddie. You don't want to do the dog around the squad room right now. Besides, Internal called and I told them you were in a hot-pursuit situation and couldn't be reached. I mean, they know that's crap, but why don't you fire on up to the Two-seven and chase their butts around for a while? I've got the Duty Captain on my ass with this one. The Spiegel kid's a tourist, so he wants the muggers scooped fast. This case isn't going to be a priority for the Two-seven. They've got troubles of their own. How's Wolfie?"

Maksins came across the large hall toward Kennedy, balancing two coffees and a pile of glazed donuts, a patrolman's lunch.

"Wolfie's okay. Am I taking him to Harlem?"

"Jesus! Wolfie in Harlem! That oughta be interesting. Sure, take him along. Tell him Sorvino wants him to do a lineup with those Angel assholes. He's supposed to bring his witnesses in whenever he can swing it. Eddie, you keep him out of trouble up there. Wolfie's a nice kid but he's got an attitude about the blacks, eh?"

Kennedy looked up at Maksins, who was devouring a donut and smiling at a brace of PWs behind the desk.

"Hey, Wolfie. We're goin' down memory lane."

Stokovich laughed and cut off. Maksins said, "Where?"

"Harlem."

Maksins stopped chewing.

"Harlem?"

Kennedy headed for the door. "Yeah. North of here. Remember, Wolfie?"

Down the steps of the station house, Maksins squinted into

the light, closing up behind Kennedy, and said, "Yeah, Eddie, I remember."

All the way up Eighth Avenue, Kennedy thought about Porfirio Magdalena Ruiz, and Maksins emptied and reloaded and emptied and reloaded his Dan Wesson with the zebra-striped grips and the interchangeable front sights. They switched the set to the uptown frequency when they got to Columbus Circle, bouncing over the ruts and potholes, working their way through the pedestrians milling around at the western edge of the hotel row.

The Columbus monument was surrounded by small-time coke and smack dealers, bums and winos, pushcart peddlers, undercover cops, tourists, couples. A lot went on in a gore formed by the intersection of Eighth and Broadway and Central Park South. They broke through the pack and headed straight up Central Park West. The trees and glens of the park swept by off Maksins' right shoulder. He rolled the window down and flicked off the air conditioning. A dry wind blew dust and the scent of ripe greenery, dead leaves, blue scorch-smoke from a pushcart stand, diesel fumes, horse manure, pretzels, cigarette smoke; not fresh air, not a zephyr from the coast or even a hint of salt water, but New York air, spicy and rich and close. On Kennedy's side, block after block of clean bright apartment towers went by: spotless granite facades and reliefs of robber barons, bronze casement windows hung with heavy damask, here and there on the lower floors the sheen of brass, or the fragmented scintillations of a clustered chandelier. They bounced over a section of thick metal plating, both of them holding on to the dash, as the Dakota loomed up on their left, a Victorian pile, turreted and spired, cloaked in its own light and air, like a faded painting. They drove at forty miles an hour, taking every light, past the mansions and the apartment towers with the canopies and the uniformed doormen, the carved wooden doors, the smoked-glass doors, the discreet brass plaques, the buildings with old bronze numbers coated in verdigris, the broad walks, the little dogs in fans of five tugging and yapping, dragging a young black girl in nurse's whites around the corner at 96th, the buildings failing only a little but still failing as the border of Harlem got closer, and the sunny little doorsteps got older and grubbier.

Maksins was still in a good mood. He counted off a door, a canopy, another door, three people at the side of a long black car, a woman with long blunt hair and a broad red mouth, laughing, tossing her head in the afternoon light, an old man waving to them from a bench in the shade, a Porsche, a Porsche, a Mercedes and a Porsche, a woman wheeled by a bored black maid, southbound taxis cruising at the curbline, a balloon-seller losing his hat, a blind closing, coming down slowly but steadily. Central Park West was alien territory to Wolfie. Somebody else ran things here.

At 96th Street and Central Park West the beat falters, recovers; there's another fading pile and the Porsches are falling away. The park is denser past Maksins' window. They bounce across a loose steel grid. There's a crack, a bong, a rolling boom from the roadway, and here's where Gershwin gets off, at Duke Ellington Place. They pound over the fault line at 110th Street. There's a burned-down supermarket on their left. Three black boys are kicking a burning ashcan over at the edge of Frederick Douglass Circle. Wolfie puts his piece away. He's in Harlem.

Drunk and rolling, Maksins had once driven into Harlem on his way to racket at Saint John the Divine; he'd come jolting over the potholes at 111th Street, singing "Dixie" at the top of his throat, when the rail-yard scene from *Gone With the Wind* had taken him over. He had a sensation of riding a crane, a boom, a dolly, whatever the hell they called it, up into the sky at the northern end of Central Park. Whatever the machinery, he had gone up five hundred feet and Harlem was spread out in front of him in exactly the same way that the railway station in the movie was littered with wounded Confederates, rows and rows of them in blankets, arranged in files, tagged and orderly, but wounded. Harlem had looked just like that: rows and rows of low flat roofs, set out in ranks, set down in files, all of them out of the combat, flat on their backs. Waiting for Scarlett O'Hara to come along. He had been drunk and fanciful, nor did he mention the illusion to Kennedy now, but whenever he crossed 110th Street he felt the same sensation, going up fast, seeing it all at once.

There are hills and high places in Harlem where Wolfie used to park his car and open a beer and look south toward midtown and lower Manhattan. If he set it up right, putting it at the top of Park, at the corner of 125th Street, a few long strange blocks east of the Apollo Theater, Wolfie could see the floodlit crest of the Helmsley Building all the way down at 44th Street, and behind it a dark rectangle, the Pan Am Building, the white pinnacle of the

Citicorp Center tower, the arcs and bars of the Chrysler Building, and the illuminated steppes of the Empire State Building. All around these landmarks, a compressed glittering wall of lit spires, pulsing lights, the city itself blazed away in the dark like a ship far out at sea.

That's how Wolfie had seen it, as a young cop, like a freighter at least a thousand miles away from the low flat brownstones of Harlem, as if all of Harlem were floating in the dark, floating in the wake of that receding, shining city.

Grace McEnery's front parlor had a woven rug on the plastered wall, an American Primitive scene cranked out by a computer-driven loom in Pittsburgh, endlessly generating blurry and confused echoes of Edward Hicks and Winslow Homer. The rug had been nailed to the plaster above a vinyl couch the color of an old tangerine, and there was a carpet on the floor beneath a spindly Danish table with rubber caps on its legs. At one end of the room there was a kitchen, scrubbed and spotless. A hall led away toward the rear of her ground-floor flat to three small boxlike bedrooms, each with a single overpainted window covered with a rusted mesh screen. Her bedroom had a crucifix above the bed, quite a fine one, in carved rosewood. The Christ figure writhed on it in pious counterfeit pain, far less convincing than Grace McEnery's hands.

"My boy is not home," she said to the two detectives standing in the door. "He has gone to my sister's place in Great Notch—that's near Little Falls? In Jersey? He left on Monday morning, took the bus from the Port Authority. I can't remember just when he was supposed to call me, but if you want you can call me back later, I can let you know the bus he took?"

Grace McEnery had dense and gleaming black hair which she wore in a scarlet kerchief, pulled so severely back that it seemed to stretch the skin at her temples. She was young, perhaps no older than thirty-five, but she was growing heavy in the face and hips from eating foods too starchy and too cheap—canned macaroni, canned spaghetti, cheap white bread and pasta from the Sloan's store—making her food stamps last at the expense of the body she used to have. She was still beautiful, and she looked directly at the policemen, speaking carefully and calmly, not shaking more than one would expect. Whenever she forgot about them, her feet would tap restlessly on the table leg, but when she became aware of this she compressed her lips and tightened her body again, angry with herself.

The detectives at the 27th had been having a bad day when Maksins and Kennedy pulled up—a break-in at the General Grant Houses, a nurse raped on her way to Saint Luke's Hospital, and a number of smaller collisions around the precinct area. They'd been only too happy to let Kennedy and Maksins go over alone to the McEnery flat on West 114th. They knew Dennis fairly well. He'd been arrested by the precinct Street Narcotics Unit guys for some minor drug offense and a few felony assault raps. He hadn't made much of an impression on any of the detectives, but they all remembered his older brother, whom they referred to simply as Apollo. A good-looking kid, said one of the men, leading a hand-cuffed girl out of a holding cell. Could have been a great defensive end. Went to the same school as the Perry kid, who'd been shot by a cop.

Kennedy stopped at the door. "What, Exeter?"

"Shit, no," the man said. "P.S. One-thirteen. Perry was in a grade ahead. Funny how the shit turns out up here. Perry goes to Exeter and gets shot a block from home. Apollo could have been anything he wanted, even gone to Exeter. Everybody wanted to go to Exeter in this neighborhood—any kid who knew the Edmund Perry story. But Apollo had to be a shmuck. He blew his shot at ABC grants."

"That's still open, isn't it? His case?"

"Yeah. But there's a lot of stuff happening. The Task Force has it in their book, but I think it was somebody from the Bronx, one of those Cuban wackos. Good luck with the mother. And go easy on her, will you? She's a nice lady, had a lot of bad luck."

Kennedy and Maksins knew Mrs. McEnery was lying, but there was something about the room and the way she held herself that made Kennedy want to be as gentle as he could. He stood and listened for a good five minutes, letting her wind down, letting her do what she could for her kid. Maksins was less sympathetic. He radiated supressed aggression and impatience so clearly that Kennedy asked him to go and talk to the old man sitting in the back bedroom, listening to an old Philips radio and drawing wetly on a scorched Medico pipe. Maksins thumped off down the hall. As soon as he was gone, Kennedy raised his hand, palm out, and came closer to the woman on the couch.

"Mrs. McEnery, we know your boy's a good boy. The way we see it, he probably got into something he couldn't control. Now you know and I know that he can't just go off to Jersey because his youth worker has to see him every week and he has to tell her when he goes, which didn't happen. Now all we want to do is talk to him, maybe he had nothing to do with the . . . incident."

Kennedy had not told Mrs. McEnery that there was a John Doe lying on a gurney downtown and that her son was their prime suspect in the death. He had found over the years that it was better to deliver bad news in small doses, so that people didn't get too hysterical.

"I'm telling you that my son is so in Jersey! You can ask his Uncle Ray! He was going to tell his worker but he couldn't get through to her, her phone was busy, and when he went over to tell her she was out of the office."

"Can you give me your sister's phone number? If your sister can vouch for the fact that Dennis was at her place yesterday evening, then that's the end of it."

"She don't have no— She doesn't have any phone right now. They're having some trouble with the lines."

"Then how was he going to phone you?"

"He was going to use a phone next door."

"Can you give me your sister's address? I'll have a State car drop in and talk to him."

"She's not in right now. That wouldn't do any good."

"Isn't she expecting your son?"

"Yes, but they were going to go for a drive. My son had to go out there because he was supposed to drive the car—they had to go for a drive and—"

Kennedy shook his head slowly.

"And so Dennis was going to . . . He had just got his license, you see . . ."

She was looking for something in the detective's face, some sign that he wasn't bad bull, some reason to believe that there was a way out of this for her son. When it came down to the two of them sitting in her place with the sound of the kids playing stickball in the street, car horns and radios playing, the day outside clear and bright, you could see that she was coming apart.

This was why Kennedy didn't hate the blacks, and why most of the street cops in the NYPD talked a rougher game than they played. You couldn't sit on a chair in a woman's front room and wait for her to give up a second son without making a connection with her. You could hate a people but you had to be working on a Fiberglas heart to hate the one in front of you. Every day of his life Eddie Kennedy had a chance to resist his humanity and save some of his strength to take home with him, and every day he couldn't do it. Grace McEnery, looking at him out of thirty-five years of a life Kennedy could never really feel, saw this quality in him and it broke her. She stood up, seemed about to run, twisted her blouse under her hands, made a move to sit down again, and began to cry silently, from the throat at first, and then more deeply, until her body was shaken and wracked with the force of it. Kennedy waited a moment, his head down, feeling oddly false, as if he had stolen something of value and was here to make amends. The sounds of a broom sweeping back and forth across a wooden floor came down from the apartment above them. He looked around the room, at the Hitachi color TV and the Marantz stereo system, at another schoolboy photo of a young black man with a fine-planed open face, a bright insolent smile—a beautiful boy, really, too old to be Dennis. It had been framed in what looked like sterling silver. The rest of the room was austere and barren. The couch had been patched with tape over both of the armrests, skillfully and with care. Maksins coughed at Kennedy from the hall. At the sound, Grace McEnery raise her head again. When she saw Wolfgar Maksins standing in the room, his face a flat mask, holding a picture of her youngest boy, she gathered herself with a deep breath.

She spoke only to Kennedy. "He never came home last night. He said he was going to go to the Cosmo to see a movie. I don't like to let him go out all the time but he's almost grown now. He's a good boy, but what's he going to do, hanging around on the stoop? He's got no job. I can't keep him home all the time."

Maksins broke into the speech. "Where is the kid, ma'am? It's better for him if you just tell us where he is and we go get him. Somebody else gets him, they may not be so easy on him."

She looked desolate, ashamed at what she had to say.

"I don't *know* where he is, officer! He just never came home last night at all!"

"Lady, you let that kid—a record like he's got—you let him run around all night long? How'd you know something bad hadn't happened to him?"

She had no answer for that. The trouble was, she did know that something bad had happened to him. And she knew he was running from it.

They watched her as she got her nerve together.

"What was it? What are you after him for? Did he hurt somebody?"

Kennedy spoke up, to head off something vicious he could feel building up in Maksins. "Ma'am, we don't know that for sure. We just need to talk to him. Do you know if he had any friends, any place where he might have gone, somebody who would give him a place to sleep?"

She was a tough woman. Kennedy could see her gathering her strength. How was it that a boy, two boys, could grow up with this kind of a woman for a mother, and both go so wrong? One dead, perhaps another going to Attica. How about a woman like Veronica Perry, a power in the PTA at the public school the kids from 114th Street attended? That woman had put her whole life into her kids. Grace McEnery was another in the mold, and it had gone even more badly for her sons.

"Yes, I know who he'd be with. He's always hanging around with a boy named Denzel Willoughby. They hooked up together when Dennis was at Rikers last year. I told him not to be hanging out with that child. He's a bad child and he was just going to get Dennis into trouble."

Maksins was making notes. Kennedy kept her attention, trying to keep the connection. The feelings against police ran deep and permanently through Harlem. No one gave them anything, no one talked to them, and anyone who did was often driven out of the area by the anger of her neighbors. Even a woman who lost two sons.

"Do you know where this Denzel Willoughby lives, Mrs. McEnery? Could you give us an address?"

"No, he never would say where he lived. I know Dennis went there sometimes. I think it was up on a Hundred Forty-fourth Street, in a project up there."

Maksins asked her if it might be the Drew Hamilton Houses.

"Maybe. It was a project up there, but I don't know which

one. But if Dennis is in trouble I can tell you right now that it was
none of his doing. That other boy, he's a mean child, never had
any use for him at all."

"Can you remember what he looked like?"

"Bad-looking boy, always preening himself and lifting weights.
He had lumpy skin and he was always getting into fights."

"He had lumpy skin, ma'am?"

"Yes, he has some kind of skin disease. Uncle Ray says it's
heredity, like that."

Kennedy nodded to Wolfgar, who went outside to the
car to get Farrell to search the NYSIIS lists for a Denzel
Willoughby. As he left, the gray-haired older man who'd been
sitting in the bedroom came into the room and sat down beside
Grace McEnery. She wound her hand in his. He pulled on his
pipe and sat next to her without speaking, staring at the floor, one
foot resting on the other, his other hand laid flat along his thigh.
There were heavy lines in his face, and his eyes were hidden
under thick white brows.

An incongruous sense of social obligation led Grace McEnery
to introduce the man as Raymond Washington. Kennedy leaned
forward to offer his hand. The man did not look up and made no
move to take it. Kennedy drew back again.

Maksins called from the door. "Eddie, we've got an address
on the Willoughby kid. Come on."

When Kennedy got up to leave, the old man followed him
out to the detective's car. There were people on every stoop.
Maksins was leaning on the driver's door of a blue-and-white
marked NSU, talking to a hard-faced white sergeant with mirrored
aviator glasses and a gunfighter's moustache. Three younger officers, one of them a pale-blond woman, not much more than a girl,
were sitting in the NSU car.

Kennedy waited for the old man to come down the steps,
spilling ashes from his pipe, moving as if his joints were locking
up. He got to the bottom step, sighed heavily, and stared about at
the people on the block, and the people leaning out of upper
windows, and the knots of surly black teens gathered in small
groups up and down the sidewalk.

Kennedy, sensing that the man wanted to say his piece away
from the mother, lit a cigarette and waited for him.

When Raymond Washington did finally raise his head, somebody from across the street called him an oreo. He paid no attention. "You goin' after the boy now, Detective? You goin' send that cracker you got with you after him?"

The man made no attempt to lower his voice. Maksins was easily close enough to hear, although he showed no sign. Kennedy said nothing.

"Grace, she don't have a bit of sense about that boy, but you got to understand he growed up here, he be seein' all the street dudes with pockets of cash, with Cadillacs, with suits on. His older brother, he was a street boss around here. Grace is a good woman, but no kind of good woman can keep a man out of trouble around a Hundred Sixteenth Street."

Maksins got into the detective's car and slammed the door hard. Kennedy shrugged at the old man.

"Mr. Washington, if the boy shows up around here, or he gives you a call, will you tell him to come in? He's got to come in—you know that. There's a call out on him. They'll be looking for him. It's a dangerous thing, up here. The cops are going to be nervous about him."

"No, sir, I won't tell that child to come in. And don't be shuckin' me, Mister Detective. You'll put a car on the block and wait for him to come home. I just askin' you, you keep that partner of yours off that boy. I see him, nothin' make him happier than using that big old piece of his on Grace's last child. I don't think that boy's a lost boy yet, but I tell you, you let that man kill her boy, you might as well come back here, put a bullet into her and be done with the whole family! Yessir!"

And that was that. He turned and began to work his way back up the steps. Kennedy watched him go. The old man's braces were attached to the waist of his worn-out pants with safety pins. His heels were worn to the uppers.

When Kennedy got into the car, Maksins accelerated away, forcing a group of black boys to jump out of his path.

"Shit, Eddie. You can be a real pussy sometimes!"

"Yeah, Wolfie? Fuck you too."

There was a strained silence in the car all the way to the corner. When Kennedy looked back he could see a crowd of boys around the McEnery flat. In Harlem, there is no good reason for talking to a cop, not a single one.

"Dancing shoes," said Kennedy, mostly to himself. Maksins slammed on the brakes.

"What shoes? Eddie, what the *hell* is the matter with you these days?"

Kennedy didn't look at his partner. "Mr. Washington, the old guy. He was wearing a pair of black patent-leather dancing shoes. You know, like they used to wear at the Cotton Club, in the movies?"

Maksins said nothing. He pulled away with a snarl.

There was no one home at the Willoughby apartment in the Drew Hamilton Houses on 144th Street. Although they had sent out a radio call for a Dennis McEnery, both men knew that life in the precincts up here was busy enough without taking on the work of a pair of alien DTs from Midtown. They had some hamburgers at a White Rock which Maksins insisted on eating inside. He leaned up against the windows of the place, his jacket undone, with a pair of Serengeti sunglasses on, working his way through the hamburger and staring at every black kid who came into the place. The reaction was always the same. They'd bop into the restaurant talking fast, laughing with friends, jumping and pushing each other, and then one of them would notice the two white men standing beside the door; he'd shove another, the word would go around, and they'd all shut up tight. Maksins liked the effect. He seemed to have an inexhaustible reserve of dislike for blacks. Kennedy took this shit for about three minutes, and then he went back out to the car, got in, closed all the windows, and turned on the air-conditioning. Cops with attitudes pissed Kennedy off.

The sergeants' test. The god*damned* sergeants' test. The New York Police Foundation, the black police brotherhood called The Guardian Society, the Chief of Patrol, the Office of Equal Employment Opportunity, the Mayor's Office, the Affirmative Action people, the good fairies, the little people, and the fucking Dallas Cowgirls had spent years trying to develop a civil-service test that did not discriminate against ethnic minorities, specifically against black recruiting candidates. The muscle for this program came from the 1980 federal court decision of Judge Robert Carter, who had ruled that not only did New York City discriminate against minorities, but that the bias was entirely intentional. Kennedy had no real argument against this. New York City is now, and always has been, a constellation of dark stars, warring factions, competing elements. Here in Harlem you had Spanish Harlem, Black Harlem, Puerto Rican Harlem, Italian Harlem, gang wars, turf struggles. The same thing went on all over the five boroughs. It even went on in the midtown area, in places such as the diamond district, where orthodox Jews had established a monopoly that not even the Mafia had been able to counter, and in Wall Street, where Harvard M.B.A.'s saw to it that nobody else got a Bass Weejun in the door without the high sign from a Phi Beta Crimson.

Judge Carter had ruled that one out of every three new recruits should come from a minority, and that all subsequent promotions within the NYPD should accurately reflect this quota. The trouble was, one out of three minority members weren't passing the tests. So, naturally, The Guardians, the brass at One Police Plaza, and the man from Gracie Mansion decided that rather than chase after a better class of recruit, perhaps by improving the inner-city school system, they would simply lower all the standards for getting into the Force.

The idea seemed to be that if minorities weren't getting past the recruiting standards, then the recruiting standards were at fault. Which, in Kennedy's opinion, was partly true but not wholly true.

Most of the experienced officers in the NYPD, including many of its blacks and Hispanics who had fought their way on to the force and up into the hierarchy the hard way, on the strength of their guts and their skill, felt that police work should not be treated like a democratic institution. The Police Force maintained order and enforced the laws of the land. This activity was *not* something the average senator or city councilperson could do. It required a basic set of physical, mental, and moral skills. If a recruit didn't have the size, the education, or the moral character to do that job, then the recruit shouldn't get the job.

The clash came when the minorities pointed out, with some historical justification, that it was precisely *that* bit of reasoning that had kept the downtrodden down and trodden-upon for lo these many years.

Kennedy's father was an Irishman from Armagh. He knew the Troubles well, and he'd grown up at war with an occupying army that was a declared and ruthless oppressor, the Black and

Tans, enforcers for the British occupation. Kennedy grew up
hearing stories of the Irish revolt. The similarities between Belfast
and Harlem were not lost on him. But the parallel broke down on
the difference between Ireland and New York City. In spite of
what many civil rights activists felt, Kennedy believed that the
NYPD was *not* an occupying army, or the tool of a brutal regime.
New York City was, in a cop's world, a very tough town, with
some extremely vicious people carrying on their businesses in it,
and what a city like this needed wasn't an ethnic hiring quota. It
needed good cops.

If you could *get* good ethnic cops, then as far as Kennedy,
and most of the reasonable cops on the force, saw it, may God
bless you. But don't for Christ's sake hire midgets, or twits, or
cokeheads, or petty criminals, which had happened now that the
prior criminal record of a recruit was *not* an automatic disqualifica-
tion. Kennedy hated to see what had happened to the reputation
of the NYPD in 1985. Like a lot of cops, he felt that the OEEO
and Judge Carter's ham-fisted approach to minority hiring had led
directly to the disgrace of the Force. It had also led to an
increase in outrages like the Internal Affairs Field Associates and
their grab-bag entrapment war against the whole patrol and detective function. The brass at One Police Plaza didn't trust the
quality of recruit it was being forced to accept. They responded by
hiring them, and then setting informers and spies at work among
them. It was a lousy situation. Kennedy was hardly surprised that
there was so much bitterness in men like Wolfgar Maksins.

Funny thing was, Wolfie Maksins reminded Kennedy of his
first partner, Al Weeks. Now there was a bitter man. Kennedy
had gotten the guy as a partner mainly because nobody else with
any pull at all would take the man on. Weeks liked to fight. If he
wasn't fighting with a punk or a psycho in the Bronx, he was quite
ready to go after a fellow cop. He wanted only one thing: let the
cop be white. He and Kennedy had their night on the roof of a
tenement off Fordham. Hard to say what it was over. Kennedy just
got tired of being called a mick, or a honky, or an ofay, or a faggot.
Tired of being fucked over just because of the color of his skin.
Afterward, they'd had a drink and a sweat at the police club.
Weeks told him a few stories about being a black cop. Guy had a
point. But.

A friend of Kennedy's who worked in the personnel office had

sent him an OEEO internal report that showed black representation
in the Detective Bureau, specifically in the gold-shield ratings,
was averaging out at twelve percent, and even higher when the
Detective Bureau lost nine hundred officers after the 1975 financial crisis—a very high average.

Here in Harlem, and in the Bronx, Kennedy's experience had
led him to believe that people in need didn't care very much
about the color of a cop's skin. What they did care about was the
officer's ability to do what they asked him to do.

There had been one final bit of bullshit affecting the general
problem of race wars in the NYPD and on the streets of the city
itself. It was generally believed that white cops were far more
willing to shoot black people than were black cops. That was one
of the main reasons for the quota system in the first place.
Stokovich's squad room library included an internal stat sheet that
listed shooting-board investigations during the late sixties and
early seventies. They showed that one out of every thirty-eight
black policemen had shot and killed someone during this period,
as opposed to one out of two hundred and fifty white cops. A few
more than nineteen hundred black police officers had shot forty-
four black people. Thirty thousand white cops in this same period
had accounted for only sixty-four black deaths and twenty Hispanic
deaths. The stats got a little muddy when he considered that black
policemen are usually assigned to the roughest areas, but the
point had some validity. The whole affair had been dealt with in a
Police Science journal article published in December 1981, in
which a researcher named James Fyfe had demonstrated that
minority officers are more likely to have been involved in a fatal
shooting than any white officer. Stokovich was using this report as
justification for his prejudice against black female detectives. Which
just goes to show that there are lies, damned lies, and statistics.

Kennedy decided the thing was a bag of snakes and turned on
the police radio to listen to the sound of Harlem until Maksins got
tired of intimidating school kids.

*"All right, Six Adam, ahh, they're not giving any description
on this but according to the caller there's a man on her fire escape
and he's waving a dead bird at her, K?"*

beep . . . beep . . .

"Ah, Six Adam to Central, he's waving a what at her?"

"Eight Frank to Central, we have a call-back?"

"Nah, Eight Frank, no call-back."

"Six Charlie to Central, K?"

"Six Charlie?"

"Ah, we're ninety-Z, Central."

"Oooh, not for long, Seven Charlie."

"Two Eddy to Central, K?"

"Two Eddy?"

"We're hearing a ten-eleven at three thirty-two West a Hundred and Twenty-fifth Street."

"A what?"

The dispatcher was a young black woman with a heavy Bronx accent. She ran the net with an iron hand. Kennedy tracked the hectic cross-talk while he updated his Spiegel case notes. The time was 1533 hours, and whatever the schools were doing to slow down the crime rate in Harlem was going to be officially over in a few minutes. Maksins was talking into his portable. He had probably left it turned up while he ate his hamburger. Look at the guy, Kennedy thought: six two, an easy two hundred pounds, a weight lifter who looks like an ad for the Third Reich, a punk brush-cut and a piece of weaponry under his arm that could punch a hole through a concrete wall, talking into the radio and staring out the plate glass at Kennedy. If he could ever get over his reflexes, he'd be a good cop someday.

"Five Charlie, that was no cardiac, that was a seizure. Can we have a bus at One Thirty-Seven East a Hundred Twenty-ninth Street, apartment seven?"

"Five Charlie, ten four, the bus is on the way."

"All units, on the Hudson Parkway at the tollbooth; she's reporting a black male with a gun, a possible EDP. He's harassing the people in the cars there."

"Emergency Services, Central, we're on the parkway. We'll take that call."

"Roger, ESU, we have a call-back on that. She says there are shots fired, repeat, shots fired. All units respond."

"Central, was that the Hudson Parkway or the Hudson Bridge?"

"Ah, it's from the toll sergeant at the Hudson Bridge. She's reporting that shots have been fired. Stand by, I'm on a landline.

. . . *(Some static here, and the sound of an open carrier, agitated voices, and a siren whooping and falling away)*

"ESU to Central, we're on the Parkway. We'll take that call—no further, no further!"

"All right, ESU, slow it down. All units, slow it down. Emergency Services is on the scene. No further."

"Three Auto Recovery to Central."

"Three Auto?"

"Central, one of the people we're looking for is a sixteen-year-old black male last seen on the Bronx end of the Hudson Bridge going south into Harlem. We had units of the five-oh and the five-two in pursuit. We're going to take that gun run at the tollbooth too!"

"Three Auto, that's a possible black male EDP and shots have been fired. I have a complainant and a call-back on the landline and she says that they have a man down. Approach with caution, Three Auto. Emergency Services is on the scene."

"ESU to Central, we're not on the scene yet. Have you called for a bus?"

This cross-talk was suddenly interrupted by a rapid high-pitched beeping on all channels. Kennedy saw Maksins push himself away from the wall and head for the door of the White Rock.

"All units, all units, we have a Signal Thirteen at the emergency room, Harlem Hospital, Lenox and a Hundred Thirty-fifth. Shots fired. All units respond. . . ."

Shit! Holy hell could break loose up here in three minutes. Kennedy was backing out of the White Rock parking lot as Maksins jerked open the passenger door and clambered in.

"Eddie, where are you going?"

"There's a Thirteen at Lenox and a Hundred Thirty-fifth, Wolfie! What do you think I'm doing!"

The radio was crackling and firing with taut, edgy cross-talk from units of the Two-Six, the Two-Eight, and the Two-Five. Every time a car got the air you could hear the sirens blaring in the background of the transmission. Even Street Crime Units and Neighborhood Stabilization Units were answering the citywide Code Thirteen, which means "officer needs assistance." Coupled with a "shots fired," it was a combination guaranteed to galvanize every field unit in any nearby precinct. Kennedy had hardly pulled out onto 145th Street when two RMPs from the 32nd Precinct went looping by him on their rims.

"Jesus, Wolfie, they're coming down from the three-two! Belt up, will you?"

Maksins reached over and put a grip on the steering rim. He shut the radio off with his right hand and pulled Eddie's portable out from under the briefcase on the bench seat between them. "It's fucking *off*! Kennedy, they were calling us from the bureau at the two-seven. One of their SNAP guys says he saw the McEnery kid going into the Olympia Quad about two hours ago."

Kennedy felt a warmth shooting up the back of his neck. What *was* he doing? This was no RMP and he wasn't any patrolman from the 28th. The Signal Thirteen had just canceled his brains. And here it was again, the out-of-step sensation he'd been having all week. Maksins was watching him warily.

"Fuck, Wolfie, you're right. Sorry. The Quad's on the B'way at a Hundred and Seventh. It runs all day. Figures the kid would rack up there until dark and try for his block. Did the SNAP crew bag him?"

Maksins straightened up and belted in. "Nah . . . they're running some op against a banker around the corner. They say not to come in like stormtroopers—just take the kid quiet or we'll fuck up their collar."

"Two hours past? Have they seen the kid come out?"

"No, but that doesn't mean he hasn't. Come *on*, Eddie, drive, will you? You see the guy in that NSU car, outside the McEnery broad's apartment? Yeah? Well he says the McEnery kid is always hanging out around a Hundred and Sixteenth and he's got a crew who play slow-pitch at the diamond in Morningside Park. If he's not in the Quad we'll do a Hundred and Sixteenth Street and shake up some of the shits over in the park. They'll drop a dime on him. These people have no balls."

Feeling a mixture of anger and embarrassment, Kennedy took it out on cabbies and pedestrians all the way down Adam Clayton Powell Boulevard riding the gas and the brakes and saying little to Maksins. The wide street was lined with boarded-up shops and graffiti-covered walls. There were plenty of people about, all of them black and Hispanic, mainly young kids of several mixtures walking in and out of mom-and-pop stores, sipping Coca-Cola, throwing the Frisbee or playing with a hackey-sack ball. On

Seventh the latest trend was preppy, and most of the black teens
were wearing white Bermuda shorts and lime-green Izod shirts.
At a basketball court five lean black boys hung on the chicken-
wire fencing and catcalled at the DT car as it went racing past,
Kennedy pounding the horn with his fist, making the siren yelp
whenever a car wandered into his path or a gang of black kids took
too long to cross at a light. By the time the two detectives reached
Cathedral Parkway they were in a very bad mood.

The Thirteen at Lenox and 135th Street had drawn RMPs
from all over Harlem. There were no detective units around to
give Maksins and Kennedy a hand at the theater on Broadway,
and neither man felt much like waiting. They flipped out their
shields at the booth, pushing their way past a lineup of black
teens. There was no way in the world anybody would have taken
them for anything but cops.

The Quad was running four films on a Monday-to-Friday
matinee schedule. The detectives looked at the show cards for the
various screening halls. *Rambo* was running in the first, *Brewster's
Millions* in Two, *Secret Admirer* in Three, and *Desperately Seek-
ing Susan* in the last room. It wasn't hard to make a choice.

Screening Room One was close to capacity. *Rambo* was drawing very well even on a slow Tuesday afternoon. There were no
white faces in the crowds in any of the rooms. Maksins stayed at
the head of the ramps, covering the exit doors, while Kennedy
tried to slide down the side aisle toward the front of the hall
without attracting too much attention. If it hadn't been for the
action on the screen, he'd never have reached the midpoint. The
70-millimeter camera was lingering on Stallone's latissimus dorsi
as some devolved lout in a butch-cut cranked a current through
him. Stallone was writhing and flexing magnificently, to the apparent delight of the teenage crowd in the hall. The girls were
screaming, the boys were cheering, and nobody in the room was
paying much attention to the obvious jake tippy-toeing down the
sticky carpet in the marijuana-laden darkness.

The hall worried both men. It had a couple of exits down
beside the screen, and it was full of people. If Krush was in here,
and armed, he could make one hell of a mess out of the theater,
cause a panic with a couple of shots, and stand a pretty good
chance of getting out in the aftermath. Kennedy walked slowly

and looked very carefully at every black male in the place, trying
to make that eidetic connect-the-dots matchup on Dennis McEnery
before McEnery realized there was a DT in the room. Maksins and
Kennedy had looked at the CATCH photo again just before they
got out of the car. If he was in here, Kennedy would know him.

But, Jesus, there are a lot of similarities in faces. There's a kid
with the right build, popping jujubes like Quaaludes, mesmerized
by the screen. But the ears are wrong, the lobes are connected,
not extended and full the way McEnery's ears are. And the nose is
flat and wide. What about the kid in front of him? Tall, clean
lines, the right age. A moustache? Is it real? Yeah, it's real. Okay,
this one, six seats over, with his arm around the girl? No, the
head's wrong. Too heavy in the face, too.

Kennedy ran the internal scan along every seat and down
each aisle, making the process as mechanical as he could, resisting
the urge to leap from one to the other. This one? That one? He
was close to the final eight rows now, and he was getting some
attention from the crowd. Well, that's all right now, thought
Kennedy. He was close enough to cover the front, and if the kid
ran back toward Maksins he was in for a thumping at the top of
the ramp. Heads were turning all over the theater now, eyes
widening in recognition, and a low murmur was starting to run
through the kids. Kennedy got to the end of the aisle. The screen
swept away off his shoulder in a vast distorted landscape across
which abstract lines and colors split and formed, broke apart and
clashed again while the solid thump of a heavy-caliber machine
gun made the speakers rock above Kennedy's head. Five young
kids a few rows back started to stamp their feet. Fine, thought
Kennedy. Raise some hell. Let's scare this kid into moving.

The stamping was spreading over the room now. It grew
into a booming. There was a motion out of place up there to the
right, about halfway back. A face had dropped down; something
was jostling a couple. A popcorn bag flew up in the air; a voice was
raised, a high-pitched falsetto. There!

Dennis McEnery exploded out from the cover of a row of seat
backs, leaping up into the aisle in a pinwheel of long legs and
flailing arms and a wet white flash from his eyes as they caught the
light from the screen. He gaped at Kennedy for a moment and
then pelted up toward the door at the back.

"Go for it, bro! Fuck you, assholes!" The crowd was on its

feet, yelling and chanting. Kids were crowding into the aisles as Kennedy pounded around the bottom of the theater and came up after McEnery. All he had to do was drive him into Maksins, who would be covering the upper exit.

Now the room was chaos. Faces and open mouths, cursing and pushing into his vision, kids laughing at him. The foot-stamping grew louder. Three heavyset black males got out of their seats and ran into his path, blocking his view of the fleeing boy. Kennedy backhanded one boy above the ear. He went down. A second man caught at Kennedy's jacket. He could feel someone fumbling for his gun. This was getting crazy. He pivoted on his right heel, with his elbow up. He could feel bone on bone as his elbow took the youth in the cheekbone. Kennedy put his right hand down and brought out his gun. While he had no intention of using it, he had no intention of losing it either. The third boy decided that it was the better part of valor to get interested in the movie again. Other kids got out of his way, opening up a section of the aisle for ten feet. Kennedy saw a rectangle of white open up at the top of the aisle. It filled up immediately with Wolfgar Maksins. The McEnery boy skidded to a stop, sliding in the grease and the spilled Coke on the floor. He turned again, showing Kennedy wide white eyes full of feral intensity and shock. It crossed Kennedy's mind to bring the gun up and tell the kid to stop, but the boy was showing no weapon, and the place was too crowded and too unpredictable. Let's hope Wolfie sees it that way, thought Kennedy, bracing for an impact with the McEnery kid, now less than three rows away. Wolfie puts one into the McEnery kid, he thought, that slug won't stop until it blows out a searchlight on the Empire State Building.

McEnery hesitated less than a tenth of a second. Up he went, a muscular, a superb leap really, landing on the balls of his feet along the line of seat backs, dancing and weaving like a slack-wire walker, moving fast and well, trapping the DTs in the aisle, now almost all the way to the far side of the theater. The crowd gave him a sustained cheer. Maksins jumped up on the seat backs and started to pursue him while Kennedy turned and raced toward the front of the theater, thinking that the whole goddam chase was coming dangerously close to vaudeville. Kids were backing away from all of them, sensing that the cops were getting angry, not wanting to draw any fire. Two girls screamed as McEnery landed in their laps. Then he was up again, running along the tops of the seats, leaping from row to row, bobbing and dancing in the projected beam, little droplets of water flaring like sparks off his slick stretched face as moved through the cone of light, blotting out the helicopter chase on the screen. Maksins was closing in fast, moving like a wingback over the rows, his face set and grim, but no gun in his hand. God help the kid, Kennedy said to himself. He's being a serious pain here. When Wolfie gets to him, he is going to damage that boy. Maksins wavered in the cone, staggered, dropped one foot onto an empty seat, and then went down as his leather soles slid off the material. A rigid railback took him in the crotch and he fell between the rows, raging. Krush reached the exit door and was through it, caught for a flash in the outside light like a snapshot of a long-distance runner with his weight forward, on his toes, arms reaching for it, head down. And he was gone.

Maksins was back on his feet. He plowed through the rest of the aisle, shoving kids out of the way like a bull moving the *locitos* at Pamplona, bellowing curses, calling them every racist name he could think of, and he knew many.

Wolfie was out the same door, flashing the same stop-motion image, and then he was gone too. All the way to the exit door Kennedy listened for the heavy concussive boom of that goddam Dan Wesson Wolfie was pulling out as he went through the doorway. Kennedy slithered and scrambled up to the door as the crowd cheered and whooped and he felt a temptation to stop at the door and bow. He hit the door with the flat of his hand. It bounced off and back into the wall, and Kennedy lumbered out into the busy street, sweeping the cars and the crowd, checking the corners, looking hot and wild with his coat open and his shirt pulled out at the waist and his cheeks flushed from the scramble, almost in pain with the compulsion to detect that scrap of cloth, that bobbing motion, that ripple in the street scene that would tell him which way the kid had run. A clatter of metal and glass and a hoarse cry from behind him brought Kennedy around. There! A glimpse of Maksins' wide back as he plowed through a pushcart peddler at the corner of 107th, sending burning pretzels and hot coals flying into the street, sending the black man rolling. Cursing, panting, fumbling for his keys, fumbling with the lock and the door handle, Kennedy piled into the car, started it, and came around in a tight-cranked lock-to-lock pivot with his off-side radial smoking and the positraction grinding. He let the wheel race between his fingers as the cruiser came around and then he shoved the pedal right into the matting.

God*damn* god*damn* that fucking little nigger and that asshole Wolfie. This was just what Stokovich had warned him about and this was just what Kennedy had been afraid of all day, drag-assing around Harlem with that god*dam* werewolf for a partner! And when Wolfie found the kid, was he going to say, "Now, just hold up there a minute, son. We just want to ask you a few questions"? No fucking way! He was going to chase that poor little nigger until he got him backed into an alleyway or a Sloan's or the Little Flower Baptist Church and then he'd use that mothering zebra-striped 105 on the kid and he'd put a hole through him so damn big you could put your arm in and not get any blood on your cuffs.

Did Wolfie have a drop gun? Was Wolfie stupid enough to think that a drop gun was going to help anybody out of the shitstorm? You just *try* to run a drop gun past Forensic and the Shooting Board these days! No cadaveric spasm? No sign of the automatic clamp a dying man puts on anything he's holding when you shoot him? No way to tie the gun to the dead man? Adios, sonny. You're *gone*. Kennedy tried to remember if he had ever seen Wolfie with a throwaway piece. God knows there were enough of them around the station house. They took little junk pieces off shits and skells every night of the week.

"Central, this is one-oh-four. I'm in pursuit of a black male suspect last seen on foot running north on Broadway at a Hundred and Seventh. Suspect is six one, one-sixty, clean-shaven black wearing jeans and a gray hooded sweatshirt. Suspicion of felony assault. Suspect may be armed. Plainclothes officer is in foot pursuit. Any units in the area please respond."

"One-oh-four, do you need a bus?"

"Negative, Central. I'm in vehicle pursuit northbound on Broadway. I do not have the suspect in sight. I do not have the officer in sight. There are no shots fired and no one is hurt. Just get me some cars, K?"

"Ten four, one-oh-four. All units in the area of B'way and One-oh-seventh, we have a black male six one wearing jeans and a gray shirt. Wanted for felony assault. Last seen on foot running northbound on B'way at a Hundred and Seventh Street. May be armed. There is a plainclothes officer in pursuit. No shots fired. No emergency."

Three RMPs took up the call. Kennedy got the car to the next block and was pulling over to the curb to check the alleyways when Maksins called him on the radio, his voice coming in short bursts as he fought for breath.

"Eddie, where the hell are you?"

"I'm at One-oh-nine and the B'way, Wolfie! Are you okay?"

"Yeah, I'm fine. He's a fleet little shit. I'm at the lot next to the Cathedral. I lost him crossing the Parkway. Come and get me, will ya?"

"Six Charlie to Central, K?"

"Six Charlie?"

"Central, we saw a male black answering that description going into the park at Manhattan and a Hundred Seventeenth Street. You have the unit eighty-five us here, we'll do a sweep, K?"

"Central, this is one-oh-four. We'll eighty-five Six Charlie."

"Roger, one-oh-four. Six Charlie, that unit will eighty-five you. What is your present location?"

Kennedy pulled up opposite Saint John the Divine and watched Maksins ignore every car on the road as he crossed the street to the cruiser. They were rolling again as soon as Maksins slammed the passenger door, which he did with such force that the glove compartment door flipped open. He closed it with his knee, almost incoherent with rage.

Six Charlie was waiting for them at Manhattan and 115th Street, along with the same Neighborhood Stabilization car they had seen outside Mrs. McEnery's apartment earlier in the day. Kennedy pulled up next to them and Maksins rolled down his window.

The driver of Six Charlie was a black man in a crisp summer uniform. He spoke as soon as they stopped moving.

"My Recorder is on foot in the park. The sergeant says we can have the rookies and I have Six Boy and Six Frank on the far side of the park. The guy you're looking for, is he a lean sucker, runs like a deer?"

Kennedy leaned forward to speak across Maksins.

"Yeah, fast as hell. Was he wearing a gray sweatshirt? With a hood? Jeans all muddied up, like he'd slept in a ditch or something?"

The patrolman nodded. "Yeah, that's him."

The sergeant from the Stabilization Unit walked in between the cars. He leaned into Maksins' window. Kennedy could see the interior of the car distorted in the man's mirror lenses. Maksins looked like a pale mountain.

"We'll sweep the park for you. I have a Portable up at the diamond, and two cars coming through from the other side. You want to take the drive up by Columbia?"

Kennedy shook his head. "No, we'll stay here. You get your guys to do a foot sweep through if you can. Stay on the air. And remember, this kid isn't John Fucking Dillinger, so tell your guys to be cool, hah?"

The sergeant never smiled. Kennedy couldn't see anything but his own inverted reflection in the glasses.

"Sure. We'll take him out nice and sweet. You guys sure tossed the Quad, I hear. We'll catch shit from the manager for sure."

Maksins growled at this. "Fuck the Quad. You get your buddies to kick that little nigger out anywhere along Manhattan. We'll be waiting."

The RMPs broke up, heading north and south, turning into the short, crowded cross streets, rolling slowly down the blocks. The brownstones were solid all the way to the hill, stoops and trash cans everywhere, and on every set of steps a group of blacks stood, women and men, small girls with their hair in ribbons and cornrows, wiry little boys with round cheeks and scraped knees, old men and women with lips sunken in over bare gums, young girls with smooth skin and full hips, and everywhere you looked, in threes and fours, lean black youths with closed-up faces, threatening, angry, sullen, full of resentment. The buildings needed paint, the brickwork was dirty and worn, and many of the windows were covered with boards or screened in heavy wire. The gutters were choked with scraps of paper and shreds of black rubber, beer cans, McDonald's wrappers. As Kennedy drove the cruiser down a line of rusted cars on 115th Street, at least two hundred people watched them pass.

Maksins wasn't surprised when Kennedy finally pulled to a stop thirty yards west of the McEnery flat on 114th Street and shut the engine off. Maksins was breathing hard.

"You okay, Wolfie?"

He didn't answer right away. "Yeah. I'm okay. Just give me a minute, Eddie."

Here, 114th Street was busy but not too busy. The action had drawn most of the kids up toward the park. There was no one on the steps in front of the McEnery place. The cruiser was fairly well hidden in a long row of parked cars, but Kennedy had a good line all the way down to the broad triangle formed by the intersection of St. Nicholas and Seventh Avenues, and beyond that, along a cluttered, dusty, and ragged line of tenements and cars and dense, scorched, and flattened earth, the wide flat stretch of Lenox Avenue and the bulk of the Martin Luther King Towers. Manhattan was full of tightly compressed visions like this. You could see a long way in Harlem, for all the good it did you.

Kennedy looked at his watch: 1655 hours. Almost five o'clock in the afternoon. Long shadows were crawling east from the lamp posts and steps, and the light was changing as the sun went down at their backs. Some of the heat was going out of the day. A slanted shaft of sunlight lay on the north side of 114th Street, tinting all the brickwork a deep sepia, and the street seemed to be lit from beneath, as if it were burning. The two detectives sat without speaking in the stale luminous air of the squad car as motes of dust drifted in the fading day and the digital clock on the dashboard clicked off twenty-two minutes. Now and then a burst of chatter from the radio would startle both men. The search in the park was coming up empty. A 54 on 118th Street at Manhattan pulled Six Boy off the hunt, and a 30 assault call from a Portable holding two at 38 Claremont across from Barnard College took Six Charlie. At 1717, Central passed the word that the NSU car had been redirected to a meeting at the station. Did 104 want any further? Kennedy said no thanks, and cut the radio off.

Dennis McEnery came out from between two derelict buildings on the near side of Seventh Avenue and stood, blinking in the sidelong sun, scuffed, panting, covered with dirt and sweat, his skin pulled like a drumhead over his cheekbones and his jawline, his lower lip sagging and pink. He shaded his eyes with a raised hand, still holding on to the railing of the tenement beside him as if there was some kind of help for him in the connection. He was on fire in the hot yellow light, a wavering flame sixty yards from home.

Maksins made a sound deep in his chest. Kennedy held the man in place with his right hand.

"Just wait, Wolfie. Where's he going to go?"

Maksins moved his head in a tight circle, indicating the walls and the roof lines, taking in the whole long block in one economical gesture. "They'll warn him. I'm tired of chasing this little bastard."

"Where's he gonna go, Wolfie? Just be still."

Maksins wavered for a few seconds, knowing that Kennedy was right. Where was he going to run to? But he wanted that kid. Maksins told himself, sometimes, that he never liked to hurt people. And, sometimes, it was true.

Krush started to move west on the north side of 114th Street, on his toes, his hands out in front of him, an expression on his drawn, tight face that reminded Kennedy of something . . . something. Krush took another step, now staring up at the roof lines. Kennedy could see the street through the kid's eyes now, see him raking the roof lines and looking into each shadowed doorway on the block. He was staring down the line of cars now, to him a continuous chain of headlights and grill sections, fat black rubber with worn-out treads. Kennedy could hear him thinking:

Do I know that car? Yes, that's Rainy's, and that Chevy it belongs to Mrs. Parker who works at Saint Luke's and this old Pontiac here with the glow-in-the-dark crucifix hanging from the rearview that belongs to Leroy Delacorte who drove it all the way from someplace called Batten Rude or some such and this old mother yes I know you I do you're the dark-green Cadillac de Ville I had a ride in you once when my brother was alive you belong to the Barnes man who runs the dealers on 116th Street. Last year, he let me fuck his best whore she was blond, but real blond with pure white skin and little blue veins running down the inside of her thighs all the way to her knees. She said her name was Dawn and she used to be a weather girl. Well, what the hell, Krush my man, you might as well go. . . .

"Come on, kid, come on," said Eddie Kennedy, right out loud in the squad car full of hot dead air and strange liquid amber light, and at that moment, as if he'd heard him speak, Dennis McEnery stiffened his back and pushed off against the sidewalk of 114th Street, staggering as if the shove had come too suddenly. And now he was into it, up at speed within three long loopy strides, reaching for it, going for it, coming straight up the line of parked cars with the garbage-can stoops and the ruined tenement walls all around him. As soon as Kennedy put a hand on the door

latch and the late afternoon sun glinted off his gold detective's
ring, he got it all at once like a telegram from his id.

Krush came up the street fast, laying his feet down and
picking them up with a fine careless grace, rolling at the hip joints
and taking in the air through a wide mouth, gasping, racing for the
door step, sixty, fifty, forty, thirty yards from home. Is that Uncle
Ray getting out of that car? What is old Uncle Ray doing in a
car? There's the door. He was only twenty yards from home.

Kennedy had the sun right at his back when he stepped into
the kid's path, so Dennis couldn't really see who the man was. He
kept trying to make the silhouette fit into the rounded, defeated
contours of his Uncle Ray.

Kennedy stood there on the sidewalk watching two black
boys race up a line of tenement stoops into a flat sideways sunset,
the image of one superimposed and hovering over the other and
then shifting back and forth.

Kennedy shook this confusion off, just a little alarmed at his
state of mind. Concentrate, you asshole. Wake up. He heard the
side door slam as Maksins got out into the street. The McEnery
kid swerved madly into the road and tried to angle toward the
steps of his apartment. Kennedy moved a few yards to intercept
him. He watched the kid's hands but there was nothing in them.
McEnery's eyes were closing, and a sound was coming from him as
if from someone in pain. He tried to run right over Kennedy, but
Kennedy took it all in the body and chest as his arms closed
around the boy and he used all the kid's speed and momentum to
sweep him right up and lay him across the hood of the squad car.
Maksins stepped up to the hood as Kennedy pulled the boy's left
arm around behind his back and snapped on a cuff. Kennedy
could see the hammer back on Maksins' .357, but Maksins' index
finger was not inside the guard. He had it laid up underneath the
cylinders, according to the regs. When Wolfie shoved the barrel up
against the boy's neck just behind the left ear and called him a few
bad names, Kennedy knew everything was going to be okay.

Kennedy pulled out a Frielich's gun shop card with the
Miranda rights printed on the reverse and started to read them off
to Dennis McEnery. Around him in the street, people who had
been nowhere were suddenly everywhere.

Maksins was a little rougher than he had to be when he put

the kid in the back of the cruiser. Kennedy gave him all the room he needed. When he came around to get in behind the wheel he could not help but look for Uncle Ray. He was there, standing inside the patched screen door at the top of the tenement steps, watching Kennedy from the shadow, his face a cipher. He didn't raise his hand or make any motion toward Kennedy or toward the cruiser where Grace's boy sat slumped and weary in the back. But Kennedy felt something coming from the man and it was enough.

They went down Columbus as the last of the sunlight climbed the brickwork and the roof lines along the shops and cafes, and blue shadows lay in the doorways. At 72nd they pulled up in front of a David's Cookies. Maksins went in and bought a tin of chocolate chip and three coffees, which the three of them shared. The streets were crowded on this Tuesday evening—white couples pushing baby strollers; a pair of young men jogging close together; people with clothes the color of ice cream and Reebok jogging shoes, headbands, Swatch watches, smooth well-tended skin, clear eyes. Dennis slouched in the back, traveling down Columbus Avenue past the Frusen Glädjé signs and the windows displaying Giorgio Armani suits and the café where all the people who work on the ABC daytime soaps can be seen at the corner tables in the greenhouse extension; returning the stares of the hundreds of people out strolling in their pastel jogging suits or their genuine British-Army-in-Africa khaki shorts with the cotton top seams, people dragging a brace of Akitas from Akitas of Distinction or sitting at the unsteady round sidewalk tables sipping Ramlösa, worrying about the progress of their in-vitro fertilization, listening, politely bored, to the troubles somebody's two-year-old was having in his play group; passing block after block of the best and the brightest, the aggressive and the blessed and the fit, setting trends, talking their talk in the West Side drawl, taking seriously the things that are said in *Christopher Street* and *The Village Voice* and *The New York Times*, thinking of their career paths and ambitions in terms of combat and duels, preening, stroked, swollen and fat with life, oblivious as livestock, bred to be praised and preyed-upon.

Maksins ate the last of the chocolate chip cookies, and the McEnery boy slept as Kennedy cleared the tangle at Columbus and Broadway. Colored lights played over the dusty surfaces of the squad car and illuminated the faces of the men inside. Kennedy looked over at Wolfie. He had the rapt expression of a man at a movie, in a trance at the opening frames. The car pounded over the flat iron plates at 57th Street. Broadway filled the screen.

CHAPTER 8

JURIS DICTION

The comatose biker had disappeared when Maksins and Kennedy got their prisoner up the stairs and into the squad room. So had the rest of the Task Force. The Westclox over the bulletin board gave the time as 1630 hours. Fratelli had left the coffee on and there was a note from Oliver Farrell saying that Kennedy had two calls—one from Stokovich which had come in at 1500 hours, and the other from Genno Sorvino saying he'd be in the office all evening and he wanted to talk to Detective Kennedy as soon as he got back from wherever the hell he was. There was also an interdepartmental flimsy from downtown that had IAD all over it. Kennedy read this first, read it slowly and carefully, taking in every cold-assed phrase and every hidden threat, and when he had finished he felt an overwhelming need to piss. He took the note with him into the squad room toilet with the cracked mirror and the grimy wash basin and the gray metal cubicle with the doors removed so the prisoners can't ask to be allowed to crap in private. Standing at the urinal, he rested his arm along the top of the fixture and read the short, nasty little communiqué again and again until his bladder was empty. Then he folded it twice and dropped it into the urinal. The day he answered a call like that was the day he left this force.

He called Stokovich first, partly because he knew that Bruno would have the latest word on this Internal nonsense, and partly because he'd rather talk to a cop than to an Assistant District Attorney. Maksins went downstairs to get Dennis McEnery a

169

dinner, prepaid monthly by agreement with several local delica-
tessens. McEnery was lying on his back with an arm thrown across
his face, shielding his eyes from the forty-watt bulb in the wire
cage overhead. One of Stokovich's boys answered, Kennedy didn't
know which one, and then the lieutenant was on the phone.
Kennedy had never known Stokovich to refuse to take a call, no
matter when it came in. He was a son of a bitch, but through this
latest tempest in a pisspot, Kennedy had been getting the idea
that he was *their* son of a bitch. A boss who went to the wall for
his men was like the white buffalo these days: an endangered
species.

"Kennedy, you miserable bastard! How the hell are you? Do
not tell me you don't have that MacIlwhatsit kid in the cage right
now. Do *not* tell me that!"

Kennedy spoke through an involuntary grin. Sometimes there
was nothing like a line of patter to make you feel better.

"No, *sir*, I do have him. He's asleep in the back right now.
He tried to go home around seventeen hundred hours. Wolfie and
I scooped him outside his flat."

"Wolfie behave himself?"

"Hey, Lieutenant, Wolfie's okay. A little tense maybe, and
he's no Martin Luther King. But he's fine. Did good today. He'll
get his attitude under control someday."

"You think so, huh? You ever ask him about Cardillo?"

Kennedy was startled into silence.

"Yeah, I didn't think so. Him and Cardillo, they knew each
other in the Two-Eight. He took that pretty hard. Has a bitch of a
grudge against Ward about it."

"This the Cardillo who got shot in the Harlem Mosque fuck-up
back in '71? Louis Farrakhan's little office party up on a Hundred
and Sixteenth Street?"

"Yeah, that one. Get him to tell you about it sometime, but
wait till you get this perp down to Central Booking. You get
Wolfie on to that, he's liable to eat that sorry son of a bitch by the
light of a full moon. Take a note, will you?"

Kennedy cleared his pad and took a pencil out of a brass
artillery shell on his desk. "Yeah, I'm listening."

Stokovich's voice dropped, and his tone steadied. "Okay.
First, about your little MacIlwhoosis there, I got a call from our

buddy Shodiker at Midtown North Street Crime. He gave me a sheet on a weird little fucker named Ahmad something, also known as Ronnie Holloway. This Ahmad kid, he's—get this—an albino nigger. Great, huh? He's an albino and he runs a street crew on Forty-second Street. He got nailed by some Portables after he pulled a jostle operation on a pair of out-of-towners at Forty-eighth and Seventh Avenue. They pulled him out of a booth at the Show World—"

That rang a bell. "This guy, Spiegel, he said something about there bein' a racket in the basement. A bunch of patrol guys dragged an albino out of a booth and whacked him up pretty good. Is this the same . . ."

"Oh, noooo, Eddie, it must have been another albino nigger perp who was there that night. There was a convention or something. They were bussing them in from Yonkers."

"Okay, Lieutenant, so then what?"

"Well, they have this little shit on a whole mess of stuff— stolen property, jostling, resisting, wounding. He said he had AIDS, bit one of the officers, so they had to take him to Bellevue—"

"I'll bet they did."

"*And* when they get him up to the station he starts giving up every perp and skell he can think of. Anyway, in the middle of a whole lot of other shit, he gives them a pair of muggers he'd seen earlier, who he called Krush and Jimmy Jee."

"Jimmy Jee is Denzel Willoughby. Ex-Denzel Willoughby."

"Yeah, I know. I sent Farrell over to the morgue and he made the kid from his CATCH shot."

"You sent Ollie to do that?"

Stokovich chuckled into the phone.

"So, anyway, what we have here puts your guy and the victim in the same location, seen in each other's company, on the street, right?"

"Lieutenant, you think this Holloway kid'll hold up?"

"Hey, *none* of this'll hold up without a confession. I just want you to lay it on your guy at the right moment."

"Yeah, it'll help. But so far, all we have on this kid"— Kennedy dropped his voice and looked across at the holding cell— "all we can do him for is a C felony assault. We've also got him for possession of stolen goods, robbery, but I think we ought to go for second-degree felony murder under Section One Twenty-five of the Code."

"Which part? Intentional death? Or reckless endangerment? You can't get him for 'death while escaping' because the victim was a participant. And if you're going for reckless, how the hell are you going to back up the 'depraved indifference' part? What you got here, if we're lucky, maybe a B felony manslaughter, first degree. Kid was on the run after a felony assault, so they're gonna make a case for 'extreme emotional disturbance.' That's definite manslaughter. I hear Peruggio says there are no witnesses?"

"That's what he says. I think we ought to do some canvassing of the Twenty-third Street station, see if some of the regulars can remember anything. The token seller, maybe the driver—he was right there when the Willoughby kid went over. I'll want to talk to the Transit guys. If we can show that there was a fight going on, something like that?"

"This is thin stuff, Eddie. I was hoping it would come together stronger than this. Right now, you'll never get this by the DA. Even if the kid rolls over, he's going to retract the whole thing in court. You'll have to video the whole confession, and for God's sake I hope he isn't marked up, because if he's showing anything on the video they'll get us for duress."

"He's not. He's dirty—he slept outside all night. But he came in like a zombie."

"Drugs? Was he cranked up when he did it?"

"You think he'll go for diminished capacity? I can fill the place with people who'll say he was in damn fine shape when he tear-assed all over Harlem with the cops at his tail. And his uncle says the kid is not a user. Anyway, he's criminally liable for the Spiegel assault, even if Willoughby did the wet work. Frankly, I think we've got a shot at second-degree felony murder."

"Aah, Eddie. This has 'Let's Make a Deal' written all over it. But you give it a shot. And make sure you have your notes complete on his visible demeanor, because they are sure going to try for diminished capacity and you're going to have to show clearly that he was sharp and aware when he talked to you. Right now, you've got him nailed for robbery second, because by Spiegel's own account it was this Denzel shit who did the damage, and your guy was only an accessory. Shit. I was hoping this would pull together more. You see this holding up under Section Seventy in the Procedure Law? Have we got 'reasonable cause to believe'? Have we got 'weight and persuasiveness'? I don't see it."

"Are you kidding? What kind of 'reasonable cause' do you need? If we can use Holloway and somebody like the token seller at the Twenty-third Street station to put them together and if the driver can give us some support—maybe even get an Information from the driver—then he's gone."

"Well, I don't know, Eddie. Even if he confesses, we're going to have to find a fuck of a lot of corroborative testimony, and I don't see that happening. People go deaf and dumb in something like this. You're sure not going to get anybody on a Hundred Fourteenth Street to help you out, even if he did ace one of his own people. Have you talked to Sorvino yet? Maybe he can help us out."

"The Duck? He won't go for this one unless we can nail the kid eight ways from Tuesday. You think he wants to screw up his conviction ratio?"

And back, and forth. Maybe we could this? What about that? as Kennedy and Stokovich tried to step carefully through the thickets and tiger traps of Criminal Procedure Law on their way to laying a charge that had some chance of sticking. It was a typical procedure, repeated in every squad room and station house all over the five boroughs. Finding the criminal was perhaps the simplest part of the process. It was the pattern in New York for one out of a hundred felony cases actually to proceed to trial. It takes an average of fifteen court appearances to dispose of one felony charge, *and* there are close to 40,000 felony and misdemeanor charges before the courts in any single year. Going by the odds, crime does pay.

Given the sheer frequency of criminal events in New York City, the egregious business of the plea bargain—what Kennedy and Stokovich referred to as "Let's Make a Deal"—is arguably the only way in which the legal system can make a dent in the case load.

Which is just fine, if what you are after is legality, but not so fine if you seek simple and unequivocal justice. Both men knew going into it that their chances of securing charges of murder in the second degree against Dennis McEnery for the death of his accomplice were slender, but until they had made the attempt, the matter was still up in the air. There were several reasons for the attempt, starting with the simple fact that they had some free time to put a man on it. And it was advantageous for both of them to have Kennedy in hot pursuit because it gave them a way to stall the investigation of Kennedy's alleged conduct violation.

At the heart of it, they went after the case because some good could come out of the pursuit, even if charges were never laid. Dennis McEnery was going to face some charges, and this time it was unlikely that he would get a simple suspended sentence. He was now over sixteen, so this would be the first felony charge he would have to face unsheltered by Section 30 of the Penal Code, which suggests that a person under the age of sixteen is not criminally responsible for his conduct. There were some exceptions to this in Paragraph Two, dealing with violent offenses, but as a general tendency, minors got comparatively gentle treatment in the New York court system—gentleness which most police officers felt was quite inappropriate.

In the McEnery case, both Stokovich and Kennedy knew that the possibility of a murder charge, even if a conviction was unlikely, would give the prosecutor an extra card when it came to the inevitable plea bargain with McEnery's lawyer. And at the bottom of the list for everybody else, but right at the top for the detective, was the emotional and moral certitude that the kid had gone on the street to rob, that he had robbed someone, and that he had then pushed a living person off the platform of the uptown IND at 23rd and Eighth Avenue. Whether or not the kid went to jail for it, *some*body ought to fuck up his weekend over it. Most of the time, that was the only satisfaction that a detective would ever get.

There was one other factor at work in the calculus of crime and punishment, and that was the political nature of the office of District Attorney. Most DAs do give a visceral damn about crime. If they're still alive below the cortex, they feel the sense of outrage that violent crime produces in a human heart.

But the human heart plays no role whatsoever in the courtroom. In that arena, the blood is always dry and the visible wounds are either healed or buried. All that remains is the cerebral combat of lawyers on the paper battlefield of the Code and the Constitution. Whatever may have happened in the heat of the moment, whatever may have been done and whatever may have been endured, all that remains is dry prose.

So the game is played for purposes other than vengeance, and one of the prizes is reputation. Thomas Puccio rode his reputation as a successful prosecutor into stardom as the defense attorney in the media circus known as the Von Bülow trial. He was hired for the defense because of his record of successful prosecutions. He was made, as they say, in criminal court. The same forces are making national stars out of Rudolph Giuliani and Robert Morgenthau, both active DAs in the New York area.

It is hardly surprising that other Assistant DAs in the region want to secure an impressive reputation that may someday translate into an offer from a powerhouse law firm, and the best way to do it is to make damn sure you get a lot of convictions. One of the ways to get a lot of convictions is to make certain you go into court with the odds in your favor. Judges don't like to be seen as Torquemadas, so they shy away from hard, draconian sentences for grievous crimes. And they don't appreciate seeing their calendars cluttered with cases that could have been plea-bargained away. All these factors create a desire in the District Attorney's office for extra depth in the evidentiary material and for three or four different paths leading to an almost certain conviction. They see nothing to be gained in proceeding without evidence in depth. They frequently refuse cases that have only a reasonable chance of success. They want to win in court, and they want to win as often as possible.

Part of what drove Kennedy crazy about his life was the number of times he had to drag a violent criminal back in front of a judge before the son of a bitch *finally* got a sentence that would slow him down for a while.

Kennedy and Stokovich tangoed like this until Maksins came back with corned-beef sandwiches and coffee from the All-Nite-Rite-Bite around the corner. The steam-table scent and the tang of Gulden's mustard reminded them that chocolate chip cookies are not the staff of life, whatever they think up on Columbus. Kennedy took his and attacked it as Stokovich gave him some advice about the Internal Affairs Department.

"Eddie, I've talked to downtown about this and even the guys in IAD think it's bullshit. All they want is, you should come down, talk to them, tell them your side. They close the case, you go back to work. Thing is, you don't go down, then they rack you up for refusing to cooperate."

Kennedy snarled around a mouthful of coleslaw. "Fuck *that*, Lieutenant. I've been around the track on this one. I can't think of anything I said yesterday that could have offended anybody. Last year these assholes put a *captain* on my case for a full two months over a few pictures I used in a lecture at John Jay. Some female in the crowd thought they were sexist! Can you believe it? Yeah, I know you know. The point is, I don't want to give those guys the idea that I'm going to belly-down there because one of their fucking stoolies heard me say a bad word. It's the . . . the *precedent* I don't like. You already *know* all this, Lieutenant."

Stokovich sighed into the phone. "Eddie, the thing is, sooner or later you're gonna have to tell them your side. Why not tomorrow?"

"No, not tomorrow. Not next week. I'm just fucking *tired* of this shit. They haven't got anything better to do? Isn't there some wounded cop, they can go visit him in the hospital, try to get him for a breach of the uniform regs? Or maybe there's some poor putz on the Fixer at Beth Israel, he's sleeping in the box. Land o' Goshen, Bruno. It's a fucking cop crime wave!"

"All right, Eddie, you're not gonna go down, give them the satisfaction. Maybe you'll think it over tonight, you'll come up with a different attitude tomorrow. In the meantime you're doing such a nice job out there, snagging the perps and whatnot, how about you take a boo up around the Bronx tomorrow? I got some good news for you. An RMP from the Four-Oh saw a man answering Mokie Muro's description going into the Blue Flame bar at Third and a Hundred Thirty-eighth Street around thirteen-thirty hours today."

"Jesus! They get him?"

"Nah, the mopes. Said they had a perp in the back. Some Crime guys checked it out later but no luck. You get your butt up there and do better, right?"

There was a short scuffle over at Maksins' desk as he and Krush worked out a divergence of opinion about the spelling of his mother's name. Maksins was taking the kid through the preliminary paperwork.

"Look, Lieutenant, we're going to have to get this kid booked. Let me poke around the area tomorrow morning, and you get that Crime Unit car at the Four-Oh to see if they can pick up Mokie Muro in their sector. If they can't and I get nothing from the finks, maybe I'll take a spin up there in the afternoon. How's it goin' with the Ruiz thing?"

There was a short break here. Kennedy could hear the wheels going around. "Well, buddy, it's a bag of snakes, like you said. It's connected to a crank factory, and the case goes to New Jersey so the FBI is all over it. I'm trying to get them to see our boy Porfirio as something separate, but they're not going for it. I'm down to taking notes and they're telling me that when the hammer comes down on their bad guy I'll get a piece of him for the Ruiz trial."

"Sure, boss. Unless it's big enough for him to get under the witness protection thing. Do I get to hear some more of this later?"

"Yeah, as soon as I do. *Semper Fi*, Eddie. Say good-night to Wolfie for me."

Sorvino's line was busy. Kennedy and Maksins Mirandized the McEnery kid again, and pinned the Miranda card to his sheet. They listed him for felony assault, robbery second degree, and possession of stolen goods. According to the law, they could not question him about the death of his accomplice unless they were prepared to charge him with the murder, and that would require a separate Miranda reading. All they could hope for right now was that the kid would stew quietly over his unspoken crimes, and that he wouldn't feel compelled to blurt out a confession.

Outside the house the cars were packed into the narrow cross street like cast-iron bulls in a pen, bellowing and bawling, butting each other. The hoarse curses of an angry cabbie carried over the din. Evening had come down on Manhattan. On both of the river drives the cars formed a long chain of winking tail-lights, stretching endlessly up the FDR and the Hudson River Parkway, lining up at the white-tile mouths of the Midtown and the Holland tunnels, inching across the Triborough Bridge, the Brooklyn, the Manhattan, and the Williamsburg into the bedroom communities of Maspeth and Hackensack and Long Island City. The squad room windows turned a deep smoky blue under a skin of fine gray dust. The Westclox on the wall sounded off the seconds in a taut little click and the city rolled eastward toward whatever the hell the morning had in mind.

It was funny, Kennedy thought. It was funny about truth.

People behaved as if it were something you could catch in a bottle
and take to court: This is precisely what happened and that's the
guy who did it; he says he didn't but I have the truth here and it
says he did. Kennedy sat there and listened to Dennis McEnery
go over the events of the previous night in a weary, half-sullen,
half-defeated whine, and with each pass Kennedy could feel the
truth fade. There was never a crime done and a criminal caught
where the man failed to come up with three good reasons why he
could not have done it and another six to explain why he had to
do it, why it was the only reasonable thing to do. It was a bitch
just trying to keep it straight in your own mind, to remember just
what happened and who the hell did it.

The phone rang as Maksins threw the kid a pad of paper and
told him to write out the story his way, describe just how he had
been tricked by Jimmy Jee into holding on to a bunch of cash, a
gold-plated Seiko watch, and a Marine Midland credit card made
out to a James Spiegel.

"Yeah, Kennedy here?"

"Is that Detective Edward Kennedy?"

A woman's voice. Nobody Kennedy knew.

"Please hold for Mr. Sorvino." There was nothing in her tone
to support the "please." Wait or fuck yourself—it was the same
thing to her.

He waited. Where the hell did Sorvino get a secretary to
make his calls? How much staff did they have over there?

"Eddie?"

"Yeah, Genno. Since when do you rate a secretary?"

"Ms. Fremont is not a secretary. She's clerking this fall and
has kindly agreed to assist me in clearing up some critical case
loads. I'm going over a set of briefs with her right now."

Kennedy wasn't going after *that* one. "So?"

"So, I haven't been getting your summaries on anything *like* a
regular basis. That's par. But that stiff we caught yesterday, the
Ruiz case? Where do we stand on that?"

Tricksy tricksy tricksy.

Did he know and was he hoping Kennedy would breach
security? Or had nobody told him a thing, so that he was trying to
get it out of Kennedy? He was a pretty junior ADA and it was
possible that the honchos in the DA's office were kissing him off
with minor shit and keeping the sweet stuff for themselves.

"Golly, Genno . . . I don't know where we stand on that. What do *you* think? Professionally?"

"Well, it's certainly a complex one. How are you handling the jurisdictional problems?"

"That's the tricky part, certainly. We're just trying to get all our ducks in a row here, see if something bites our asses, y'know. How's it look from your end? What's the DA's position on it?"

Maksins and McEnery had stopped talking. Wolfie was watching Kennedy talk the way a man would watch another man juggle a pair of straight razors; interested but not envious.

"Well, naturally he's watching it carefully. The interest level here is pretty high. We see the whole thing as . . . linked, you know. I can't put it too specifically, but there's a definite . . . aaah . . ."

"Linkage?"

"Exactly! I don't have to tell you how vital it is that we observe the strictest security on this. Have you interfaced with Justice on this yet?"

"Not directly. We're bulletinizing them subofficially on an hourly basis, of course. But, well, can you keep this quiet? Just between us, Genno? This is pretty raw data we're getting, and I'm not sure how far it's going to take us. You'll have to keep this close. I mean, if it surfaces outside Intelligence, I'm going to need deniability, you follow?"

"Are we blue-skying it here? Are we into a covert op situation-wise? You can tell me, Eddie. I mean, we're getting the briefing from the federal side, but you know how it is, you like to read off as many probes as possible. What are you getting from Intelligence?"

Kennedy picked up a piece of the wrapper from his corned-beef sandwich and compressed it noisily next to the phone.

"What was that, Genno? Genno, is this line . . . secure?"

Maksins laughed outright. Kennedy waved him down.

"Christ, Eddie! Aah, well, I mean I'm calling from the office. I think the lines are . . ."

"Okay, Genno. Sorry to overreact there. You ought to know what you're doing. What I'm hearing is that the Ruiz thing is just the state-side end of it. This thing could go all the way, investi-gatively speaking. We're into loose-cannon territory here. A lot of people are getting pretty nervous. I'm going to give you this,

Genno, but if it gets back to me, we never had this conversation, understand?"

"Yes, Eddie. You have my word."

"Okay, Genno. This is strictly unofficial. I'm getting this right off the Phoenix system, but it's beginning to look as if this thing goes deep deep deep into the whole Nexus project. You understand, my data is strictly down-link from the AT and F guys, and the spooks are doing most of the field work. I do know they have a mole in place right now, but nobody outside of the Combined Task Force is seeing the hard-copy. It's at the 'eyes only' and 'need to know' stage right now."

"You really think this runs into the . . . the Nexus thing? What do you see coming out of this, consequence-wise? Should this office interface directly with State? Will there be a special combined-services task force dropped into it? My case load is pretty heavy, but if you see the whole thing taking off, well, I can clear the decks pretty fast here. Be in a go-status."

A *go-status*? "Well, you'll have to take your cues from the man upstairs, I guess. Just like us. You'll see the inside of this one before any of us at the operational level. I'd say you should be ready for them. I know the Nexus guys are getting mucho funding. They'll . . . reach out for you. That's my reading. I'd say you should hold yourself in a go-status situation until the clearances come through from the federal level. Look, I can't get into this any deeper. I know I'm way outside the protocol as it is. And Genno. . . ?"

"Yes, Eddie?"

"Code Alpha on this whole thing, hah? That's vital! That's the main position we're in. Code Alpha."

"Code Alpha? Okay, Eddie. Code Alpha it is."

"Thanks, Genno. While I have you on the landline, Genno, did you get the day sheet out of us yet?"

"Yeah. You mean the McEnery case?"

"Yeah, I do."

"Well, forget murder second," said Sorvino. "You got shit. No way The Man is going for *that* one. Even if you get a shitload of corroborative evidence, best we can give you is second-degree B felony manslaughter."

"What if we do get all that, and the guy rolls over as well? It could happen in this one. I can feel it."

Genno's condescension paraded itself as pity.

"Jeez, Eddie, you know I'd ramrod it through this office if I thought you had a hope in hell. But let's face it, we're in a *cui bono* situation. It's a matter of where's the good in it. You don't have enough makeable cases lying around? They're climbing up my ass already on the rape-homicide thing you caught last week, and so far I don't see diddly on that one coming out of your day sheets. When the hell are you going to scoop those guys—Mokie and what's his name?"

"Mokie Muro and Tinto Olvera. We've got a few leads. But I'm telling you, this one, we're close on it. Close!"

"Hey, it's a who-gives-a-shit situation. It's up to you, but I've seen this Denzel kid's rap sheet and he's no loss to anyone. Best thing you can say about him, he's dead. Nobody downtown is going to give you a breast bar for nailing McEnery, even if you can, which I doubt. Anyway, it'll be Dennis McEnery come-on-*down*! Right now, I'd be willing to saw it off at a C felony manslaughter and then where'd we be with the solid stuff you've got? You want to see the felony assault and robbery two go down the tubes on a plea bargain, just so we can stick it to the guy over murder charges that'll turn into accidental death if the defense is any good at all? No, you don't. I say, go with what you've got. Call me tomorrow. Bye, Eddie!"

Kennedy said goodbye into a dead phone.

And that was the way it went. They took him to Central Booking and did him on felony assault, robbery second, and manslaughter, along with a sidecar of related junk charges. In the next few days his public defender managed to plea-bargain the manslaughter charges away in exchange for a rollover on the felony assault. In the meantime, Uncle Ray had made the kid's bail somehow, and Dennis McEnery was back on The Deuce a month later.

Wolfgar Maksins and Edward Kennedy got the squad car back to the Task Force garage at a little after ten o'clock in the evening. Life was picking up for the Patrol side of Midtown Central. The Hall was packed with hookers and wackos the RMPs had jerked out of the 42nd Street area. Most of the uniform people were young clean-faced boys and girls, competent, confident, happy kids, a lot of Italian faces, a few blacks and Latins, one or two blonds, more women than the force had fielded a few years back. Change. You could see it.

Maksins and Kennedy leaned on either side of the precinct gates and watched the blue-and-whites zipping up and squealing away as the festivities got under way in the lower-midtown cross streets.

"Well, Eddie? You want to share a cab?"

"You packing it in, Wolfie?"

Maksins checked his watch. "I don't know. Rita's on the seven-to-seven shift in Oncology. You want to get a drink? Go to Brew's? We can snag a cab on Thirty-fourth, go straight across?"

"Sounds good. Wolfie, how about you and me get seriously pissed and you can tell me how you got to be such a weird fucker?"

"You buyin', Eddie?"

"The beer or the chicken wings?"

"Either one."

"Hey, a wing and a beer. Ten of each."

"You're the weird fucker, Kennedy."

CHAPTER 9

CARDILLO

They caught a cab across 34th Street to Brew's, a cop bar at Third Avenue. Wolfie liked the boar's head behind the long oak bar. Kennedy liked the women and the collection of snapshots of the regulars over the last fifty years.

Typical city grumblings and rough talk went around and around the room. The bartender knew them, and he wordlessly set down a Beck's and a Miller Lite, leaving the tab on a ledge nearby. He nodded and smiled, a big slope-shouldered man, white-haired, seamed and softening and slightly rumpled-looking, and like all good bartenders he knew when to hover and when to give you the room. The two men drank in silence, canted into the bar, both of them settling the right foot on the rail. Beyond the tilted and uneven slopes of the broken sidewalks, 34th Street went by like a broad black river. Pools of yellow light lay here and there over the crowd in the bar, with bulked dark shadows around and in between. The air smelled of wood polish, bitters, fresh-cut lemons, the cedar-smoke-on-ice tang of brandy in a snifter a few places down. Someone at the curve of the bar was smoking a pipe, an old Petersen bent; the smoker, out of the light, sent intermittent puffs of rich blue smoke into the beam from an overhead spot, where it would billow and curl and fold in upon itself, recoil, resolve into tendrils, ascending and falling away, until someone's hand or the breath from an argument would cut it in half and blow it into a haze, while the pipe bowl flared again.

They talked about nothing with a great deal of conviction for a good half-hour. Kennedy had worked with Wolfgar for close to a year now. Wolfie was a newcomer to the squad, coming in on a trial basis, promoted to Homicide, in an unusual move, while still at the sergeant's rank. He was working on detective sergeant, and it looked like he'd get it.

Kennedy, noting Maksins' favored treatment, speculated from time to time and in a disinterested way about the identity of Wolfie's "rabbi" or "angel." An influential senior officer was frequently vital in obtaining rapid promotion through the ranks. The identity of an officer's rabbi was that person's private business. Maksins had said nothing about his, and Kennedy was happy to leave it there. Maksins seemed like a good cop. He had brains and spine enough. It was his bloody-minded attitude about blacks that kept Kennedy from complete respect.

Their table came up in half an hour. They ordered a basket of chicken wings and a bottle of Freixenet and when they got to the bottom of the first basket, Kennedy said to himself: Oh, fuck it, just come right out with it.

"Stokovich tells me you knew Phillip Cardillo? That true?"

Maksins ducked his head a bit, as if something had just gone flying past his ear.

"Jesus, Kennedy. Don't beat around the bush like that. Just get it out there." He let a full minute go by, looking at Kennedy from out of those pale-blue eyes. That was all right with Kennedy. It was a fair question. If Wolfie didn't like it, that was a fair answer. He smiled back and watched a muscle work in Maksins' right cheek as he ate the second-to-last chicken wing.

"No, that's not exactly right. I saw him around the Two-Eight. He wasn't a buddy or anything like that. Just one of the older guys, a tough guinea son of a bitch, you know? Had a way about him, always happy, always ragging the desk man, never backing away from a tussle. We were the little tads—that's what they called us. The tads."

"So what happened? I mean, I know what happened to Cardillo. I got the general report. I was up at the Four-One, in the Bronx. But everybody was at Thomas Quinn and Son's in Long Island City for the funeral. You know, Foster and Laurie and then Cardillo. All the guys were getting it in those days. Like they were giving away kewpie dolls."

"Curry, Binetti . . ."

"The black guy . . . Jones? Waverly Jones?"

"And Joe Piagentini. They shot them all down in Harlem, Eddie. They were shooting them for fun, for kicks."

"I remember. When Jones and Piagentini were down, they put sixteen more rounds into them, just for keepers."

Maksins nodded, only half-listening. Few policemen will ask another any questions about his past service. It's as if their careers started the day they hit the same unit. The reasons for this vary. Sometimes it's just tact; other times it's because you never know what wound you're going to be prodding. Better not to ask at all.

"This was in '71, I think? They were looking for the black guys, the Zebra Killers? Anyway, they were staking out a place up on a Hundred and Sixteenth Street, west of Lenox. The finks had said that one of the guys who shot Foster and Laurie was holed up in the building. So they had, you know, the hard guys, the stars. Sonny Grosso and Randy Jurgenson. Things are pretty cool. I was on my way in, it was maybe around noon. What happens is, there's a Ten-Thirteen phoned in to Communications, around eleven-forty hours. They have this male black-sounding voice—he says there's an officer in trouble at one-oh-two West a Hundred and Sixteenth Street. So of course everybody hits the bricks. They do the whole number, and the closest units are there in seconds, right?"

Kennedy knew most of this story. What he knew very little about was Maksins himself. He made the right noises and let Wolfie tell his story. Maksins was calm, telling it with no apparent anger or intensity. He spoke as people speak about events that took place in another century.

"So, one-oh-two West a Hundred Sixteenth Street is—tah-dah!—Mohammed Temple Number Seven, a Muslim office building they've turned into this Black Muslim semi-religious, semi-political hangout for their people. We had trouble all the time, in and around that place, and a lot of the street shit we were getting was a result of the speeches and the talk coming out of this Louis Eugene Walcott character, a real firebrand with that gotch-eyed look in his right eye, his hair all afro'ed and all this bandy-cock rooster flyweight arrogance coming off him. He *hated*. You tell me I hate the blacks—buddy, you haven't *seen* hatred until you've tried to enforce some bylaw or make some drug collar on a Hundred Sixteenth Street in those days. And along comes this

Walcott guy—he was calling himself the Reverend Louis Farrakhan by that time—he'd be on the street with his bodyguards, walking along in that funny little stiff-legged way that street guys have. We *bad*. I'm the *baddest* motherfucker you ever *did* see! You know all that black bullshit."

"Yeah, I've seen Farrakhan. Stages big rallies at the Garden. Saw him on *Donahue*—Phil is trying to get him to admit he said the Jews had a 'gutter' religion. Farrakhan, he's bobbing and weaving: No, sir, I believe I said 'dirty' religion. As if it made any goddam difference."

"Watch him talk, Eddie. Who's he remind you of?"

"Aah, Wolfie! He looks like every asshole who runs for public office. I've heard this black Hitler shit before. Hitler was a heavy-hitter if there ever was one. Farrakhan's about as much like Hitler as Butterfly McQueen."

"Maybe. He said—I think it was last year—he said Hitler was 'a great man' and some crap about Hitler 'raising Germany up from the ashes of defeat.' What does he think about the Jews, Eddie? How about 'Hymie Town'? And when that Coleman guy, the black reporter, put that story out, Farrakhan puts his 'Fruit of Islam' enforcers on the guy."

"Jesse Jackson is the guy who said 'Hymie Town,' Wolfie. Not Farrakhan."

"Okay, okay. So who jets off to Libya to hit Qaddafi up for a few bucks, calls him a great leader? None other than our little buddy Louis Farrakhan. Who's calling the rest of the country a nation of 'white devils'?"

"I'm just saying the woods are full of assholes, Wolfie, assholes of every stripe. I can name you six white assholes I hate just as much as this Farrakhan guy without going outside the Manhattan telephone directory. Don't build him up like that."

"You want to hear about Cardillo, or what?"

"Yeah, I want."

"Anyway, because of the Foster and Laurie stakeout, there's a lot of tension in the street, because, you know, they're always doing that: calling in a Ten-Thirteen, a false alarm, just to smoke out the surveillance guys and the perp gets a chance to boogie. So you can't ignore a Code Thirteen, but the precinct RMPs are also supposed to not make too much of a fuss and blow the stakeout thing. Anyway, they get to the Temple, answering a Code Thirteen, and there's a whole mess of black guys standing just inside the doors. They won't let them in, right? Well, the guys, they freak out. Here's a Ten-Thirteen, an officer in trouble at this address, and now they've got all these black dudes jerking them around on the steps. As far as the guys are concerned, there could be a cop getting killed right then, right inside the doors. This is no time for chitchat with a bunch of niggers."

"Probable cause?"

"That's the *whole* argument, right there! In any other situation they would have had probable cause to go inside and check the place out. But because this Farrakhan guy has got all of Harlem boiling, we're supposed to stand around and wait for the Muslims to let them in. If the Thirteen had gone down at the building next door, or the Arco station on the corner, they would have gone in like the cavalry and nobody would have said boo about it later."

"But there was some noise, wasn't there?"

"The Muslims say no. Our guys say yes. I don't give a shit either way—there was a noise, there wasn't a noise. The point is, you get a Code Thirteen, you go in, you look, and if anybody tries to stop you, down they go. Fuck them. If you can't be sure that a Code Thirteen is going to bring the rest of the guys running, no matter where you are, no matter how deep inside somebody else's property, then they have no right to ask you to do the job. It's your safety net, your ace in the hole. What else have you got?"

"So, there either is or there isn't a noise, and the uniform guys say whoops, excuse us. In they go, and up the back stairs. They get to the second floor, and *pow*, they're up to their asses in crazy black bastards. Guys are jumpin' on them from everywhere. Dropping down out of the sky.

"The fight goes back and forth. It breaks up into small groups. People are yelling and going down. The sticks are out. Meanwhile, out in the street, of course, all the black militants are getting the word around. The supervisor sees a potential riot building. That was the big fear, of course. Watts, Chicago, Harlem, the Bronx. Riots had everybody shaking down at One Police Plaza.

"The blacks get our guys back to the front door. There's a big tussle here. Three of the guys—Negron, Padilla, and Cardillo—they get cut off in the scramble.

"The doors get slammed shut, and the uniforms are back outside. They kick in the plates and out come the pieces. Shots go up into the ceiling, warning shots.

"You're sure about that?"

"Hey, Forensic was all over it. Bullet tracks, angle of incidence, the whole thing. This wasn't just a cover-up. You think if the guys had wanted to shoot into that pack, they couldn't have killed a few black guys? They had their own men in there, three of them anyway. No way were they shooting into the crowd. They just wanted them back from the doors.

"They get back inside the building, they find Negron and Padilla, they're okay. They find Cardillo on the floor with a bullet in him. Dying. He bails out later at Lenox Hill and they find a police slug in him. His gun? Well, it's in handgun heaven. He's got powder burns, stippling—he's been shot from up close. You tell me, if he was shot by his own men, who were all by this time out in the street, one hell of a long way from Cardillo, then how come the powder burns? And where's his gun? Or did he shoot himself in panic? Some of the Muslims said he committed suicide when he got cut off. Well, whatever they say, I know, and all the guys at the Two-Eight know that the Muslims took his gun and shot him. He died and that was that."

"Not exactly, Wolfie. There's a hell of a scene in the streets. They called it a Ten-Forty-five and upped it to a Ten-Forty-six. Over the next couple of days, while your guys were holding some of the Muslims, all hell breaks loose in Harlem. Naturally, everybody at One Police Plaza is shitting themselves. Jesse Jackson, Rucker, and this Mr. Farrakhan work the crowd up, demanding their rights, demanding that the Muslims the NYPD is holding be released. Calling them 'political prisoners.' That's what I remember most about it, Wolfie. We all thought it was going to spread into the Bronx. Harlem was ready to go. It was a hairy three days. The whole force was on its feet."

"Yeah, Eddie. All that shit happened, and what comes of it? Does anybody talk about Cardillo? The papers are all going on about did we have a right to enter a religious temple? Did we *have* to be so brutal? Couldn't we have asked for permission? Why did we feel we had to violate the freedom to worship?"

"Farrakhan met with the brass, didn't he? As the leader of Mohammed Temple Number Seven, he was the man in the middle, wasn't he?"

Maksins pushed his plate away and drained his wineglass. "Yeah, he was the man. It was his mosque and we were holding his people. The cop who died shouldn't have been there. Let My People Go."

Kennedy could feel some of his own anger at the mosque shooting coming back to him. It was at once strange and familiar. It was in his nature to push these things down deep. There seemed to be nothing else to do with them. The man who shot Cardillo wasn't going to walk up to the gates of the Two-Eight and offer himself to the balance.

"Your beef here, Wolfie, it's not just about Farrakhan, is it? I remember who was the Deputy Commissioner then, just as well as you do. I know who told the Two-Eight to release the Muslims and to back off from the whole thing after he'd talked to Farrakhan and Jackson."

"Yeah, so do I. Oddly enough, another black guy. Benjamin Ward, now our revered leader."

"It's not as simple as that, Wolfie."

"Yes, it is, Eddie. They took his gun and they shot him; he died, and they walked. It's as simple as that. Ward thought he was going to have a riot if they didn't. He had all the black honchos on his case. Jesse Jackson. Dudley Rucker. And Farrakhan."

"You're saying he was in a conspiracy with them?"

"No, no, I'm not. But they blew it. They rolled over and let those guys fuck the department over, and they let them kill a cop without doing a goddam thing about it. And now Ward's the Commissioner, and he's busting white cops all over town. You figure it out, Eddie."

"What white cops? Those SNAP cops at the One-Oh-Six? You think they didn't do it? They didn't zap those black kids with that stun gun? C'mon, Wolfie, grow up!"

"Eddie, you know as well as I do that the dealers and the pushers in that area have been using those stun guns on each other ever since they came out. You can *buy* the things for eighty dollars up on Forty-second Street, right over the counter!"

"You're saying the SNAP guys would *never* rough up a dealer to make their numbers?"

"No . . . no, I'm not. I've danced a few shits around up on the roof, bounced them off the pigeon coops. I know how it works. Maybe they did it. Maybe they had the heat on them because of

the numbers, the collars they had to show. Nobody's talking right
now about what it used to be like around the One-Oh-Six, about
how the dealers were almost a union around there. There was so
much dope on the street that the dealers were getting political,
jerking around with community action groups, getting representation. School kids were nodding out all over the place. The SNAP
program hit those bastards where they lived. Maybe some cops
did get rough with those guys. So how was this supposed to have
gone on for weeks and not one of the Field Associates makes his
secret call to Internal downtown about it? You can count on it that
if Internal had gotten even a hint about torture in the One-Oh-
Six, they would have come down on the place like Airborne. It
would have been raining slicks all over Ozone Park."

"Hey, Wolfie. Isn't that what happened?"

"No. There was nothing until that Davidson kid goes on TV
with the burn marks. And then the junkies come out from under
everywhere, squealing about brutality."

"Times change, Wolfie. Suspects are golden now. They walk
around in the station house, it's like they have this special glow.
Everybody walks on his tiptoes around them now. You can't ask
them questions unless you're going to charge them, and you can't
charge them unless you've Mirandized them, and you can't
Mirandize them unless you can ask them questions, which you
can't ask unless you've Mirandized them, and you can't Mirandize
them unless you're going to charge them. Make one mistake, it's
your shield and your pension. Violate the guy's rights, you're sued
in civil court. Every move you make, you know a pair of suits and
a judge are going to spend a couple of days talking about how they
could have done it better asleep. Cops are the only people in
America, when you're on trial, you're *gone* until you can prove
you're innocent. But you're after the wrong crowd, Wolfie. You're
wasting your time if you think the black guys are going to change
their tune. Would you?"

Maksins had a battery of objections, but Kennedy just raised
his voice and rolled through them.

"In New York, in America, you've got what? Three, four
hundred years, we've been jerking the blacks around. Even Lincoln said the blacks were a damned nuisance. We'd have been a
lot better off if we never dragged them over here. But we did,
Wolfie. Your trouble is, you still think life is supposed to be fair.

Farrakhan doesn't give a shit about fair. Neither do The Guardians. What's going on here, it's a balance. We fucked the blacks and the Latinos over for a couple of hundred years. Now it's their turn. They've got the liberals; they've got the press; they've got the timing. We're up the tree and here they come, yapping and snapping. And there you are, Wolfie, there you sit. Six three, two hundred pounds, thirty-four years old, blue eyes, blond hair, pulling down forty thousand a year plus overtime for a job you'd do for free if they'd ask you. Got yourself a Dan Wesson three fifty-seven with interchangeable sights. You can shoot the nits off a gnat's nuts at a hundred yards. You've got a wife—she's got a body could give a yak the trembles. You're wading through all the strange pussy a man can handle every night Rita's on the late shift. And all you can do is whine about how the blacks don't appreciate you and the faggots don't appreciate you. The whole ACLU would like to unscrew your head and puke down your neck."

Wolfie managed to smile over that. Kennedy couldn't see why. It was true. "You'll keep your sergeant's rank, Wolfie! You're a good cop. Your only problem is you want justice, and you're not going to get it. So fuck it. It's ten cents a dance, buddy. It's a tango in Roseland. It is what it is, Wolfie."

A beeper went off in Maksins' coat pocket. Heads at the nearby tables turned while he fumbled it out and shut it off. He pushed his chair back and stood up.

"I can see how you got your grade money, Eddie. Maybe you're right, too. Maybe there isn't anything we can do about the blacks and the ethnics. They're going to get their way. Maybe it's time they did. But there are a lot of cops around who aren't as reasonable as you are, and they don't give a damn if the minorities were jerked around for three hundred years. They don't think they ought to pay for something that happened before they were born. And you tell me, Eddie, as a cop: How *is* the Department doing these days? Are we the good guys or the bad guys now? And if we're the bad guys, you tell me why. Get me a depth charge, will you? I'll call in."

Maksins was full of surprises. Kennedy had been inclined to dismiss him as just another racist cop, but cop racism was rarely a free-floating evil, rising out of vapor. It often came from a personal experience of injustice, some particle of genuine truth around which generalized feelings had collected and solidified. For Wolf Maksins it had been the unavenged killing of Phillip Cardillo and the role Benjamin Ward had played in the aftermath. For Kennedy it had been the growing gap between the reality of violent crime in the 41st Precinct and the position taken by civil rights activists who seemed to value nothing other than political advantage. The Four-One had been a war zone, a lawless outland where the only safe place for the women and children of the territory was the parking lot in front of the precinct gates. Rapists, addicts, killers, pimps and outlaw bikers, hookers and zombies living off adrenaline and violent nihilism preyed on the rest of the South Bronx. They had a reason for calling it Fort Apache, a reason as incomprehensible to the rest of the world as the true nature of the war in Vietnam. The Four-One had gotten trapped outside America, outside the rules. There wasn't any law in that neighborhood. There was just your gun and my gun. No lawyers, no judges. Nobody from the ACLU. A war zone.

If we're the bad guys now, you tell me why.

Maksins was right. In 1985 the NYPD had become the bad guys again, the thugs and brutes, the peril of the city. It started with Rudolph Hays, a black plainclothes cop who had shot and killed an innocent woman named Sharon Walker over a trivial traffic dispute. He had pulled out his gun and shot her in the back as she tried to run away. December 9, 1984.

On January 3, 1985, Officer Joe Vacchio shot and killed Darryl Dodson on a gun run, a report that a man had been seen carrying a weapon. Dodson turned out to be holding a bunch of presents for his mother. Vacchio was charged with manslaughter.

February 24, 1985. Officer Mervin Yearwood was charged with criminally negligent homicide when his revolver accidentally discharged during an arrest, killing a boy named Paul Fava.

It got worse as the year went on. On March 15, on the eve of the Saint Patrick's Day parade, *the* major NYPD event of the year, an RMP driven by Sergeant Fred Sherman struck and killed an elderly Park Avenue psychologist named Hyman Chernow, and injured a doorman. The RMP slowed enough to be identified, and then it sped away down Park toward the Helmsley building. It took a citywide search to bring Sherman out into the light, a career sergeant with a history of traffic violations and alcohol problems.

Next it was Perry Novello, the off-duty officer who got into a dispute with an ex-girlfriend at a Greek restaurant. He assaulted Martha Medina. Before any other cops had arrived, Novello had beaten and handcuffed her boss, Jacob Koumbis.

And then, on April 17, Mark Davidson, high school student in the Ozone Park area of Queens, called a press conference to show the cameras several pairs of match-head-size burns on his stomach and back. His lawyer alleged that the burns came from a hand-held electric-shock machine, called a stun gun, and that it had been used on him during a torture session in the basement of the 106th Precinct. A few days later, additional allegations came from two small-time drug dealers in the sector. After this story hit the news, the national press and every activist group in the New York State area descended on One Police Plaza. Ultimately, Benjamin Ward managed the firing, the transfer, or the forced retirement of every official in the chain of command leading from the 106th to Headquarters.

On April 27, 1985, Commissioner Ward laid down the law to 327 ranking officers of the NYPD during a closed-door meeting at One Police Plaza, at which he promised that no captain would get promoted if his subordinates had a large number of brutality complaints registered against them. He asked for more discretionary powers under civil service regulations in order to be able to dismiss or demote questionable men. And he brought charges of "incompetence" against the 106th commander, Captain Allen J. Houghton. He also threatened charges against the precinct's Integrity Control Officer, Lieutenant Stephen Cheswick.

Ward also tried to get some distance from the SNAP program he had instituted in response to city pressure, claiming that the SNAP cops who were charged with torture were not "an authorized part" of his own Street Narcotics Apprehension Program. Kennedy thought that line was a tad coy.

In the meantime, a lot of ancient horrors clanked back onto the political stage of New York warfare. Carol Bellamy, the City Council president, running against Ed Koch in the mayor's race, asked for a special investigative commission into the NYPD, an echo of the hated Knapp Commission hearings of the early seventies, and Governor Mario Cuomo asked for an FBI task force to conduct its own investigation. The phrase "a blue wall" of silence got headlines. Civil rights groups asked for new hearings under ex-Knapp ramrod Roy Goodman.

And by April 30, one of the best-loved police officials, Chief of Patrol Hamilton Robinson, the third-highest ranker in the NYPD, had resigned. Robinson was widely thought of as competition for Ward and Ward's cronies, and many of the older men in the force interpreted his resignation as the result of opportunism and back-stabbing on the part of Ward and his clique. The spiritual collapse of the NYPD was just about complete by September of 1985.

Maksins' question was valid. Were they the bad guys? It looked like it, and judging from the press and the cloud of civil action parties fluttering over One Police Plaza like God's own fruit-bat nightmare, everybody in the country had turned against them.

Publicly, few members of the Department had much to say about the scandals. Privately, experienced hands such as Bill Abromaitis, the head of the Honor Legion, blamed politically mandated quota-hiring programs and the Big Mac financial collapse. Detectives like Bruno Stokovich and his boss, Richard Nicastro, blamed the lack of military service in new recruits. Everybody had an opinion about the state of the NYPD.

Like every other member of the Force, Kennedy had felt the sense of personal humiliation that comes when your own service disgraces itself. It seemed fairly weak to point out that so many officers had lived up to their jobs in the same year. Out of roughly 25,000 members, there had been a total of some 6,000 complaints filed, half of which were for brutality. Aaron Rosenthal, the Deputy Chief in charge of investigations into Complaint Review Board charges, had privately circulated a list of 300 officers against whom there were multiple charges filed. As far as Kennedy and most of his friends were concerned, the numbers were almost insignificant, considering the size of the city and the number of violent incidents that the NYPD has to contend with every year. Kennedy had read a report from downtown which estimated that the total of serious criminal incidents the NYPD would have to deal with this year would probably round out at a record-breaking 625,000. That worked out to something like 40 criminal incidents for each serving patrol officer, of which there were over 15,000. That was 40 head-to-head clashes with criminals ranging from drunken bar brawlers to professional button-men and coked-out psychotic killers.

And every one of those clashes had taken place out there in

the streets, in the basements, on the rooftops, in the alleys, in
that hidden land where the lawyers and the reporters never had to
go, where the stakes were literally mortal and the room for hesitation and uncertainty no wider than a neuron, no more durable
than a synapse. They were on you in seconds, and over you in a
heartbeat. And whatever you did, no matter how frightened or
how brave you were, the issue would always end up discussed in
the club-room serenity of a court of law, by men and women who
met for drinks when it was over, detached, privileged, and protected acolytes of cold-blooded Justice, who didn't know, and
didn't care, about you or what you had been trying to do.

Pointing to the thousands of police officers who did what was
required of them in anonymity should not have struck Kennedy as
a weak defense, but in the political and media combat of New
York City, the old saying was true: If you're explaining, you're
losing. The NYPD was losing.

"Hey, Eddie. Earth to Eddie!"

Maksins was standing over the table, a dark silhouette against
a ceiling spot.

"Buddy, you look like hell. What were you thinking about?"

Maksins sat down with a tray of drinks, two tall glasses of
draft beer and two shot glasses of Canadian Club. He picked up
one of the shot glasses and held it over his beer glass.

"Well, I gotta go back to the grind, Eddie. They just pulled
my witness out of a Dumpster at Seven-oh-two East Fifth. He's got
his cock stuffed into his mouth. They think his hands might be in
Queens. We can kiss Daphne bye-bye."

He dropped the shot glass into the beer and raised the draft
to his lips, taking the whole thing in a single swallow, finishing
with the shot glass upside down between his even white teeth. He
exhaled, thumped the table, clapped Kennedy on the shoulder,
and stood up with his hand in his jacket pocket.

"You want to come along, Eddie? Kolchinski'll be there. You
can bum a deck of smokes and generally do the dog around the
crime scene, maybe piss off another mole?"

"I'll pay, Wolfie. Put it away. No, I think I'll go home. Bruno
wants that Muro thing jumped on. I've got to get the papers
caught up tomorrow and then go up to the Bronx. This means
you'll be packed up tomorrow?"

Maksins stopped a few paces away, thinking.

"Yeah, I will. The Angels are asking for it—they'll get it now. Things were just ticking over. But when they start taking out Grand Jury witnesses, it's a new game. You're not going up there on your own?"

"No, I'll snag somebody. Maybe I'll get Frank—he's good company."

"Yeah. Frank's okay. Eddie . . . I'm sorry if I rubbed you a little raw today. You were right about that kid. It wasn't worth it."

Kennedy lifted up his shot glass and blessed it.

"What is, Wolfie? Give my regards to Kolchinski."

Maksins was gone. Kennedy killed his drink, feeling just a little lonely. A woman smiled at him as he looked around for a waiter. Her face was familiar. Irene . . . Eileen . . . something. Very dark hair, big eyes, and pale skin with a network of good lines around the eyes.

Elaine. That was her name.

"Elaine?"

"Eddie. You look lousy. Come over here and tell me why."

Elaine was a caseworker for Human Resources, so they had a lot in common, including the good sense not to talk about anything remotely resembling their jobs on a fine fall night at Brew's.

She talked with detachment and irony about her last Yuppie stud, a broker for Chase Manhattan who had "bi-coastal goals" and the ethics of a piranha. Kennedy told her about the Nexus project, playing Sorvino's part up to and including his Westchester accent.

Other people came in, friends of Eddie's from Ryan's, off-duty uniform guys from Midtown South. Around midnight they were heavily into a discussion about Daniel Perlmutter, the Giuliani aide who had stolen a half-million dollars' worth of heroin and cocaine from the evidence vaults to finance his infatuation with an actress named Stacy Hunnicut. Then there was the Alex Liberman bribery scandal to deal with, and the rumors of corruption in the Parking Violations Bureau, and the growing power of Russian Jewish criminal conspiracies, and the fraud charges against Sallie Mathis for illegal key-charges collected from welfare tenants. Elaine contributed some stories about mismanagement between the owners of the Carter and the Holland hotels and the Manhattan Human Resources agency. Welfare cases were being warehoused in the Carter and the Holland at room rates approaching $2,000 a month. The rooms were roach-infested, crawling, filthy horrors. Babies were being sodomized in their cribs. Children were coming to her with venereal infections of the lips. A mother was caught renting her seven-year-old daughter to addicts at the Holland. They had ended up talking about their jobs after all.

Elaine's last name was Farraday and she lived in a co-op in the East Sixties, only a few blocks from Kennedy's building. They walked home up Second Avenue, past the shuttered stores, stopping for a while at the promenade in Tudor City, watching the Secret Service cars prowl around the UN neighborhood, enjoying the fleeting illusion that it was still 1935, believing through an act of will in the lyrics of Cole Porter, choosing their blocks carefully, talking quietly and easily about the drought, about the mayoral race, about Sidney Sheldon's latest.

She was taller than Kennedy by an inch, perhaps two. Her black hair was heavy and glossy. When she started a sentence, she would look down, taking in a breath, making a gesture with her right hand, a gathering-in motion. Kennedy watched the way the streetlights changed the contours of her face. He altered his pace to match hers. Feeling a sense of daring, he took her arm at the corner of 57th and First. He was still holding her left wrist and she had laid her fingers along the top of his hand as they crossed the broad concrete space beneath the Roosevelt Island tramline. The air smelled of hot coffee, popcorn, exhaust fumes, dead leaves, muddy curbstone pools. Cabs and cars rushed by, other couples followed a few paces behind, or passed them going down Second with their heads together, disputing, intent, connected. Content.

Under her canopy, in the bright-blue light from a courtyard statue, she offered him coffee. He said thank you but no, he really had to go. She withdrew imperceptibly, warming only a little when he asked her if she wanted to go up to the Catskills for the weekend. She said she might—would he call her on Friday afternoon? Yes, said Kennedy, he would do that.

Eddie felt it was better to sleep alone. His nights were not the nights he wanted to share with anyone.

Calvin Jackson was standing out in front of Kennedy's apartment building when Kennedy came down the street. He had a garden hose in his hand and he was playing a soft stream of water over the glass doors and the terazzo floor under the canopy.

"Hey, Jackson!" Kennedy called to him, absurdly delighted to find someone awake at this hour. "Don't you read the papers? We're in a drought-type situation here, go-status-wise!"

Jackson's smile was just a bit thin.

"Evening, Eddie."

There was a tint in the pool of water. The palest rose. "Calvin, that's blood. What happened?"

"Rats, Eddie. I found one here, t'other over that way. By the tree. Fearsome fight, I guess. Look."

Jackson pulled a carton out from the shrubs. Two large brown rats lay in the bottom, clotted and torn. Brown incisors caught the light, a sickly wet sheen. And there was blood on one torn muzzle. Tiny slivers of black fur lay up underneath the rows of teeth, along blue gums.

Jackson looked at him apologetically. "I checked your apartment, Eddie. Hope you don't mind? But he ain't there. He ain't nowhere."

Kennedy stopped looking for Dudley around seven in the morning. There were just too many places where a hurt cat could go, too many window wells and Dumpsters, crates, stoops, shrub rows. If he could make it home, he would. If he couldn't make it home, then he wouldn't.

Jackson met him in the lobby with a mug of hot black coffee and a promise to keep his eye open for Kennedy's cat. Kennedy thanked him and went back up to his apartment to shower and change. He knew when he opened the door that Dudley was not there.

CHAPTER 10

WEDNESDAY

Oliver Farrell was the only man in the squad room when Kennedy labored up the stairs at 0800 hours on Wednesday morning. Farrell liked to keep his coat off in the squad room, so that he could show off his shoulder holster. The sight of Farrell fussing about the common room—sorting out the interdepartmental mailbag, cleaning out the coffee maker, setting it up to brew another ten cups of a coffeelike substance—incongruously suggestive of a solicitous aunt, put Kennedy into a slightly better frame of mind. It held up through a half-hour of Farrell's talk as the man wandered through the last twenty-four hours of station-house life, rattling on discursively about things Kennedy didn't give a damn for, occasionally dropping into sententious, sepulchural tones, touching upon matters that Kennedy cared quite passionately about, but not in any way that Farrell could understand, and from a body of experience unguessed-at.

There was mail for Kennedy. A peremptory summons from the Detective Division, instructing Kennedy to present himself at the Bureau offices at 1000 hours on the following Tuesday, to be interviewed by representatives of the Office of Equal Employment Opportunity with regard to "certain allegations of racist and prejudicial statements" which were "alleged to have been made by Detective Kennedy," such complaints having been registered with the Internal Affairs investigators, so on and so forth . . . the essence of which quite clearly suggested that he had better present his ass downtown on time, and with his hat in his hand, to discuss

199

the matter, or face "such disciplinary steps as may be considered appropriate" by Kennedy's superiors in consultation with the Departmental Advocate's office.

Kennedy found a note from Maksins taped to his phone.

Eddie . . .

Got cracked up a bit last night. Rita does not know. She's asleep until two this afternoon. Can you give her a buzz at 1430 hours? Tell her I'm on a surveillance detail but I'll be home around dinnertime? Don't let Farrell call her. He always makes it sound like I'm out screwing around. I'm getting some X-rays and a tape job, and I'm supposed to hang around for an EEG and some tests. I'll see you in the house later.

Called you at four this morning. No answer. You finally notice that number with the black hair? She was staring at the back of your head all night.

Thanks.

Wolfgar.

P.S. No, I can't call Rita myself. I can't talk too well with my ribs all banged up. She'll think I'm either shot or getting laid. Be a buddy? OK?

"Farrell! What the hell happened to Wolfie last night? What's this shit about getting his ribs taped up?"

Farrell looked up at him from the pages of the Green Book, over his glasses, slyly ingenuous.

"Well, shit, Kennedy. We tried to reach you all night, but you were out screwing around as usual. They eighty-sixed one of the Angel witnesses last night. Stokovich got the DA's office to come up with a warrant and they punched a raid into the clubhouse on Avenue D. The whole nine yards. ESU brought the ram. Wolfie and the lieutenant went in after them and it looks like Wolfie caught a tire iron across the ribs. It took Stokovich and two of the ESU guys to drag him off this biker, big as Vermont. Wolfie fucked him up pretty good. They say the guy's gonna lose his eye. They called from Complaint Review. That Conroy character, the corporate lawyer for the Angels? He laid a brutality charge on Wolfie, along with excessive force, abusive language, a whole bunch of shit. Gonna look pretty hinky on his Performance

Profile. Personnel is already looking at his charge rate, so he's gonna have the shoo-fly brigade sitting on his head. Conroy is talking civil suit, damages, maybe lay an assault charge. Loony tunes, Kennedy!"

"The boss was in on it? Bruno went through the door?"

"That he did, Eddie. This Angel thing, the Grand Jury is going to take it all the way. The Strike Force is onto it. Anyway, the lieutenant took it personal when they whacked the witness. Nobody was supposed to know about him, but somebody decided to take him out anyway, just to be on the safe side. Oh, yeah, I have a message for you from the lieutenant." Farrell fumbled about in his center drawer, flipping out old cigarette packs, note papers, crumpled file folders, his thin white fingers riffling through the mess, nicotine stains showing between the index and second fingers of his left hand. "Here it is."

Kennedy took the paper. It had been folded as if it had been put inside an envelope, but there was no envelope. Farrell had probably opened it, destroying the envelope as he did so. Information was Farrell's stock in trade, his source of influence and his value to the squad. It was typical of him to conceal the news about Maksins' injury and to open private communications. Kennedy had gotten used to it. It was Farrell's sense of theater. Maybe the man was a lightweight, but he wasn't an intriguer. He just liked to know things, to be on the inside.

Eddie.
You are going to have to go see the OEEO people on Tuesday. There's no way around it. I tried to get the boss to shitcan the hearing. I said you would settle for a command discipline and that would be it. But the IAD guys have their noses out of joint over you not coming in when you were told. I said you were in hot pursuit, but they say that racism in the department is a cancer and you have to clear the air.

I did find out who the complainant was. It was Bergman. An unidentified MOS reported you as using racially prejudicial language at a crime scene. "Grossly abusive" is the line I like best. You're supposed to have said "Hebe cocksucker."

You pissed off Sergeant Bergman when you went

over his head about the ACU man, Stradazzi. Downtown knows this is a bullshit charge. Bergman lays at least three a year.

But you have to be there. That is the best I can do. If you don't show up, I can't help you.

Stay in the office today. I'll be in at 1300 hours. Do some paperwork, why don't you?

Stokovich.

He folded the letter up, picturing the encounter they had in mind for him. In one of the round-table rooms downtown, the fluorescent banks buzzing away over their heads, Styrofoam cups all around. Two college kids in gray two-button suits, pale-blue button-down shirts, black socks, black penny loafers, one of those Manhattan power club ties, a yellow background with tiny red paisley patterns. There'd be a notebook out, and one of the gold-shield gophers from the Detective Division. The two college kids would have only a few minutes. They'd convey solicitude and urgency, and when they looked at you they'd have this look Barbara Walters gets when she wants to ask you if it's true about you liking to fuck helpless bunny rabbits: the puzzled frowning expression that says, hey, this is so painful for both of us, and if you just unburden yourself to me, why, we'll all feel *ever* so much better.

"So, Detective Kennedy, we have a complaint here from a Sergeant Bergman where it says you called him a 'Hebe cocksucker'—I believe that was the phrase?" Then he'd look at his roommate with a quizzical expression.

"Yes, Randolph, that's what it says here. A, ahem, a 'Hebe cocksucker' was the phrase. Hhmmph!"

Kennedy would say, "No, excuse me, I think it was *dildo*. I think I called him a dildo."

"Really? Reeeally? A 'dildo'? Well, Sergeant Bergman maintains that his source testifies that the words, your exact words, were 'Hebe cocksucker.' Nobody said anything about 'dildo,' did they, Randolph?"

"Not a word, Carter, not a word."

"Goodness," says Randolph.

"Goodness," says Carter.

"Goodness," says the gold-shield gopher.

"Well," says Randolph, "which was it, Detective Kennedy?"

"Which was what?"

Randolph will ice up a little here, just around the edges of his tan. Carter will adjust his ankle holster.

"This is a serious matter, Detective Kennedy. Racial slurs and prejudicial attitudes are *not* going to be tolerated in this department!"

"Goodness, no!" says Carter.

"Goodness, no!" says Randolph.

"Here's my tin," says Eddie Kennedy.

Well, one good thing had come out of all this nonsense. Kennedy was prepared to bet a year's vacation pay that the mysterious mole who had lodged the original charge was none other than the charming and eager and helpful Officer Brian Harris, the young First Officer on the scene at the Ruiz killing.

Knowing who one of the precinct moles was did not make Kennedy's day, but it helped a little.

Kennedy put in five unbroken hours on his paperwork backlog, on updating the response report for the Willoughby investigation, on collating the Forensic reports, on the Toxicology reports, on the index-card system, on the assignment sheet, on the case-file folder cover notes, on summaries for the DA's office, on the Response Report Investigator's interview summary and the verbatim transcript of his conversations with Grace McEnery, with Dennis McEnery, with Uncle Ray Washington. He organized the protocol for the Willoughby post-mortem, and verified the IDs and shield numbers of the morgue attendants who had taken the remains of Denzel Willoughby to the M.E.'s office.

He went over all his notes from the field investigation and the details of the pursuit and capture of Dennis McEnery and the times at which key events took place. The exact circumstances of the Mirandization, the actual card used to Mirandize the boy, and the verbatim responses of the boy to the procedure—all of this had to be included, clearly and accurately, in the official report, the chronological diary of the progress of any homicide investigation.

Since the Ruiz case was no longer his direct responsibility, Kennedy was only required to furnish a complete description of his movements and his activities in connection with the case. He had already broken down the various people involved in the case into a series of three-by-five index cards, each card carrying the name, the homicide case number, the address, the response report number, and the relevance to the investigation.

All information from Kearny's Crime Scene Unit had to be organized, notated, filed, receipted, and tagged with an evidence number.

There were also additional comments to be entered concerning cases not currently under full-time investigation. Kennedy had primary responsibility for about twenty of these, as the Detective Investigator responding. Stokovich was the Detective Supervisor, and all the cases were ultimately his responsibility, but it was up to Kennedy to update and review all his open cases whenever new information became available, or whenever he had the time for a simple reassessment of the events.

The work went well, and Kennedy found it calming.

It appealed to the clerk in him—all those stuffed brown files covered with notations in black ink, annotated and alphabetically filed, duly entered into the Green Book, cross-referenced to Evidence Storage, flimsies of the DA Summaries included, receipted, invoiced, triplicated, quadruplicated, deceptively tidy accumulations of humanity's most untidy proclivities.

He had been aware of men coming and going as he worked. Deke Fratelli came in around noon with two Hispanic males in handcuffs. They fought him halfheartedly when he put them in the holding cell, taunting the room in gutter Spanish, calling the men *maricones* and *lajaras* and *camarones*—which for some reason meant "detectives," although the original Spanish word meant "shrimp."

There was a department mythology to the effect that the Hispanic gangs called the cops *lajaras* because of a legendary patrolman out of the Two-Five whose name had been O'Hara. The story held that O'Hara was such a ferocious bull that all the people in Spanish Harlem went in great fear of him, and that whenever he was spotted, the children would run up the block before him, crying "O'Hara! O'Hara!" and that after a while the word became *lajara* and applied to any uniform officer of the Two-Five. After a while, the name spread down to Alphabet City, to the Marielito and Puerto Rican population in the Lower East Side.

Deke Fratelli tossed a bagel over to Eddie. Fratelli was looking extremely "GQ" today. Like most NYPD detectives in

Manhattan, Fratelli dressed to kill. He had his navy-blue Gianni Versace on today, with a wrinkle-shirt to match, and a linen tie in a smoky-blue tone. The shoes . . . the shoes were amazing.

"God, Deke! What the hell have you got on your feet?"

Deke smiled his slow Sicilian leer. It started with a crease in the right corner of his mouth and then he'd let it move to the left, a sardonic undulation revealing capped teeth as white and as even as convent tombstones.

"My Mauris? Blue lizard, Eddie. Got them at Leighton's up on the B'way. You like?"

"Deke, you're a vision. Thank god I'm sitting down. How'd it go with the Gypsies?"

"They were there. That place. The Holland—Eddie, it's a hellhole. They had kids living in the bathroom, along with the food. They were using the toilet for a sink. Another family was living in the main room. The kids were wearing cotton balls in their ears, so the roaches wouldn't get inside. When we turned over the dresser to check the bottom, Frank gets about a zillion fat little brown roaches all over his arms and his hands. Drops the dresser on his foot, comes out of the bedroom and heads straight for the elevator. I had to go back to the car and get him. He *hates* roaches. But we nailed the husband and there's a bunch of them squatting in the DAMP project, in the basement. I think we've got them. They had all the stuff right there, in those skirts with the sewn-in pockets. Weapons all over the place."

"The murder weapon?"

"Forensic's got it. The initial word from the M.E. is that the weapon is appropriate to the wound. But there's a hilt print, and even I can see that it matches right up. Latent prints all over it too. They're *gone*, Eddie!"

"Where's Frank?"

"He'll be along. He's down at the lab. There's a lot of narcotics stuff, and some forgeries, and we're trying to lift a latent off a twenty-two. It's not a murder weapon, so we'll get Tyranski to drop it in the acid bath for us."

A booming laugh came up from the stairwell, followed by an exchange of insults. Bruno Stokovich filled the doorway, resplendent in a navy-blue pin-stripe suit, black shoes glittering, his custom shirt as white as cocaine, a raw-silk tie in regimental stripes, knotted just so, hard up against his thick muscular neck, grinning ferociously at the squad room like the father of all cops.

"Ten-*hut*, you faggots! Your sun has arisen and yea verily I shineth upon your asses even as we speaketh!"

There was a scattering of applause as Stokovich charged through the desks, obviously delighted with himself, clapping the men on the shoulders, dispensing affectionate curses, walking heavily on his heels, sending subterranean tremors across the dingy tiles.

He stopped at the coffee machine, shaking the contents, holding it up to the light as if he expected to see something floating in the thick brown liquid. Satisfied, he poured out a cup into his personal mug, a large Toby jug with the face of a pig. He headed for his inner office, waving Farrell away. When he reached the door, he put a large hand around the molding and leaned back into the room.

"Kennedy! I got you Robinson for the Muro thing. You and Frank, get us that Mokie kid, eh? Have you been over the response report?"

Kennedy patted a file box on his desk. Stokovich dipped his head. "Okay, Eddie. You wanna talk about anything? You think about that meeting?"

Stokovich's tact could have sunk the *Coral Sea*. But it was honest concern, for all that.

"I got the note, sir. I'll have to kick it around."

Conflicting emotions played across the lieutenant's uncompromising face, like sea birds soaring across a rock cliff, settling finally into a cheery go-to-hell grin.

"Hey, I sense progress. *Semper Fi!* Back to work, girls! Graduation is only days away!" He closed the door behind him with a punctuating thump.

Even the prisoners had shut up when he arrived. And they stayed quiet until Deke brought them out to take their statements and deliver them to Booking.

Kennedy had brought most of his paperwork up to scratch and the interdepartmental courier wasn't due until 1600 hours. It was close to 1400 hours and Kennedy was having some trouble with the file box in front of him. The trouble wasn't with the box itself. It was the case inside it. Adeline Muro. Rape-homicide Case Number 114/09/85.

Perhaps Calvin had heard something about Dudley. That call took up a few minutes. The doorman had kept watch for the cat all day. There had been no sign of him. He was sorry. Maybe if

Kennedy wanted to call back around dinnertime? Dudley always showed up at Jackson's desk around dinnertime because he knew Jackson could be touched for a couple of potato chips. He kept a bag behind the counter. Sour cream and onion flavored.

That, plus some additional notations that were suddenly deemed indispensable for the Ruiz file, and a note to Charlie Marcuse about his copy of *Gunshot Wounds*, Vincent J.M. DiMaio's new textbook on forensic ballistics, and a number of other housekeeping matters brought Kennedy to 1430 hours. It was time to call Maksins' wife, Rita.

"Yes, hello?" A ruffled, sleepy feminine voice. Very much like Trudy's. She'd speak to him from under her pillow when he brought her a cup of coffee in the morning. It would be a voice just like that, with the sun coming in through the blinds, soft slatted light rippling across the rumpled bedclothes, rising to her hipline, and when he sat down at the edge of the bed, Trudy would slide closer under the covers, insinuating an arm around his waist, pulling herself in to him. She'd be lying on her left side and she'd open one startling blue eye, her blond lashes catching the sun, on fire, above a parabola of flawless cheek. A delicate excursion of fine blond hairs rested in the hollow of her temple, shading into a deeper wheat-toned gold where her hair thickened and grew dense, smelling of cigarette smoke and shampoo, a painfully evocative scent now.

Kennedy felt a pang of guilt. These were indecently familiar thoughts to be having near another man's woman. Kennedy's feelings about fidelity and honor between mates was profoundly Old Testament, absolutely nonnegotiable.

Rita and Trudy were thoroughly tangled in Kennedy's mind by the time he managed to wake Maksins' wife up enough to listen to his message.

"He's what?" An undertone here, sliding into peaks, a jagged reading on an oscilloscope. She was wavering between suspicion and panic, as Maksins had anticipated. She had reasons. Kennedy himself had called her up once or twice, backing up one of Wolfie's lies while Wolfie wound himself in damp sheets and spilled champagne at some midtown hotel.

"He's on a stakeout. They're watching some bikers right now. He asked me to call you because he can't get to a phone."

She didn't believe him. There was some resignation in her

reaction, which was a dangerous sign. Anger was fine. Resignation was fatal. Well, that was Wolfie's problem. The asshole.

"You're right, Rita. That's bullshit. The fact is he caught a boot in the rib cage last night and he's over at Bellevue being taped up. Wait." Kennedy flipped through his Rolodex until he got the number. "Here's Admitting. Give him a call. No, no, don't worry! He's fine. He just didn't want you to worry!"

She hung up without saying goodbye. Kennedy thought to himself: Wolfie, you'd better not be lying to me as well, because if you're not at Bellevue, your marriage is in the toilet. And don't ask me to lie for you anymore.

While the squad room chatter rolled around the room and the typewriters thunked laboriously down an endless beltway of forms and carbon copies, Kennedy pulled a switch-blade from his desk drawer and slit the tape on the top of the manila case holding the Muro crime-scene shots. He tipped them out onto his desk, like a deck of tarot cards, overlapping, glossy black-and-white and color 8 × 10 prints of Adeline Muro. Her eyes held a startled expression, as if she had seen wonders. The open staring face floated like a dusky tropical moon above the devastated terrain of her body, a pulpy ruin where no shadows softened the record, driven off the body by the photographer's flash, to gather in the hollows and depressions like blackbirds.

Looking at the scene, Kennedy found himself thinking about Pete Garibaldi and the way he had died, the unkillable invincible madman of the Bronx Street Narcotics Unit, and his funeral, and his wife, dry-eyed, white around the mouth, and the thing she had said to the rest of them.

They were a street crew, all of them boys really, in their twenties, athletes and hardcases. They had a simple task: street surveillance and interception of small-time heroin and smack dealers in the South Bronx. It was easy and simple work, in the way high steel work can be easy. The trick is not to look down and to keep your eye on your work. Because it was dangerous. They were getting in between an addict and his needle, a bad place to be. The addicts were as unpredictable and as feral as wild dogs, scored down to the bone by their habit. Even the tamest could come up off the sidewalk with a knife. It had happened just often enough to keep the crews on their toes. They ran the dealers and the bankers from one part of the Bronx to another, clearing this street only to find them turning up somewhere else, in another bar, at the back of another clubhouse, in a different vacant lot.

Pete Garibaldi was the sergeant who ran the squad, a beefy Calabrian cop, swarthy and crude and vital. He wore a mammoth black moustache, like a pair of black bull's horns, so wide it stretched beyond his ears. And he was strong, unearthly. Kennedy had seen him pick up a Volkswagen full of addicts and set it on its grillwork, with his cheeks bursting and the deep-blue veins popping up all over his neck and forearms. He'd taken one of the baseball bats the crew used and beaten that car into an ashtray, with the dopers inside quailing and crying, scuttling from one side to the other as that bat came down and the paint chips flew, Pete Garibaldi laughing and raging around it while the crew leaned on the pursuit cars and passed around the Coca-Colas.

The method was simple and crazed. The man in the observation post would radio the pursuit team, waiting out in the street in confiscated cars and old Department wreckers. They would take the handoff when the dealers came out of the bar and they'd follow them until they were in the right spot. And then they'd land on them, six to eight guys in a crew, wild men, with the guns out, bellowing. Usually the pushers would be paralyzed by fear. Sometimes there'd be a fight.

The best way was to close up on the dealers in the pursuit cars, one in front and one behind, until they all reached a light. Pete Garibaldi was the bat-man. He'd be out first, jumping up on the hood of the dealer's car, swinging that bat into the windshield. The dealers would sit there, too stunned to move, while Garibaldi pounded their window into fragments. The rest of the crew had the shotguns out. It took seconds. It never failed.

Afterward, if it was a good bust or the end of a long surveillance, they'd all go back to Garibaldi's house in Maspeth. There'd be hundreds of red-hot chicken wings and chicken-fried steaks, kegs and kegs of Coors. The girls would show up later, and they'd push the rugs back and dance to Garibaldi's Wurlitzer with the bubbles in the pipes and the toffee-colored panels. They'd listen to "Ain't That a Shame," and "Since I Don't Have You." Booker T. and the MG's doing "Green Onions." The Platters sang "Only you can make this change in me / For it's true you are my destiny / When you hold my hand I understand the magic that you do / You're my dream come true / My one and only you. . . ."

Garibaldi put red bulbs in all the table lamps, changing his rec room into a bar in a movie, where Kennedy danced with a girl named Holly in the red haze, feeling the ribs of her bra, feeling her body working underneath the dress, burning wherever their hips touched or their thighs moved against each other, spinning her in the red haze until the room rolled like the diadem of a Ferris wheel, spinning in the long summer nights.

It was death in a boy's world, a childish world, but no less dangerous for that. They lived a kind of Vietnam in the south Bronx, experiencing the same wild exaltation wrung from the nerve's tightest twisting.

Kennedy could still smell the cinammon and gasoline interior of the van the night of the Crotona Park buy. The dealer played with a butterfly knife, *shick-kah-shick* in the dashboard light. His ratboy did the acid test on their kilo of cocaine. By now Kennedy was sure the buyer was crazy, so far down the cocaine highway that he was never coming back. He radiated a hunger for the in-and-out of killing, as some men do, a hunger for the loopy fruits of somebody else's belly to come sliding out across his wrist, and the blood to run. They knew he'd killed a man in the yard in Attica and another man in Union City. They wanted him off the streets. Kennedy gave the signal and his crew came out of nowhere. Pete Garibaldi took the windshield out, laughing, and the ratboy came up with a cut-down Winchester over-and-under from someplace near the glove box. The interior of the van rang like a big bronze bell, once for each barrel. Pete Garibaldi flew backward into the dark, riding the plumes of flame at his chest, with that look on his face, the shock and the sudden comprehension mingling with arterial blood and tissue as he sailed backward onto the grass with the pink mist settling down around him.

His father wanted the ashes sent back to Reggio, so that's what happened, but the Department gave him honors at Cypress Hills, on a hot humid August afternoon. When the ceremony was over, the men in the squad drove Garibaldi's wife around the cemetery until they reached the driveway in front of Cypress Hills Abbey. The Abbey was closed, the massive bronze doors frosted with verdigris. Creepers and vines covered the huge stone walls. It seemed to float a few feet above the earth, on a miasma rising up out of the steamy black earth and the strangling vegetation.

Kennedy felt the heat on his shoulders as the crew stood in a circle around Garibaldi's wife. She listened to their sympathetic talk for a while, and then lashed out at them, spots of white on her flushed cheeks, her hands held tightly together under her breasts.

"You're children," she said, and Garibaldi was the worst, and he died playing a boy's game for nothing worth having. A stupid, empty, silly death. You're fools and asses to play such stupid games. Where was the good of it? Did the drugs go away? Did the streets get better? Did anybody care? Why die in such a trivial way? Where's the honor in it? Where's the glory now? Pete's dead. I'm alone. You say you're my friends, and in a year you won't know my first name. You're not men. You're nothing.

It was the timeworn women's lament, but none of them had an answer for her. Women look at men from a great distance, no matter how close they might feel to their husbands and brothers. The women Kennedy knew had pulled even farther away during the last ten years. They had shed the round flesh of the girls of Garibaldi's basement. Now they were lean and sinewy, and cord-bound at the heart as well. Men had lost them, of course—men who promised to take care of their women and then failed, willfully and relentlessly, proving nothing to the women but the durability of their faithlessness. He looked around the squad room at the detectives talking, working, typing, and ragging one another. The walls were covered with drawings. The commander had a picture called "Sitting Duck" pinned to his door, a cartoon duck in sunglasses, holding a drink, staring up at the wall behind his right shoulder where two bullets have smacked into the concrete. There was a circular for a retirement racket on the filing cabinet, "Farewell to Cash," and a dancing elf. The place looked like a team locker room, a boy's clubhouse.

Women rejected babies and fought for careers. They wore heavily padded-shoulder suits, stalking around in the Manhattan streets like Mafia button-men, in lavender sneakers and sweat socks. They swore like dragoons at you across the roofs of cabs. The television was littered with women as cutting as blades, wearing headbands, pumping iron, running the board-room meetings; models with Fiberglas lips like the flank of a Ferrari struck threatening postures and glowered into the camera. Everywhere you looked, the women bristled and strutted like Prussian duelists and the men sank into languorous androgyny, pouting at each other under blunt shocks of razor-cut hair.

Women walked and talked in daily contempt for the values of Kennedy's era, imagining, perhaps rightly, that times were different now. It wasn't clear yet just what the women proposed to put up in the place of all those fallen values. As far as Kennedy could see, they had no new ideas. Just the usual naked lunge for power and privilege.

Kennedy found himself thinking about Elaine Farraday, the caseworker for Manhattan Human Resources. He didn't know her well, but he knew her territory, the Holland Hotel, the Carter, the George, Hell's Kitchen, Tenth Avenue, the Lower West Side. In a sense they both worked the same acreage, and they saw the same things festering there.

Perhaps every lean and self-absorbed parasite on either side of the gender line had a counterweight like Pete Garibaldi and Elaine Farraday, someone who lived a good life far away from the well-lit avenues of midtown, in a thousand little combats with poverty and the inevitable violence that comes out of it. Perhaps you had to be a child to think it was still worth doing.

It wasn't a widow's hard words or the contempt of sheltered and self-absorbed ideologues and careerist harpies that put the strain on Kennedy's dwindling reserves of humor and compassion, nor was it the senseless death of Pete Garibaldi. There it was under his hand, in full color, the undeniable proof that the world was not nearly as safe or as civilized as they thought it was on 57th Street or Columbus Avenue.

A neighbor had heard Adeline Muro's baby crying all night, in a sunken brownstone in Alphabet City. She had knocked on the door when the sound persisted. Finally a number of the tenants had forced the lock to Adeline Muro's two-room apartment. The television was on, tuned to static, in a room with an iron bedstead and a crib beside it. A naked two-year-old was standing in a filthy diaper, still crying. The bars over the window had been forced inward. Whatever the woman may have owned that had the slightest street value had been taken. Whatever it was, it hadn't been enough to satisfy the jackals who had come in through the window. They had taken out their frustration on Adeline Muro.

She had been beaten and stripped, and apparently beaten again, and then they had raped her, repeatedly, stifling her screams with a Pampers pulled from a crib-side box. The woman had fought back. They found blood and skin under her nails. So they had tied her up and gagged her and gone back to it, with an atavistic, witless, vile intensity far beyond any atrocity the animal world could show, bestiality uniquely human. It had gone on for a long time, while one man had rested, wandering around the apartment, fumbling through her closets, tossing her possessions into the center of the room. For some reason they did not kill the baby, probably because a backhand blow had been enough to knock it unconscious. Then they had turned Adeline Muro over and raped her again. Then they sodomized her. Then they used a kitchen tool on her. And after they had exhausted their invention and squeezed themselves dry into her body, they bound her up with towels and hacked her throat open. As a kind of afterthought, they sliced off her breasts.

Frank Robinson had gotten to the crime scene an hour after Kennedy had arrived. There had been something new in Kennedy's face and it must have worried Robinson, because he had dragged him out of the confusing welter of detectives and crime-scene workers in that hot, airless, and unbearably scented room. Out on the street, Robinson had poured a coffee for Kennedy from a flask in the back seat of his squad car.

Kennedy had been speaking in a monotone about the Behavioral Science Unit of the FBI at Quantico. He had been musing to himself, in a flat voice, that the FBI had proven the likelihood that the killers would still have the woman's breasts when they were caught. Robinson, looking for something to say, caught between embarrassment and compassion, brought out the old sustaining delusion, heard in every squad room and every cop's bar from Yonkers to Raritan Bay.

"Come on, Eddie . . . lighten up. You think she was still in there, by the time they did that? No way, buddy. She was gone, God bless her. She was far away."

CHAPTER 11

DUDLEY

A woman pedestrian had been run down by a delivery van on East 34th Street, backing up the traffic. The driver of Kennedy's taxi, cursing, fought the dust and diesel smoke and a hundred other cars to get a half-block eastward on 34th. An EMS bus took the sidewalk around the jam-up, opening a gap in the pedestrian wall at Park Avenue South and 34th Street. The cabbie cranked his wheel hard, bounced over the curb into an illegal left-hand turn up Park. Kennedy, leaning forward to keep his shirt off the sticky back section of the seat, saw the Church of Our Savior coming up on his right as they neared East 38th Street. On an impulse, he told the driver to stop there. He climbed out onto the wide walk and stood in front of the huge sandstone facade, trying to remember if they heard confessions at 1730 hours on a Wednesday afternoon.

Kennedy's Catholicism had declined to the status of an empty social gesture many years before, shortly after the introduction of the English Mass. His Latin had always been sketchy, so it came as something of a shock to him to hear the translation of invocations and pleas that had seemed so majestic in an indecipherable tongue, and yet were revealed, in English, as commonplaces.

But the cathedrals retained their power. When Kennedy pushed open the wooden doors, he felt thirty years slipping away into the colonnaded interior. The same amber light filled the scented space. Stained-glass panels graced the clerestory. The stone floor breathed the same old soothing silence. His footsteps echoed in

the church as he made his way up the center aisle toward the
sanctuary, where a forest of pillars and arches flew upward in a
rush into the buttressed dome. In the tenth pew on the left, taken
out of habit, he made no attempt to pray. The lights were off
above the draped confessionals, which was just as well. The last
time Kennedy had tried to make a full confession, he had been
quite disappointed when the half-grown priest had stopped him
only a minute into his litany. He had worked some ten years on
those sins, and he felt they called for something better, or worse,
than the Stations of the Cross and a couple of laps around his
Rosary beads.

He came here now and then, in times such as these, to try to
resurrect some of the old consolations of Catholicism, that evil
comes from Lucifer and Leviathan, in this case from Asmodeus,
and not from someplace far more frightening, from someplace
much closer, completely inescapable, congenitally damned.

When he found himself counting the posts in the Communion
railing, he got up and strolled back down the aisle toward the door
and the hectic midtown streets. At Pershing Square he gave
himself up for damned and used his buzzer to warn the competition off an air-conditioned cab. When it pulled up in front of his
apartment building's canopy, he could see from Calvin's face that
there had been no sign of Dudley.

Holly had talked him into going down to the shelter to get a
pet in the first place. He went along with it just to humor her,
although he was privately determined that they'd be back at his
apartment in a couple of hours with nothing more petlike than a
couple of chili dogs from the pushcart vendor at the corner of 74th
and Second Avenue.

The shelter had been an animal oubliette, row after row of
wire cages holding ragged dogs and moth-eaten cats, even a rabbit
and a couple of mongooses. Mongeese? They'd never resolved
that question.

The place had a steamy density to it, dog's breath and closed
spaces. It had been winter, and the shelter was overheated and
dank. Holly had run from cage to cage, going predictably and
nauseatingly gaga over animals Kennedy would have backed over
laughing. She was convinced that a pet would go some distance
toward improving Kennedy's tendency to brood. A bird, a dog,

even a kitten, might help turn Kennedy, and Kennedy's ruthlessly neat apartment, into a more malleable, and marriageable, commodity. Kennedy, who loathed any dog that couldn't bring down a bull elk on the fly, had visions of being stroked and cajoled into bringing home some hideous triumph of decorative genetics. He'd have to take the little brute for walkies on rainy nights and at half time in the Super Bowl.

That wasn't really fair to Holly, who knew him better than that. She did favor small dogs with big eyes, but she spent a lot of time talking to a couple of Samoyeds and a Rottweiler, for his sake. Kennedy moved away, and something snagged his coat sleeve near a rack of small cages.

He looked down and there was a long furred arm attached to his best leather jacket by a fan of lethal claws. The arm was connected to what was, obviously a hydrophobic cat, a damn *big* hydrophobic cat, as black as midnight, glowering at him from the cage, filling it with ill-will and murder, baring his formidable fangs, emitting a low and sustained hiss like a damaged bagpipe. Kennedy, unable to get the cat to release his jacket, moved in closer to negotiate with the beast. In a blindingly fast move, the cat made a lunge with its other forepaw and actually caught Kennedy's jacket by the lapel. Now trapped at the cuff and the lapel, Kennedy tried to pull away and the damned thing tried to drag him into the cage. They got into quite a tussle over it, back and forth, until Kennedy put a foot against the stack and shoved backward. His coat gave in several places. The big black cat withdrew into the cage, tatters of leather coat hanging from both forepaws.

"You son of a bitch!" Kennedy had bellowed. "You're a dead cat, you little bandit." The cat had only snarled back, all white fangs and defiance in a flare of black fur. An attendant came running. Apologies were offered. Somebody mentioned that the cat was a disagreeable brute who was headed for that great litterbox in the sky, Monday next. The sentence got to Kennedy in some odd way.

Holly was patting a gray mongrel the size of a grizzly and calling out to him. Kennedy moved to within a safe distance and tried to get a better look at this doomed monster.

He was *big*—that was one thing. He'd be a handful for Holly's woolly mammoth, maybe. There was something in the cat's big yellow eyes that reminded Kennedy of Pete Garibaldi, the late demented leader of the now-scattered narcotics unit. The cat had settled down into a sullen indifference, half turned away from the cage-front, watching Kennedy over one bulked shoulder. Beneath this cage, five white kittens tumbled over one another, and above it a cocker pup sat staring down at Kennedy, its head slightly tilted, one eyebrow raised, a sliver of pink tongue sticking out over its baby teeth. Kennedy felt the dog's look.

"What do *you* think? You think this bandit ought to go to the green room? Hah?" The cocker raised its other eyebrow and reversed the head tilt. Kennedy put a hand up against the cat's cage, tentatively, ready to snatch it back if the cat made any move. It blinked at him.

"Your card says you're Dudley. What're you in for?"

Nothing.

"Nothing? Yeah, you wuz framed." He could see the cat's ears, as chewed and ragged as a wino's pantscuff. And he had several whiskers missing. And scratches above both eyes. Charmless, lethal, grumpy, and unregenerate. He called the attendant back, indicating the cat.

The boy, a Puerto Rican in a lab coat, had tried to talk sense here.

"You makin' a mistake about this one, sir. Tha's a very bad cat. He have mark up all the girls. He don' like girls very much." He nodded toward Holly. "The lady, she's not goin' be very happy with him. Anyway, I thin' he's got bugs but I can' get close enough to give him no medicine."

"I'll give him his medicine. As long as he's not sick? No distemper, or anything like that?"

The boy shook his head ruefully. "No sir, he ain' sick. He's jus' a mean machine. You wan' him, sir, I get him ready for you. You sure you don' wan' one of those guard dogs? The lady, she's got a nice Labrador cross over there?"

Holly came over at that point, taking in the cat and the look in Kennedy's eyes. "Eddie, I thought you hated cats. You can't want *this* ugly bugger? At least go for a kitten!"

The attendant came back with leather gauntlets and unlocked the cage. The cat was up on its toes, looking for blood and battle.

"Holly, this is the one I want. Look at him! He doesn't give a damn if I like him or not. That's my kind of pet. Hey, Holly, if it'll make you feel better, we'll buy the dog too. I think this cat is hungry."

It took a year for Kennedy and Dudley to learn how to get along with each other. It took less than a month for Dudley to make a name for himself on the block.

In the following ten years, Dudley broke his right foreleg jumping onto a moving car. And then again, jumping out of the second-story window with his leg in a cast. Not to mention about a hundred minor wounds, and the time, three years back, when Dudley had cast a pall over Kennedy's first evening at home with Trudy the dietician by leaping up on the bed at a critical moment, cursing his cat-curses, sitting on Kennedy's shoulder, staring down past Kennedy's neck as Trudy, gathering, cresting, wild, opened her eyes at the sound and saw a huge black cat looking down at her with his left eye torn out and dangling by a vein.

Ten years later Kennedy was seeing little Dudley-clones all around the Upper East Side, many of them living in much better circumstances than the original Dudley or his owner, riding around in the back windows of BMW 320i's, sauntering along Lexington Avenue sharing leashes with scoliotic *grandes dames* in Russian sable, even once at the window in Alo Alo, lapping at cream in a Baccarat flute.

Yes, Dudley had left his mark all over the neighborhood, a legacy of bandit cats and bounders who could still be seen along the roof lines and behind the best windows in the area. It had been a privilege just to room with that cat.

For Homicide cops, there are killings and then there are atrocities. Most of the cases, citywide, are depressingly ordinary, in the sense that no great passion, no abyssal evil, shows itself in the deed. People get knifed over Seiko watches in the basement of a parking garage, left to drain into the pavement underneath their Mercedes. Or they turn up shot over a five-dollar heroin deck, or stabbed for their Vuarnets on Lenox Avenue. Domestic tensions exact their price, many times delivering up a killer, drunk, stoned, or merely maudlin, lying in a far corner of a peeling basement apartment in Chinatown, bloody to the wrists, whining about his rights while his common-law wife leaks into a Woolworth bathmat. Bar squabbles, grudge fights, simple juvenile machismo, childish fits of silly pettiness send half-grown

boys into death struggles over parking spaces or the affections of a
wacked-out hooker in the back of a wrecked De Soto in a junkyard
near Jamaica Bay. Husbands throw their pregnant mistresses off
bridges or slip them into the current at the foot of Roosevelt
Island. Floaters bob in the wake of the garbage scows, purple and
festering, fed upon by catfish in the pilings along the Hudson. A
flower bed in Long Island City sprouts too quickly in April, and
the sniffer-probes catch the vapors of a moldering child three feet
down in the gritty clay, her schoolbooks beside her, a stocking still
knotted around her neck; fibers convict the parent next door, who
has concealed a record for child abuse in another state from his
wife and children for thirty years. Little black boys turn up
slaughtered and eviscerated, cannibalized and burned, in a litter
of white feathers and black candle-bits, in a sunken basement in
the South Bronx, sacrificed for Voodoo gods, John the Conjure
Root, Walk On Golden Splinters, or the Gris-Gris Man. A three-
year-old girl turns up wrapped in a green garbage bag on a rooftop
in Harlem. A young girl is raped and killed in Manhattan; the
black man accused of her killing snarls into a video camera and the
television news team delivers his contorted face as the detectives
lead him to a squad car. He says the bitch was asking for it and he
gave it to her. Close to two thousand killings in 1985, and over
two thousand in 1986. The streets and parks and rivers send down
corpse after corpse, a moving beltway of bodies, and any case that
takes too much time or too much manpower threatens to back up
all the cases coming down after it. The "grounders" they catch on
the fly, solving them in hours, off a shortened bat, firing the facts
into home plate. The "mysteries" get as much time and manpower
as they can find for them—more if the media are hounding the
mayor, or the bodies are piling up too fast in an area marked for
commercial development, like the Times Square blocks or Trump's
Television City or the Amex complex.

Most of the time, homicide work is business as usual. They
do what they can, what is possible in the real world. Each detective brings something personal to an impersonal art, and responds
to different atrocities in varying ways. Three kinds of murders
draw blood from all the Task Force men: the child-killings, of
which there seem to be an endless variety, from simple brutality
to kiddie-porn deaths and sexual predation; the death of any law

enforcement officer; and rape-homicide atrocities such as the Muro killing.

You could always tell when the squad was viscerally engaged by one of these cases. The mood of the squad room changed. There was no small talk. Off-duty men came in without being asked. Case loads got juggled; court dates were negotiated around it. The whole four-precinct area got involved in the fieldwork. Uniform men volunteered for canvass duty. Plainclothes cops shook up all their finks, registered and unregistered. The Crime Units clamped down on all the minor operations, making life in the blocks intolerable until the criminal community pushed the quarry out into the middle of the street. Interagency experts were called upon for counseling. Stokovich would sit for hours in his study at home, poring over journals or forensic psychology or ballistics charts, leafing through old case files, trying to get some perspective on the thing. Life in the task force got very concentrated, precise, grim.

It got grim on the streets as well. A certain amount of low-level crime goes on in every precinct area, some prostitution, a crap game, even some drug dealing. Cops don't like to shut it all down, because most of their tips and information come from these people. But if the precinct gets an idea that a killer is being sheltered, or that there's not enough help, then the hammer comes down.

A lot of talent had been involved in the Muro case. Robinson and Kennedy had the primary responsibility, Robinson as Recorder and Kennedy as the case man. Kennedy had attended the autopsy, overseeing Charlie Marcuse as he took vaginal and anal swabs from the corpse. There had been several distinct bite marks on the victim: one very clear one on the abdomen, a few inches above the pubis, and another one, less distinct, on the neck. Marcuse had used a cotton swab to take wipings of the skin around these bite marks, to provide data for a forensic serologist to develop later. If the killer, or killers, had been secretors—people whose blood type was evident in their semen and saliva, and about eighty percent qualify—then this evidence would provide support for related evidence. It wasn't conclusive alone, but it helped in those cases where an Assistant DA wanted as much backup as he could get before taking a man into court. There would also be blood cells in the semen. Marcuse had combed out the pubic area as well, collecting a number of hairs that had been left there during the rape. Forensic technicians could make very detailed observations about the age, diet, race, and sex of a suspect, based on pubic hairs.

A forensic odontologist had gotten photographs of the bite marks, black-and-white and color, taken with a centimeter rule in the shot. Additional facts could be developed from bite mark evidence, and unlike serological data, bite mark evidence had been accepted in New York State courts as final and conclusive proof of guilt. There were so many variables in bite size, in wear-patterns, in fillings and occlusions, in the pattern and distribution of teeth, that bite marks were as good as a clear latent print in a court of law. Other psychological factors could be inferred from the clarity of the bite. Had it been delivered in a frenzy, or was it the product of a slow, sadistic attack? The clear detail of the bite mark on Adeline Muro's belly suggested a deliberately sadistic assault, a contention supported by the fact that the degree of bruising and tissue destruction proved that it had been done while the victim was still living.

An attempt had been made to lift latent prints off the victim's body, especially from the areas around the neck, the inner thighs, and her wrists. A Crime Scene technician who had been trained in the Kromekote film technique had performed the operation at the scene. But latent prints were useless unless a specific suspect was under investigation. The FBI Latent Print Section in Washington can only search for similarities in a few areas. There is no computerized filing system that can be tapped into for some magical whole-system check. The search must be directed by name and FBI print number.

But a latent print will nail a suspect, once the man has been taken into custody, and a latent print found on the victim is as conclusive as an eyewitness. It's one more item that a DA can use to convince a jury.

The brutality of the attack, and particularly the mutilations, had prompted Stokovich to contact the New York office of the FBI, to get some advice from the Behavioral Science Unit. The BSU team had been interviewing serial killers for several years, gathering data in an attempt to develop a profile of the typical mass killer. The unit had been involved in the Atlanta child murders, as well as the Ted Bundy sexual homicide investigations.

It had also been useful in providing the British police with some projections about the likely domestic patterns and personality problems of the Yorkshire Ripper. That and a hundred other smaller incidents had allowed the unit to offer a forensic resource to any police force with an interest.

The Muro case was an isolated incident, not part of a series of similar attacks, so there was no way in which Stokovich could have persuaded the Department to make an official request for their help. But he did know one of the FBI field men, and he got access to some advice through the old-boy network.

In the meantime, Kolchinski, Fratelli, and several plain-clothesmen from Patrol had conducted a major canvass of the apartment block and the streets and alleys surrounding it. They paid special attention to the apartments across the back alley from the Muro apartment, where people had a clear line of sight into the room where she had been killed.

Patrol officers had conducted the initial interviews, merely asking whether or not anyone in the area had seen or heard anything during the hours surrounding the attack. If the officers got a positive response, which was rare, then they would flag that sheet for the attention of the Detective Division. Out of 343 canvass contacts, the officers had found only seven people who had, or seemed as if they *might* have, relevant information.

A full afternoon and evening shift had been devoted to the Muro case. Physical evidence had been taken by the Crime Scene men, and other blood, semen, hair, and tissue samples had been gathered during the autopsy. The canvass had generated some possible witnesses, and Stokovich had some data concerning the mutilations. At 2345 hours, about sixteen hours after the First Officer had arrived at the scene, Stokovich pulled his Task Force back to the squad room for a conference, to see what they had, what they needed, and what it all meant.

During the conference, while the tired men slouched in chairs or leaned against the walls, and the coffee machine popped and hissed, Stokovich took each team through their actions, making notes in a steno pad.

He knew that serology and the rest of the forensic work was going to take a few days to come together. What the team was looking for at this stage was some anomaly, what the textbooks call "the stressor" in the recent life of Adeline Muro. They were hoping for some unusual occurrence—a fight with a boyfriend, the loss of a job, a new acquaintance, something ordered from a store—anything at all that could suggest the first contact with her killer. Experience had taught them that very few cases of sexual assault took place between absolute strangers. It was a depressing truth that the most likely suspects in any sex killing were members of the immediate family and close associates. The nearest and the dearest. So the first hour of the conference was devoted to analyzing what had been discovered about the last week of Adeline Muro's life and the people who had been in contact with her during that time. Somewhere in that record there might be a clue to her death.

They got the first clue when Kolchinski and Wolf Maksins reported that Adeline Muro's husband was serving a sentence for drug trafficking up at Rikers. He was a known associate of several drug runners in Alphabet City.

Fratelli had discovered that Adeline Muro had been making regular purchases of medicinal antiseptics from the Comprehensive Health Services.

Kennedy observed that Marcuse had not found any signs of disease in the victim's body.

Stokovich noted that the Crime Scene Unit had detected at least five varieties of fingerprints in the primary crime zone: some plastic, some visible, and a couple of latents. Kearny had suggested, off the record, that it looked like two of these sets of prints were from a small child and a young woman. The other three types were typical of adult male prints.

Maksins came back from the phone with the name of Adeline Muro's husband, a Rubio Joaquin Muro, DOB 05/21/48, with a history of drug and weapons offenses. He was a Cuban who had come across during the great exodus in 1980, when Castro had cleared his prisons and insane asylums and set them all afloat for America from Mariel Harbor.

Robinson presented a Manhattan Human Resources case card in the name of Hermenegildo Muro, DOB 09/06/58, and a CATCH sheet on the man, listing his a.k.a.'s as Zaka, Loco, and Mokie. The card had been found in the spare room.

A Mokie Muro was listed on Rubio Joaquin Muro's sheet, but improperly, as an a.k.a. The different dates of birth suggested a simple error in filing.

The M.E.'s preliminary report, phoned in to Kennedy in the afternoon, had hinted at two types of semen in the victim's anal and vaginal canals. And it had been the feeling of the odontologist that there were *two* distinct bite patterns on the body.

And the material under the nails of the victim was definitely human skin and blood, type AB, which matched the blood type found in one of the semen samples.

Kolchinski had been on the phone to the clerk at the Health Services clinic, and she confirmed that Adeline Muro had been concerned about hepatitis and how infectious it was for children. The paramedic had suggested certain antiseptic procedures and cautioned her against sharing drug paraphernalia. The Muro woman had become angry, insisting she was not a drug user and never would be.

Kolchinski had asked the clerk if there had been any other person named Muro diagnosed as having hepatitis by the clinic. After the need had been explained to her, the woman had pulled the name of Hermenegildo Muro from the files. Hermenegildo was also being treated for the pre-ARC phase of AIDS, which he had contracted during a homosexual liaison with an unidentified Hispanic male. The clerk could not ascertain the name of this third party, nor did she have any idea who could.

The paramedic had concluded by stating that she had inferred from the Muro woman's manner that there was some degree of tension in the house, arising from the hepatitis and ARC diagnosis of Hermenegildo, and her concerns for the health of her child.

Kennedy quoted from a Crime Scene note, indicating that while there were definite signs of tool-work and force applied to the security bars and window moldings of the fire-escape exit, there was a thick layer of undisturbed dust and mud on the middle flight of iron stairs, which made Kennedy believe that no one had climbed up or down that fire escape in the last few days. The drought, which had been in effect all summer, had left most of Alphabet City coated in dust, and a recent rain had only served to turn the top layer of dust into a thin, delicate shell of mud. Anybody using the fire-escape stairs would certainly have broken that shell.

Robinson contributed the statements of one of the canvass sources, who had said that Adeline Muro had recently broken off *"relaciones amorosas"* with a man named Fuentes, a delivery driver for a midtown service. Fuentes was nowhere around, and Robinson had put out a call for him.

Robinson also quoted from an interview report wherein a next-door neighbor had recalled a "very bad fight" that had taken place between Adeline Muro and "that boy Mokie." The neighbor was uncertain as to the exact date of the fight, stating only that she "had heard through the walls a most angry word" and that the boy Mokie had moved out of the apartment the following morning.

Another witness had reported that a "blue car, an old junker" had arrived on the same morning, and that a "fat man" had helped Mokie to take a few possessions away in the back of that car. The witness could give no better description of the car or the vehicle, nor could she remember the license number.

An addict who had been sleeping in the stairwell recalled that a very angry man had come out of Apartment 7C a few days before. The addict thought that the woman had called that man Miguel or Michael, or something similar.

Robinson closed by saying that some legwork had developed a first name for the ex-boyfriend, an employee of a bicycle delivery service whose name was Miguel Fuentes.

The conference broke up after Stokovich summarized things, assigning Robinson to check out Miguel Fuentes and detailing Ben Kolchinski to put a fire under the forensic serologist to get the decision on those blood, semen, and tissue samples as soon as possible. In the meantime, Kennedy and Fratelli could go out on the street and talk to whatever finks and addicts they could put their hands on. And he'd put the word through to Street Narcotics and to the Anti-Crime Units to put some generalized heat on the various numbers dealers and drug traffickers in Alphabet City until somebody came forward with something helpful.

Nothing worth noting had come out of the finks—either the tame ones or the casual informers that Kennedy and Fratelli had on their strings. The NYPD maintained a system of registering their informants, and each detective was required to report any consistently reliable source to the Intelligence Division for approval as a confidential informant. A source was considered to be a potential informant if he had given reliable information about a crime or a pending crime more than once, and if he had asked for money, court consideration, or had a prior criminal history. Once he was approved by the Intelligence Bureau, the confidential informant was given an ID number, made up of the precinct he had been developed in, his file number, the squad that had developed him as a source, and the Criminal Bureau number. This ID number was used to code a complete case file on the informant, and any member of the Department who could show a reasonable need for that informant could apply, through his C.O., to the Intelligence Division for access to that informant. It sounded like a great system. It was a disaster.

The reasons why it was less than efficient were complex, but the bottom line was that no one who makes money by turning in his very lethal buddies is likely to jump for joy when he hears that the Police Department, of whom he is not overly fond, has written his name down somewhere in a computer and that any boss in the city can dig it out and go see him any time of the day or night. Notoriety such as that can make you suddenly dead. Since most informants know, deep in their hearts, that even the cops who run them don't like them very much, they tend to dry up when they realize that the NYPD has put them on a list.

And detectives don't like to have to share the sources they develop, especially since some of these sources know as many damaging things about the detective as the detective knows about the fink. If a strange cop can ride into the neighborhood and get permission to rattle another cop's private finks, many times without the presence of the man who ran that fink, then nobody is safe from the prying eyes of the Internal Affairs Department. Registration of informants was seen by many detectives as just another way for the slicks at Internal to throw their weight around. The basic rule in the detective brotherhood was that a man's fink was his private property, and you had to ask him *un*officially if he would do you the honor of allowing you to relay a few questions, through *him*, off the record, to his own fink. The result was that most of the confidential informants filed with the Intelligence Division of the NYPD were either well-blown old hacks, or minor shits thrown to the computer because they were of little real value to the detective who had developed them.

Over the weekend the serologist called Kolchinski at home with the news that there had been two secretors involved in the Muro case, and that one of the secretors had type AB blood, which corresponded to the skin samples taken from under Adeline Muro's nails.

And Maksins' fink, a small-time break-and-enter man whom Maksins had turned into a pretty good source in exchange for a few dollars a crack and a word in Sorvino's ear over a Criminal Facilitation beef, reached Wolfie with the news that Hermenegildo "Mokie" Muro had been sharing a needle with a shooter on Avenue D and that shooter had told Wolfie's snitch that Mokie was "seriously pissed" with his cousin's "cunt wife" for throwing his ass out in the street and that he was going to do something about it.

Other than that activity, the men of the Task Force spent the weekend cutting their lawns, playing with whatever children they were fortunate enough to have visitation rights to, or simply lying around their apartments tossing rubber mice at their cats, if they had one. That's what sensible cops do on their days off, and they don't give up their days off easily.

On Monday afternoon, while Kennedy was watching Charlie Marcuse remove the internal mechanisms of Porfirio Magdalena Ruiz, Miguel Fuentes was giving Frank Robinson a very convincing alibi for his whereabouts on the night Adeline Muro was killed. He had been in an 84th Precinct holding cell for trying to kick a dollar out of a computerized blackjack game in a bar on Flatbush Avenue. It checked out, and Miguel Fuentes was crossed off the list.

The brownies turned out to have cited a battered 1967 Ford Fairlane for sidewalk parking outside the Muro apartment on Thursday, September 12, the morning after (all the best witnesses had stated) Adeline Muro had the big fight with Mokie Muro. The computer gave a registration for the Ford Fairlane, owned by one Salvador Olvera, showing an address on Myrtle Avenue. Salvador Olvera came up on the CATCH system as a small-time drug trafficker with the usual range of penny-ante charges, one anomalous bust for public lewdness and another odd beef—consensual sodomy. Stokovich was surprised to see the charge. The Supreme Court had declared that charge unconstitutional, although it was still technically on the books. The act must have been so outrageous that the arresting officer had laid the charge anyway.

And consensual sodomy seemed to fit the pattern. The Health Services paramedic had reported that Mokie Muro was having a homosexual relationship with an unidentified male. The color of Salvador Olvera's Ford Fairlane was listed as blue. Salvador had the a.k.a. of Tinto, along with a couple of other Hispanic nicknames, including Reina which was Spanish for "queen."

The gestation period for the ARC stage of AIDS was considered to be something like three years, so this Olvera guy, homosexual or no, could not have been the source of Mokie's disease. For that matter, there were enough addicts with AIDS in Alphabet City to give half of Manhattan a good shot at AIDS through their needles, so the ARC thing didn't really count for much.

The FINEST net had sent around the intriguing notation that a male prostitute named Jesus Rodriguez had been found in possession of a cameo with an inscription reading *"para mi corazón Adelina."* It resembled one of the articles a neighbor had described as Adeline Muro's personal and most treasured belongings. But Jesus Rodriguez had been released on his own recognizance, through a mixup in Communications, and nobody in Midtown North seemed to know where the kid was now.

And finally, Stokovich's FBI buddy had gotten back to him with the reading from *his* buddy in the Behavioral Sciences Unit at Quantico. The fact that Serology had found *two* types of secretors in the victim's body did *not* fit the usual pattern of sexual assault that they had formulated. It was rare that the kind of man who vented his rage at women by mutilating them in a sexual manner could actually perform sexually with a woman. They were usually impotent, and did not have normal sexual lives at all. So the removal of portions of the body did not seem to fit with the obvious traces of two sexually functioning males. He had added, however, that this was only a reading from a distance. If a second murder developed, Stokovich was to be sure to contact Quantico directly.

Thanks, Bruno had said, but the sarcasm was lost.

When Wolfgar Maksins made contact with the addict who had shared a needle with Mokie Muro, the man who had heard him talk about his cousin's "cunt wife," the addict was too sick to talk. He needed a hit before he could remember anything. So Wolfie bounced him around in a stairwell until he felt better. When things settled down a little, Maksins acquired the additional information that Mokie had talked about his friend who was a striker—a recruit—for a motorcycle gang in the Bronx. Mokie had said, through a fog of cheap crank and a couple of Quaaludes, that he was going to go up there and be a striker too. That was all the addict could manage to get out before he got the dry heaves, and Maksins left him there, working out his problems.

When they got together again for the Tuesday morning general conference at 0845, most of the Task Force was convinced that the killers of Adeline Muro were Mokie Muro and an "unidentified third party" who was probably this man Salvador Olvera, a.k.a. Tinto. Citywides had been issued on the teletype for both men, and the plainclothes units from Midtown were keeping a special watch for Jesus Rodriguez, who seemed like the best lead so far. Units of the Biker Squad in the Bronx had been contacted about a possible sighting of Mokie Muro, but the Bronx had troubles of its own, and it was probably going to take a personal push from some of the Task Force guys to locate either of the two suspects. Kennedy had his hands full with the Porfirio Ruiz killing. Maksins had a sadistic sex killing in Greenwich Village. Fratelli and Robinson were chasing some demented Armenian bunko artists who had graduated to homicide after a knifing on Van Dam. Kolchinski was up to his bald head in a Hell's Angels investigation. Natural velocity was pushing the Muro case into the background until the Ruiz case led Kennedy into a brick wall because of the Strike Force operation against some major drug dealers. Stokovich had already decided to hand Kennedy the 23rd Street jumper, which he thought was a grounder, and then turn him loose on the Muro case. Eddie Kennedy didn't know it, but Stokovich looked on Kennedy as his "silver bullet," his absolute best man when it came down to bringing in a running man. It was the thing Kennedy did best. His case work was textbook perfect, but out on the chase he had something extra, a sense for where a man will go when he's running for his life.

Kennedy pushed himself away from the kitchen table. The readout on his microwave maintained that it was only a few minutes after ten in the evening. Kennedy felt as if it were the last hour of the last day in the universe. But the Muro case, rough as it was, had its own power as well. By the time the Force had come to the tentative conclusion that their best bet for the killer was Mokie Muro and an accessory, the inquiry had taken up the time and energy of three hundred people: the patrol officers who responded to the call, the Communications people who relayed the word to the Task Force, the Crime Scene technicians, the DA's office, Charlie Marcuse and his people, the EMS bus crew, the Forensic lab technicians, some people at the FBI, several platoons

of the 9th, duty sergeants, Anti-Crime Units, Street Narcotics
Units, assorted finks and snitches, secretaries, clerks, telephone
operators, a Health Services paramedic, some people over at
MHR, detectives from Midtown North and Midtown South plainclothes divisions, Intelligence. The television image of the lone
man doggedly pursuing his maniacal quarry through the Dantean
landscape of night, alone, opposed at every step by stupid com-
manders and witless patrolmen, rumpled and sodden with weariness . . . well, it was mostly laughable, except for the "rumpled and
sodden with weariness" bit.

Kennedy stood in the middle of his living room, weaving
slightly, seeing his apartment through the distance of emotional
exhaustion. This is it, Eddie. This is what you're working for. An
eggshell shag rug, a burgundy leather and brass couch with a
matching leather armchair, a low black marble coffee table, two
Orient Express lamps from a mail-order house in San Francisco, a
framed diptych print of the Brooklyn Bridge, a low black lacquer
credenza with a Panasonic stereo system in flat black metal, satel-
lite speakers in the bedroom, about seven hundred hardcover
books, mostly secondhand from the Barnes and Noble Annex
down on Fifth Avenue, historical fiction, a set of encyclopedias
and the complete mail-order line of Franklin Mint Books, God
help him—the "quintessential bourgeois library" was how that
dragon lady from Barnard had described it, just before he put her
out in the hall. A thirteen-inch Sony Trinitron with a remote
control so he could turn the sound off when that godawful commercial for Grind came on, or yet another searing investigative
exposé. He had three suits in a closet in his ten-by-twelve bedroom, a blue single-breasted, a gray double-breasted, and a brown.
Three sport jackets, various slacks and jeans, his dress uniform,
socks and shirts and ties in the shelves above it. A round kitchen
table with fake-walnut veneer; four matching chairs, tubular aluminum, with padded seats, one of which had been shredded by
Dudley; and a half-full litter box behind the bathroom door.
Typical of the little monster. Bail out and leave Kennedy with the
cleanup.

It was funny how your life just happened to you, Kennedy
was thinking. All his life he'd been making plans and working for
one thing or another. The Academy, then his Gold, then Grade
Money. A better apartment. Maybe someday a wife, a kid. Some

of it he'd gotten. The rest of it . . . He couldn't place the day, the year, when he'd given up on that part of the plan. Now he was fat and forty and tired, and the thing he missed most wasn't even human.

Kennedy woke up during the weather report. Storm Field was the weatherman for this channel, something no one in Manhattan seemed to find odd, and he was talking about a major storm front moving in to the East Coast area, promising celestial brimstone later in the week. Kennedy sat up on the couch and rubbed his eyes. The vision of a heavy storm ripping up Fifth Avenue along Museum Mile, scattering the brittle old ladies, maybe a cyclone sucking up all the Shih Tzus and pekes and Sharpeis . . . it had some appeal, he had to admit. Pack it in, Eddie. Bedtime.

He found Dudley on the floor of his bedroom closet, lying on his favorite Harris tweed sports coat, on his side, torn up and clotted but still breathing, just barely breathing, and far too hot to the touch. His fur was dull and matted. When Kennedy picked him up, blood ran from his mouth in a viscous strand, like pulled toffee. Dudley's eye was almost completely closed, but he was watching Kennedy, as if to say, So, Eddie, what's happening?

A few frantic phone calls later he had located a vet on the West Side. The cabbie got into the spirit of the thing, screaming through Central Park, honking at the limos, keeping up a running commentary on why cats are the best pets in the universe, while Kennedy held the carton full of Dudley on his lap and watched for a blue-and-white. If they tried to pull him over, he was goddam well going to get a police escort for *this* run.

CHAPTER 12

THURSDAY

"So what was it? Was he there all along?"

A UPS van cut away from the curb, crossing two lanes of Eighth Avenue in a kamikaze maneuver. Robinson, who was looking at Kennedy and not at the road, saw Kennedy's expression and slammed on the brakes, spilling their briefcases and their suit jackets onto the floor in the back seat. Horns and curses erupted all around them, but the brown van kept moving until he hit a cab and bounced off that. Kennedy picked up the radio.

"One-oh-four to Central, K?"

"One-oh-four, K."

"Central, you've got a Ten-Fifty-three at Eighth and Fortieth Street, by the Port Authority. A UPS van just clipped a cab. They're out of the cars and it looks like they're going to scrap over it."

They were. The uniformed driver of the UPS van pushed the cabbie up against his car. The cabbie lashed out with a boot, catching the UPS driver in the crotch. Traffic stopped dead in a knot, windows were rolled down, and angry red faces popped up as people said inaudible things at the top of their voices. A crowd of black teenagers was gathering on the sidewalk to cheer the combatants, who were now grappling and scuffling in a wrestlers' tango. Within seconds the intersection was locked up solid with trucks and cars. A ten-speed delivery boy hurtled through the morass. Somebody opened his car door and the boy rode right into it, flying over the top in a cartwheel, packages and radio flying, too, then bouncing off the hood and disappearing between the cars.

"Roger, one-oh-four. Do we need a bus?"

"You do now, Central."

Kennedy put the receiver down and turned up the air-conditioning. "What was the question?"

Robinson offered Kennedy a cigarette and lit one for himself. "Dudley. Was he in your closet all the time?"

Kennedy shook his head through a cloud of smoke.

"No, I was all over that place. The son of a bitch must have come in through the screen while I was flaked out on the couch. I found some blood on the window ledge, and there were muddy pawprints all over the toilet. He crawled in, got himself a drink out of the can, and then sacked out on my jacket in the closet. I was looking for a shirt to wear for the morning and there he was."

"He gonna make it?"

Kennedy didn't answer immediately.

"Well, I don't know, to tell you the truth. The vet says he's infected, and he's lost all kinds of blood. He has rat bites all over his neck and his belly. Could be he's got something from them. The vet cleaned him up, shot him full of antibiotics. The poor bugger's on intravenous right now. I have to phone him later."

"How're the rats?"

"How do you think?"

Robinson chuckled. An EMS bus came whooping out of a cross street. Some brownies were waving the lead cars through the intersection. Overhead a pale sun glowed in a thin gray sky. The air smelled of ozone and burning bread.

"Is that the Portable? Up there?" Robinson was pointing at a blond PW waiting on the curb on the far side of 42nd Street. She had a hand up, shading her eyes, and she was looking down Eighth, squinting into the smog. Robinson blipped the siren a couple of times and bulled the squad car around a taxi. The driver swore at them as they went by his window. Kennedy shot him a finger. He got one back.

The policewoman was very young, no more than twenty at best, with a solid little dancer's body and midwestern features, eyebrows as pale as the sky overhead, and a flush in her cheeks as if she had been running and had not yet caught her breath. She was talking before Kennedy got his window all the way down.

"Are you the guys who wanted this Jesus Rodriguez kid? They told me to hang on to him for you. Which one's Kennedy?"

"I am, ahh, Officer vanDongen. Where is he?"

She pushed her cap back, showing a thin line of sweat along her forehead. "My partner's holding him inside here. You want him in the car?" She was standing in front of a grubby little theater called the Show Palace, a gay strip joint alternating porn flicks and live performances.

Robinson, in a falsetto trill, said, "Well, what's *on*, you bitch? Let's see, *Bullet, Pick Up*, and *Preppie Summer*. Golly, I just don't *know*, Eddie. What do *you* wanna do?"

"Easy, Frank. No, we'll talk to him inside. He might be a little tense out here in the street."

They found Jesus Rodriguez sitting on the floor just inside the darkened lobby. Through a set of padded doors, they could just make out some kind of stage performance in progress. A hot-pink spotlight was moving slowly up a pair of oiled and naked legs. When it reached an erect cock thrusting out from a sequined jockstrap, Robinson and Kennedy lost interest quite suddenly. Jesus Rodriguez was crying.

"Okay, Officers. Can you give us a little room here?"

The PW's partner was a black patrolman named Sweet. He stepped away from the Rodriguez boy and went over to his partner. Kennedy pulled the boy to his feet.

Jesus couldn't have been older than sixteen, a dark-eyed Latin exotic, with smooth tanned skin and heavy purple eye shadow around his gray eyes. His mascara had run badly, so he looked a little like a trapped raccoon. He spoke with no trace of accent, wiping his hands compulsively down his thighs, stepping into and out of his high-heeled slippers as the detectives talked things over with him.

His story was fairly ordinary. He had been working the cross streets above 42nd, not making a great deal of money. Monday nights were always slow. Tinto Olvera had come along in a Lincoln Town Car . . . yes, it was a rental. Budget Rent-a-Car had a weekend deal and he had just kept it over the limit. No, he hadn't seen the rental sheet anywhere. It was two-tone, light- and dark-blue. Blue interior. Tinto was a regular customer. Jesus knew what he liked. They had driven over to the 30th Street Terminal yards. Jesus knew a spot over there where you could relax and not be disturbed. After it was over, they had gotten dressed and instead of the money, Tinto had offered him this cameo. There had been a bit of a spat over that one. Jesus liked cash. But Tinto had cried a little, saying he had no money but that he loved Jesus and would Jesus not take the cameo, even as a gift? As a security deposit? But he wasn't to show it to anyone. In a few days, Tinto would come back with cash. They would get together again.

"Was he with anyone?"

Robinson's voice was hard-edged. It frightened the boy. He started to cry again. Robinson softened his tone, putting a hand on the boy's cheek. "Look, we know you're not involved. You're not in any trouble here. All we want to know is, was Tinto alone?"

The boy nodded, rubbing his hands along his thighs.

"Can you reach him, if you want to? Have you ever been to his place? Has he ever given you a number?"

A nod. A tear. "Yes, he has."

Bingo. "Do you remember that number?"

He didn't. He had never been able to remember numbers.

"He said he'd see you again. Did he say when?"

Soon. The rubbing got more rapid. Tears came faster.

Kennedy broke in. "You're sick, hah? You need something to make you feel better?" The boy turned to Kennedy as if he were the materialization of an archangel, shining in glory. Yes, he was so sick. Could they help him out?

"Hey, you help us, we help you." Kennedy held up a five-dollar bill. "The number, Hay-soos?"

It was . . . no, he couldn't remember. Kennedy held up another five. It was coming to him. No, not yet.

Frank Robinson reached across and backhanded the kid into the wall. He bounced off it and collapsed to the sticky carpet, wailing and sobbing, one hand up along his cheekbone, staring up at the detectives with his dark eyes wide, his cheeks running with tears and black streaks of mascara, a slender ribbon of mucus looping from his nostril onto the Ralph Lauren polo shirt with the embroidered horseman galloping across a cotton field.

"Did that help?" said Robinson, as soft as sleep.

Budget had no record of a Lincoln Town Car being rented out to anyone by the name of Salvador Olvera. But there were several two-tone blue Lincolns still out on rental. They would run a check on all the credit cards for each Lincoln rental, but that would take some time.

Kennedy set them to it, and sent out a notice on the FINEST that the Detective Division was very interested in any two-tone blue Lincoln Town Car with a rental plate—a Z number. Any units observing such a car should stop it and approach with caution. They included an updated description of Salvador Olvera and Mokie Muro, and stressed that although the men were wanted, it was not necessary to terrify every poor son of a bitch who was driving a blue Lincoln Town Car. Just pretend it's a traffic problem or a tail-light violation.

The telephone number belonged to a Brooklyn commercial establishment called the Ducky Donut Shop, at Palmetto and Myrtle. Frank Robinson pulled the car over at a pay phone on Delancey Street and borrowed some change from Kennedy. While he was in the booth, Kennedy got a patch through to the squad room and told Farrell to tell Stokovich, when he came in, that they were going to take a run out to Olvera's address on Myrtle and then fire along to a place called the Ducky Donut Shop. Farrell told Kennedy that there had been no report from any of the Bronx units about Mokie Muro, but that Farrell would ride them all hard until somebody up there got his thumb out of his ass and did some real honest-to-god police work.

"You do that, Ollie," said Kennedy.

Robinson got back behind the wheel, chuckling to himself.

"So who are we today?" said Kennedy.

Robinson fished out a leather card case and riffled through a collection of business cards. He had over a hundred of them, all in good shape, from about ten different businesses. Most detectives made it a point to scoop up a handful of business cards whenever they got the chance, from insurance firms, brokerage houses, real estate agencies, the EPA, Manhattan Human Resources. Robinson held up two quietly impressive cards from a New Jersey law firm. "Let's see, I'm Edward Carlson and you're Dennison Woodruff."

"What did you say to them?"

"Hell, I just told them that we were trying to find a Mr. Salvador Olvera and that we were acting on behalf of the New York State Lottery Division."

Kennedy took his card. "Did they say they could get a message to him?"

"They said that if he came in they would have him phone our number. Very Spanish voice. It didn't sound as if they were surprised to get a message for him."

"What number did you give?"

"The lunch-room phone. Let's call up Ollie and tell him who he's supposed to be. He likes that part."

Halfway across the Williamsburg Bridge, stalled in a jam, they got a call from Farrell saying that the clerk from Budget had called back and that three of the credit cards used to rent Lincoln town cars had been flagged by the credit issuers as delinquent, and that one card had been reported stolen out of a hotel on East 44th Street three days before. Due to a procedural error, the card had not been listed on the company's computer.

What was the name on the card?

Julian Wendell McAllister, with an address in Santa Barbara, California. The point was, Julian Wendell McAllister had rented a two-tone blue Lincoln Town Car from one of the Budget hotel offices on Saturday afternoon, and that blue Lincoln had not yet been returned to the depot. It was now being listed as stolen, and a citywide was going out on it.

Kennedy and Robinson sat in the squad car listening to the radio cross-talk from the 84th Precinct and staring out over the slate-gray surface of the East River. Downstream a thick yellow fog was riding low to the water. The feathery fan of the Brooklyn Bridge and the hard shadow of the Manhattan Bridge came through a sheen of hazy air.

"God, this is an ugly bridge," said Robinson.

"Is it?" said Kennedy. "I never noticed."

Brooklyn greeted them as they swept down beside the elevated BMT lines: WELCOME TO BROOKLYN USA. The bridge dumped them out into a vast crowded landscape of small wood-frame houses, endless neighborhood blocks of dusty scrub trees, peeling wooden billboards, a maze of tiny streets and avenues looking more like a New England slum than something this close to Manhattan. It was a tired-looking area, as if it hadn't seen anything of the boom money that was transforming the Manhattan skyline, or, for that matter, any of the boom money from the *last*

time around either. The BMT rode on an elevated rail line all the
way along Broadway, covering the street like the hull of a massive
iron ship, looming over block after block of spray-painted storefronts, spray-painted wooden fences, spray-painted tenement walls,
all of them crowding right up to the curb line in the permanent
twilight of the elevated. The line was marked off by a receding
vista of paired steel pillars supporting the elevated railway, each
pair coated with indecipherable spray-painted gang slogans: ZAKA,
ZIGGY NINE, POWER, I HEART MY GUN, RAMONES, BABAY, RUFFIO,
COPS DIE, KOCH FOR QUEEN, KNICKS, the words overlapping,
shining up through one another, wrapped around one another,
dripping down into one another, wearing away from on top of one
another, the product of years and years of pointless dedication.
Here and there a less anarchic hand had painted scenes from
Caribbean dreams. Opposite the Bushwick Tire Service someone
had rendered an abstract fort with a degree of art to it. Beyond
that someone else had set up a hubcap business in a vacant lot
surrounded by wire fencing. Three liquor stores sat in one block,
each a squat little bunker wrapped in sheet metal and chicken
wire, and inside there were shotguns under every countertop.

A dirty sun burned in smog. The two detectives spoke little
as they cruised up underneath the elevated. Now and then some
kids would wave at the DT car, or send them a finger. Mostly the
street life was just that, boys hanging out with girls, mothers
shopping in the Woolworth's or the Red Apple in baggy print
dresses and open-toed sandals, heavy-hipped Spanish ladies with
glittering black hair and full bodies and broad Indian faces. Now
and then a side street would flash by and the detectives would
catch a glimpse of a trellis heavy with hot scarlet roses, children
playing in a yard, grandparents rocking, in the violet shade of a
black-and-white striped awning, on a seat taken from a car. Wisps
and fragments of rapid talk reached them, girls laughing, a radio
set in an upper window sending raucous mariachi music into the
dusty street. Gangs of hard-looking boys played basketball on a
crumbling court or jacked up a car on cinder blocks and passed
tools up and down.

People did what they could with what they had, and like most
of the people in New York, they lived good lives and had good
kids. There were worse places to be than Queens or Brooklyn.

"Olvera's place is around here somewhere, isn't it?" Robinson was pulling over to the curb.

"Yeah. The guys from the One-Oh-Four have already checked out his home address. It's just up the road here. What do you have in mind?"

Robinson shrugged. "Maybe he's homesick? Maybe he wants to come back to get a fresh shirt? Let's give his place a toss."

Salvador Tinto Olvera had obviously cleared out of his apartment over the shoe store on Myrtle. The door was standing open at the top of the rickety wooden stairs leading up from a littered back lot. They went up carefully nevertheless. Life was full of surprises.

Although the place showed signs of occupancy—nails in the walls where pictures had hung, and a greasy smear on a wall above a rectangle of dust—it was obviously empty now. The whole apartment had been painted white, and it still appeared strangely antiseptic in the earthy riot of Brooklyn. There was nothing in the cupboards, nothing on the floors in any of the closets. Nothing anywhere.

Down in the back lot a shopworn terrier watched them with morose disapproval as they poked around in the bags and boxes. Robinson managed to do this without ever touching anything with his hands. His fear of insects was under control but palpable. Kennedy straightened up with a thin white cardboard box in his hand. Inside there were four Styrofoam cups and a wad of dirty tissues. The outside of the box had some lettering, half-obscured by muddy water. THE DUCKY DONUT SHOP.

"Coincidence?" Robinson did not take the box from Kennedy. Kennedy smiled at him.

"Probably, but let's go see this place anyway."

The Ducky Donut Shop was in a decent little block around Myrtle and Palmetto. They parked a hundred yards from it, near Wyckoff.

"Busy little concern, hah, Frank? Who looks more like a lawyer? You or me?"

Robinson laughed. "Nobody in *this* block is going to believe in a black lawyer. *You* go."

The Ducky Donut Shop was clean, friendly, and full of chatter as Kennedy pushed open the greasy glass door. A group of black kids in the corner gave him a glance and then went back to their sodas. A young Latino male was standing behind the counter, polishing a carafe. Kennedy cleared his throat to get the boy's attention.

"Good afternoon. My name is Woodruff. Here's my card. I wonder if you can help me?"

The boy took a while to work through the text on the business card, and when he did he still looked skeptical.

"Yeah, wha' you wan'?"

"Well, we're having some trouble locating a . . ." He made a major production out of checking in his pockets for a slip of paper, meanwhile smiling at the counterboy in a nervous way. "So *hot*, don't you think? Yes, here we are. My Spanish is a little rusty, but his name is Salvador Olvera? Do you know this name?"

There had been no flicker of recognition on the boy's placid face. "You call before? This morning?"

Kennedy managed to look perky. "*Yes*, that's right. I know *someone* from our office was supposed to call."

"Wha' you wan' him for?"

"Well . . . it's a matter of *some* importance, of a private nature. I'm sure you understand?"

The face shut down. "I don' know him. You got the wrong place. Maybe is someplace else. You wan' a donut?"

Kennedy twisted one hand in the other.

"You have no idea who he is? I've been misled, I suppose. Pastor Robles, at the mission—he said that I should look here."

"You from Pastor Robles?"

"No. I mean, he *sent* us, but . . . You see, we're acting for the New York State Lottery Division? That's *all* I can tell you. But it certainly would be to Mr. Olvera's advantage *if* he could contact our office. Can I leave the number with you?"

"No, you don' have to. I didn' know who you was talkin' about for a minute. You lookin' for Tinto—he's stayin' with his mother."

There had been no listing for any relative of Salvador Olvera in the CATCH and NYSIIS records. Kennedy raised his eyebrows and his face brightened. "He *is*? Do you happen to have that address? Or I could have you call her?"

"No, I got it. Jus' a minute." He disappeared through a back door. Shit, thought Kennedy. He's rabbited. But the boy was back in a short while, holding a scrap of paper.

"I can' read the writin' . . . eighty-five somethin'."

Kennedy took the scrap of paper. It was an address in Woodhaven. Close. He took his card off the counter.

"I certainly want to thank you. You've been very helpful. If Mr. Olvera comes in, will you give him this number? Please tell him to ask for Dennison Woodruff." He waited while the boy wrote out the number, suppressing his impatience. The boy looked up when he had finished and smiled at Kennedy. Quite a friendly smile.

"You thin' there is a re-war', a rewar' for findin' him? You tell him, when you spea' to him, i' was Paco, at the Ducky Donut Shop, who give you the number. Maybe he wan' to give me somethin' for helpin' you?"

"Certainly," said Kennedy, pushing the door open. "I'll be sure to tell him that. It'll mean a lot to him."

Sometimes it comes together just like that. Most people aren't good at running. They leave a trail of paper notes, credit card slips—sometimes they even give their friends a forwarding address. It's denial, that glitch in the medulla that keeps telling them that everything is going to be all right and that there's no *way* they'll ever get caught. You're doing fine. Cancer can be beaten. Forget your troubles, come on get happy. It's not that they never see it coming. They just don't *believe* it.

When Kennedy got back into the car, Robinson had received a call from Farrell. The Lincoln Town Car had been found, abandoned but otherwise in good shape, in a bus-terminal lot at Merrick and Jamaica Avenue. Brooklyn Auto Squad had spotted the plate and fired the notice right in to the Task Force.

Kennedy hadn't been to Brooklyn in a while. Robinson reminded him. "Eddie, that's where the BMT bus line stops, isn't it? By the terminal, at a Hundred-Sixty-eighth Street?"

"Yeah, so. . . ?"

"So, Eddie, the BMT line practically runs right through that street."

"*This* street?" Kennedy held up the scrap of paper.

Robinson smiled indulgently upon him, full of forgiveness and Christian tolerance.

"Yes, Edward, my son. Through *that* street."

"Holy shit," said Kennedy.

"Don't blaspheme, my son," said Robinson.

Woodhaven is a lush and sleepy little village shaded by fine old trees, pushing up against the southern border of the Forest Park Golf Course and Cypress Hills Cemetery. It's a well-settled neighborhood of small brick or wood-frame houses on rising slopes leading up to the green hills of the parkland. Many of the houses have brightly colored aluminum awnings and tiny green squares of trimmed lawn, set off by slanted bricks and populated by plaster horse-holders and garden gnomes.

They pulled up in front of a neat little house in a row of neat little houses. Geraniums and alyssum lined the flagstone walkway. A rococo soffit in shell-pink echoed the carved shutters. The awning above the porch was pink and maroon. You could have shot billiards on the front lawn. The place dreamed in the afternoon light and the air was rich with the scents of new-cut grass and barbecued steaks. A steamy humidity lay over everything, thick and cloying, a Louisiana Delta afternoon, with cicadas whirring in the leafy oaks and bees nodding in the blossoms.

They got out quietly. Robinson walked down the white gravel driveway toward the back of the house. Kennedy climbed the front stairs. A chipped Fiesta ware cup filled with black liquid sat in a pattern of rings on the porch railing, next to a rusting lawn chair. Kennedy put a hand over the cup. He could feel heat rising out of it. He unbuttoned his suit jacket and knocked on the screen door. It clattered in the frame. The heat boiled up around him.

A curtain twitched in the broad front window. A mushroom face, puffy with ill will, peered out at him, small black eyes set deep into unhealthy flesh. Kennedy knocked again, less politely.

The inner door was wrenched open and a massively fat woman filled the space from molding to door lock, blocking the interior darkness. A tiger-striped tabby kitten popped out from behind her and skittered down the steps. The woman looked at Kennedy for a long moment, as if to blame him for the escape of her pet. Her head was covered with the wispy remnants of gray hairs; her eyes were dull black stones pushed into the doughy material of her face. Her body beneath the huge print dress pushed everywhere, and folds of flesh rolled at her wrists and her ankles. She kept her hand on the doorknob and spoke in clear unaccented English.

"Yes. What is it you want?"

Kennedy showed her his badge. "We'd like to talk to your son, ma'am. We know he's here."

"And *who* might that be? I have no son." A scent was coming from around the woman as the cool air from the house leaked away. It was the smell of a cage or a pit.

"Salvador Olvera. We have information that says he is staying at this address. May we come in, ma'am?"

Her control wavered a millimeter, showing in a slight loss of her clear English pronunciation. "I wou' li'—I would *like* to see a search warran', if you have one."

"Never mind, Eddie." Robinson spoke from the driveway. He had a short fat man in handcuffs, a sagging bag of a man in a powder-blue safari suit, pouting and defiant and utterly defeated, looking up at Kennedy.

Kennedy stepped backward away from the doorway, not taking his eyes off the woman. Just because she was old and fat didn't mean she was harmless. "Come on out into the light, lady. Where was he, Frank?"

"On his way over the back fence with his Adidas bag and a ham sandwich. And guess what's in the garage, only now it's just *half* blue?"

The old woman was coming down the front steps, her lips tightening into a crevice in her floury face. She caught the kitten by a flowerpot and lifted it up to her throat. Kennedy walked over to Robinson and looked down at Tinto Olvera. He looked like a pharmacist, or somebody who specialized in estate planning; there was a soft tan cloudiness to him, as if he had no real borders, no solid reality, but was only a notion of a person, dimly perceived, always on the brink of dissolution.

Robinson was beaming with delight. Sometimes it was that easy. Kennedy looked across the lawn to where the woman was standing, a fleshy pile of reproach and denial.

"Book 'im, Danno."

Hours later, working through the traffic on the Williamsburg Bridge, Lower Manhattan black and shining in the evening sky, Kennedy turned around to look at Tinto, sweating and shrunken

in cuffs, staring out at the city. Bags of his clothing and possessions were sealed and tagged in the trunk. "So, tell me, Tinto.
Was it good for you? Was it fun?"

Tinto's eyes were wet and empty. He said nothing.

"Why'd you do it, Tinto? For what?"

"Hey, Eddie. Whatever he says, it's not going to answer a
question like that. They do it because they *like* to. The rest is
bullshit."

CHAPTER 13

FRIDAY

Kennedy's hometown sits on a range of hills and slopes, separated from the island of Manhattan by the Harlem River, which cuts westward through the peninsula and links up with the broad reaches of the Hudson at a place called Spuyten Duyvil. In the early days of the settlement, crossing the river at this point involved a fair amount of risk. The Dutch said that to cross it was to spite the devil. The name remains. So does the risk.

Along the eastern shores of the Bronx, the East River curves away toward Long Island Sound, widening as it rolls past the surburban villages of New Rochelle, Larchmont, and Rye. By the time it has reached the Connecticut border it's a shoreless expanse of salt water. Beyond that the Atlantic booms and swells into infinity.

To the west, the Hudson River reaches all the way inland to the valleys and mountains of New York State, following a fold in the green hide of the earth between the Catskills and the Berkshires. It flows fast and deep from Albany and Troy, where a canal runs west to the Great Lakes, and another reaches Lake Champlain, along the Vermont border. On a map, it looks as if that whole slice of America, the vast horn east of the Adirondacks, is resting on one spearpoint of land: the rocky headland of the Bronx.

It's a very pretty place, if you know where to look. The north is best, above Van Cortlandt Park South and Gun Hill Road. Up there it's all parks and suburbs. Some of the original forest that once covered the whole archipelago, oaks as old as New York money—which is as old as sin itself—shelter some of the most impressive mansions in the state along the banks of the Hudson or in the hills above it, behind walls of tended poplars and cedar, fifty-room Tudors and Palladian Revivals, with a view across the river to the Palisades and the suburbs of New Jersey.

This is the country where the limousines and the BMWs spend the night, tended by corporate drivers, polished by hand with butternut chamois cloths and rinsed in fresh cold water that beads up on the coachwork and splashes onto the quartz-and-limestone gravel. There's usually a breeze from the broad stretch of the river. At sundown the light on the water sways and shimmers like a field of autumn wheat.

Below Gun Hill Road it changes, and the farther south you go—riding the East Side IRT twenty feet above Jerome Avenue, in a gritty, paint-splattered car with a Coke can rolling from side to side and a sulphurous light coming in through the greasy glass—the worse it gets.

The arteries running south are Jerome, the Grand Concourse, Webster, and Third Avenue. They converge as they go south, entering a dense tangled grid of hills, cross streets, scrub parks, vacant lots, stone-gray high-rises and projects, and block after block of tenements that seem always in one stage or another of the renovation waltz. They decline through the classes, until the wage earners move out and the welfare families move in, as well as the criminals that feed off that group. The tenement shows signs of wear. Windows don't get fixed. The stairs get used as urinals. The wallpaper peels away, and the plaster rots beneath it. Addicts and hookers transact in the lobbies. A fire burns unattended in a trash can out back. The building dies and the city takes it over, stripping it down and bricking it up. They put clever *trompe l'oeil* panels over rotted empty windows—aluminum sheets with painted cats sitting on a nonexistent ledge, between painted drapes; a fat black pot of posies; fake mullions. They cover the collapsed interior like copper coins on a dead man's eyes.

At Fordham Road the wreckers are taking down a block of tenements. An asphalt crew tears up the street outside the RKO Fordham Quad. Spray paint is everywhere. The schools have turned into compounds, with armed security guards in the yards. The sidewalks are crowded with aimless men, black, white, Lat-

ins, Chinese, Vietnamese, leaning on the walls of shuttered facto-
ries, cooking soup in cans over small fires in a lot full of masonry
and bent iron rods. Children clamber around in the ruined buildings, lighting fires for entertainment, sniffing butane in the basement, dashing through the traffic and the crowds, skinny, vital, as
fast and canny as jackals, in packs and singly, living without
supervision in a landscape not much different from Beirut or
Mexico City. Under the elevated, on Jerome, it's always late
afternoon. People are everywhere, on the corners, in the shops
and stores, cruising up and down in dented Camaros or glittering
Eldorados. A fine white dust floats in the air and settles over
everything: on the plate glass, on the paintwork and the bricks,
and in the yards. Every few minutes the IRT literally thunders
overhead on the tracks, cutting off the talk, muting the music from
the record stores and the bars, and the hard-packed clay vibrates
and rumbles with the force of it. This is Kennedy's hometown.

Kennedy likes to tell the story of how he made the choice
between cop and wiseguy, up in the Bronx, back in the fifties. It
had been a different Bronx then, in the days when Fordham Road
was the best thing in the Bronx. There was a lobster house by the
Aqueduct, a big rambling wooden house where people came from
all over town to savor the best brutes from Maine and the Sound.
The Aqueduct beside it was a place for strolling couples, an avenue
of shade trees lined with green wooden benches, moonlit in the
summer nights, with faint music coming from the restaurant and
the lights gleaming all the way along Fordham, the shops and
stores busy with families and kids. He had a job at the lobster
house, working as a busboy, and for some reason he was very late
that night. His father, a bulldog Irish with a fine tenor and a taste
for sentimental songs about the Troubles, ran the Kennedy home
with a ruthless rod.

So Eddie recalls running home under the oaks along the
Aqueduct, worrying about his reception, running in his old shoes,
saving his good black leather loafers under his arm, a five-minute
dash to his apartment building. There was a blue-and-white squad
car parked at the curb. He didn't stop to look it over. He took the
stairs two at a time, four flights, arriving out of breath and flushed
at the polished wooden door of his apartment. As he reached for
the knob, a gray-haired uniformed policeman came down the
flight of stairs just behind him, nodding politely as he rounded the

landing. The door was tugged open in a sweeping gesture. Kennedy's father stood in the frame, in his pleated slacks and suspend-
ers, his business shirt still crisp and white, collarless, with the
copper studs glinting at his neck and sleeves, in his slippers,
looking like thunder and lightning.

He took it in at a glance, Eddie flushed and breathless, and
late besides, and the uniformed policeman standing behind him.

"So, ye blasted devil!" *Whack!* He struck Kennedy across the
side of his head with a folded newspaper. *Whack! Whack!* Kennedy was too stunned to object, and in those days no son negotiated with his father anyway. *Whack* again!

The policeman, sensing the confusion, feeling at fault, put his
oar in as tactfully as he could.

He was only in the building to sell tickets to a policeman's
benefit dance, and the boy was innocent, so far as he knew, of any
wrong, although he had no doubt the father knew him best, and
capable of devilment he must surely be, else the father would not
be setting about the little brute so freely and with such a will, but
it must be said he's no particular devil to the police, not at the
moment, beggin' his father's pardon for intrudin', and meaning no
interference. Sir.

The lesson stayed with Kennedy all the way through the
evening meal, his father presiding unrepentant yet slightly uneasy
at the head of the table, carving the roast and chivvying his brood.
It was the police who had the power. Even his father had been
restrained by it.

Robinson and Kennedy had spent the entire morning and
most of the afternoon in a brand-new navy-blue Plymouth Caravelle,
casting about in the various Bronx precincts, talking to the Street
Crime Units and the detectives at the local Task Force, at the
48th and the 40th, trying to get some hint of Mokie Muro. The
day was hot and still. A pale sun rode high in a greenish dome of
sky. The air was dense and steamy and there was a kind of swollen
look to the sky, cloudless but thick with haze. The wind had died
away in the early morning.

Word had come in, finally, from the Identification Division,
Latent Fingerprint Section, of the FBI in Washington, to the
effect that the five sets of prints, plastic, visible, and latent, tagged
Evidence 23, 25, 32, 33, and 37, had been compared with the

recorded prints of the suspects named. The comparison prints matched perfectly with the recorded prints of Salvador Olvera, Hermenegildo Muro, and Rubio Muro. The latent prints taken from the victim had been positively matched with the file prints of Salvador Olvera and Hermenegildo Muro. Photos and hard-copy file extracts were being prepared and would be sent along as soon as the proper documentation was received at the FBI offices.

The forensic odontologist had compared the photographs and castings of the bite marks observed on the victim's torso with dental records obtained through the Health Services Department. Only one of the bite marks could be positively identified as similar enough in wear pattern, in bite radius and occlusion, and in the disposition of the incisors, canines, and molars, to the available records. The probability was, and the odontologist reserved her final decision until a casting could be taken of the suspect's teeth, that the bite had been delivered by Hermenegildo Muro.

Blood types and tissue types and semen-sample serological reports did not exclude the suspects.

Although Salvador Olvera had been Mirandized and questioned at some length, he had so far said not one word. He was being held at Manhattan Criminal Courts and no bail had been set for him. Sorvino had promised the detectives that he would do his best to insure that, if bail should be negotiated, it would be at such an astronomical figure that even Olvera's mother, who turned out to have extensive assets in T-bills and ITT stock, would not be able to meet it. The confusion over her identity had been resolved when it was discovered that she had applied for a legal change of name in 1966, changing from Olvera to Oliver. All that remained in the Muro case, aside from the usual collection of corroborative testimony and forensic support, was to actually get out there and *find* Mokie Muro.

Stokovich had issued a citywide on Mokie. Every precinct in the five boroughs had been teletyped. Mokie's description had been read out to every mustering platoon on every watch in seventy-five precincts. Anti-Crime Units, Citywide Street Crime, Citywide Street Narcotics, Vice, Robbery, and the Auto Squad were all advised to remember the description, and highway units were notified.

So were the police forces in Yonkers, Mount Vernon, and

Nassau and Suffolk counties, and the New Jersey State Police were asked to contact other New Jersey departments.

Mokie Muro was a very hot item by Thursday evening. Reports of him were coming in from every compass point. Finks were coming up with vital information all over town, none of it worth a damn. The detectives of the 46th Precinct in the University Heights area of the Bronx were asked to shake up members of the Ching-a-lings motorcycle gang. Finks in the Fordham sector got rousted from their sleep or pulled out of bars and basements. At any one time, a thousand men and women were thinking about and looking for one Latino male, DOB 09/06/58, NYSIIS M21176544, five eight, 140 pounds, last seen wearing black motorcycle boots with chains, black jeans, a ripped white T-shirt with a DEAD KENNEDYS logo under a light-brown leather vest with cowboy fringes, small triangular scar beneath the left ear, considered to be armed and dangerous, wanted on suspicion of murder. A circular was set for printing if the hunt went over the weekend.

At 1530 hours on Friday afternoon, both Kennedy and Robinson were beginning to suspect it would.

They pulled up at the curb a few hundred feet away from the Blue Flame bar at Third and 155th Street. The air-conditioning labored at FULL. A fine white dust had settled over the squad car. Now and then Kennedy would turn on the windshield wipers, just to get the film off the windshield. They had used two whole tanks of gas since they had come across the 145th Street bridge out of Harlem at 0955 hours that morning. Their throats were sore from talking with detectives and patrol officers. They had not yet eaten, and both men were stiff, hot, weary, and frustrated. Salvador Olvera had been a cakewalk, running straight and true to his only refuge. Tinto had always been a small-timer. His flight had been panicked, careless, and clumsy. His infatuation with Jesus Rodriguez had led him to a stupid indiscretion, a phone drop at the Ducky Donut Shop, mainly designed to fool his mother, who claimed she had no knowledge of her son's homosexuality. But Mokie was turning into a real pain in the ass. Literally and figuratively. Kennedy put the lever into PARK and stretched his arms above his head, groaning, feeling the vinyl cling to the sweat underneath his legs. Robinson looked as if he had been carved out of ice. Frank was leaning forward in his seat, craning his neck to get a view of something across the huge square.

Kennedy looked around the block. He saw nothing.

"What is it? You see something?"

"Yeah, the courthouse. Quite the pile, isn't it?"

Kennedy looked back across the street. Well, yeah, the courthouse. He felt a little stupid for missing the thing. It was a huge Roman-looking structure, eight stories of blackened granite, now empty and falling into ruin, but still magnificent. All around it the low flat stores and the side streets seemed even grubbier in its shadow. Latin letters carved into the face announced it: BRONX BOROUGH COURTHOUSE.

"Yeah, quite the pile, Frank." So what?

"My law professor says it's one of the finest examples of High Victorian Neoclassicism in the New York area. Too bad it's a pile of shit now. Sort of suits the Bronx, though. You know, a blasted heath. Ozymandias and all that stuff."

Kennedy was just about to say something vulgar when he realized, quietly stunned at it, that he did remember an Ozymandias. Pete Garibaldi was always quoting something about it, just after he'd kicked in a door or trashed a bar.

" 'My name is Ozymandias, king of kings: Look on my works, ye Mighty, and despair!' "

Robinson had the grace not to look too surprised.

"Where the hell did you get that from? I always figured you Irish cops only knew two things."

"Yeah? Shit floats and payday's Thursday, right? No, an old buddy of mine, he was always saying that. He'd wreck a bar or trash somebody's Caddie during a bust and he'd say to them, looking down on them, you know, standing over them with a baseball bat in his hands, and he'd thump his chest, like King Kong, and scream that line out. Kind of a weird fucker, but we liked him."

Robinson knew better than to ask who the man had been. Most of the squad had filled him in, one at a time, each man solemnly imparting the legend to the new boy in an act of initiation. Robinson had listened to the tale, respectfully, each and every time he heard it. It was only polite, and anyway, Garibaldi sounded like a good cop. Robinson would have liked him.

"You're a bit of a weird fucker yourself, Kennedy."

Kennedy looked over at Robinson, thinking exactly the same thing about the black detective.

He was a good detective, but not the kind of man you could kid easily. Frank Robinson always held something in reserve. Kennedy felt the reserve was a racial thing. He had a hard time remembering that the man was black, though. And it was a little intimidating to work with a B.A. from Columbia. Kennedy had a high school education and that was it, aside from the endless courses at John Jay College of Criminal Justice. There was word going around that Frank Robinson was in line for one of the Police Foundation scholarships to John Jay, and the guy was studying part-time for a degree in law. One of the new lawyer-cops, like Benjamin Ward. Robinson was a strange kind of cop-scholar. He tried to deal with the street by analyzing it in a clinical, sociological way. Sometimes he just gave it up and whacked a guy, as he had whacked Jesus Rodriguez yesterday. A contradictory man, moving in precise steps, thoughtfully brutal. He was said to have a Minnesota-blond girlfriend, a teacher's assistant at Hunter College. Robinson was far and away the best-educated man on the Task Force. That wasn't unusual. Statistics in the NYPD show that black police officers, male, female, in Patrol or in the Detective Division, tend to be far better educated than white or Latino officers. Considering the shit they had to put up with, it wasn't surprising.

The only thing that puzzled Kennedy was how Robinson and Wolfie managed to work together. It was one of life's great mysteries.

"You know we're getting nowhere fast, Eddie. Got any ideas? We know the guy's not with the Ching-a-lings around the Four-Six. Maksins' fink says he's an addict, so he's got to be getting sick right now. He can score anyplace in the Bronx, so that's not much of a help."

"True. What do you get from the fact that none of the units have spotted him? I make it that he's gone to ground somewhere. Staying out of sight."

Robinson agreed. "But he's got to eat. He's got to score sometime soon—unless he's got enough of a deck to see him through this week. He's been running since last Thursday."

"Yeah. What else does he like to do?"

Robinson thought it over.

"He likes to fuck boys, doesn't he?"

"So, where do you go to find a boy to fuck if you're a long way from home? Where do you go if you need to rent a boy who'll do your running for you? Pick up your smack, get you a new deck? If you're in the Bronx, where do you go?"

"Shazam!" said Robinson.

Hunts Point Market is a flatland of low warehouse buildings and truck yards, sitting on a muddy delta that projects into the East River just below the Bruckner Expressway, in the southern tip of the Bronx. Most of the produce that comes into Manhattan is delivered to and dealt with in the Hunts Point food terminals, in that grid of streets between Lafayette and Ryawa, a hundred different companies running import-and-export and transport trades. The Terminal Market is a vast complex of store and trading halls where deals are made for the supermarkets like D'Agostino's, Sloan's, Red Apple, or Gristede's. Sixteen-wheelers and panel trucks clog the roads from sunset to dawn. There's always a lineup of out-of-state rigs along Hunts Point Avenue. Every city has a place like Hunts Point, where the goods get bought and sold, the bribes get paid, the Mafia and the Latin gangs take their cut—an organized-crime culture packed with undercover agents working for various local and federal departments, the DEA, AT&F, the IRS, Justice, the Department of Agriculture, now and then the CIA and even Military Intelligence. Hunts Point was a little Casablanca of intrigue disguised as an industrial park. And since there was no shortage of weary long-haul truckers and dockworkers with money in their pockets and some time to kill before the gates opened, Hunts Point was also the hooker heaven of the South Bronx.

Whatever your pleasure, there was bound to be some creature with a high nausea threshold and no gag reflex at all who would be only too happy to take care of you, cash up front, no vice cops need apply.

They rolled into the neighborhood around 1620 hours. The place was jumping, every long barren block around Halleck and Oak Point had a collection of mini-skirted, tank-topped Madonna clones, made-up and glossed, lifting their skirts as the squad car went by, selling it in every package, male, female, transvestite, butch, rough trade, and Other. Kennedy drove slowly down Manida and back up Baretto, looking for someone he knew.

A girl close to six feet tall, with flaming blue hair, waved to him as they went by.

"*Ed*-deeee! Hey, *Kennedy!* Stop!"

Kennedy pulled over to the curb, grinning.

The girl hobbled over to the window and waited for it to roll down, resting her forearms along the doorline.

"Kennedy, you motherfucker! What brings you back up here? You want some strange change? Who's your friend? Nice lookin'. Hi, I'm Magenta, like in the color."

She reached out and took Frank's hand. Both breasts slipped out of her lavender teddy-top and brushed against Kennedy's cheek. Very fine breasts. Kennedy managed to ignore them while he introduced Detective Frank Robinson.

Magenta winked at Kennedy. She had done that on purpose.

"How do you do?" said Robinson, through a very wide grin. "Pleased to meet you. Very."

Magenta tucked her breasts back into the teddy, talking low and soft to Kennedy.

"Eddie, I haven't seen you in three months. Do you ever hear from Alvin? You tell him I want to see him soon? Are you still seeing that Trudy creature? No! Good. She was *not* a nice person. Rude! Are we going for a ride? I *love* your car. It's new, isn't it? I can smell a new car. Let me hear the siren!"

Kennedy hit the switch and bounced a fist off the wheel twice. *Whoop! Whoop!*

"I *love* it! Look at them jump!" She turned back to Kennedy and lowered her voice. "*So!* I only see you when you want to do that thing with the scarves or when you want something. Which is it?"

Kennedy went slightly red. Robinson smoothed the moment by handing the CATCH shot of Mokie Muro over to Magenta. She took the shot, pursing her lips.

"This the guy? Everybody says you're all worked up over some asshole. Vice has been real *nasty* lately. You know that guy, Eddie? What's his name? The one with the gold earring? Looks like Nick Nolte?"

"Solarski. Or Crittenden? Which one?"

"Who knows! *Any*way, he and his partner went through here last night and they just *drove* right along the sidewalk, making everybody run into the street, banging on their doors and blowing that siren. Then Solarski gets out and slaps Nunzio around. You know Nunzio—he can't take rough treatment. How's he supposed to remember which cock he's been nibbling on with some asshole vice cop slapping him around in the street? It was *not* a nice thing to do!"

"Who was he looking for?"

"*This* character, Mokie Whatsit! Had his picture and everything. Poor Nunzio just absolutely *collapsed*. And Solarski just kicked him in the face. Eddie, you have to *do* something about that one. I think he's a little unstable."

She prattled on like that for a few minutes, until a woman called her away. Kennedy drove off, angry. Bronx Vice gets energetic, starts fucking up the hookers, looking for Mokie Muro. So naturally the place was still buzzing with it the next day. The trouble was that the cops had been so rough that nobody wanted to talk to *any* new cops. Kennedy and Robinson cruised around the area, talking to young girls and young boys, the regular street trade in the market. Nobody seemed to have anything to tell them. They did a complete circuit of the place, up Lafayette, right on Halleck, and then back and forth along Drake, Whittier, Bryant, Spofford, until they were back on Baretto.

Magenta was still there, but she was holding on to a slight black male. "*Eddie!* Hey, Kennedy. Get over here!"

The kid had wild hair dyed the brightest orange and a bright-yellow sweater over Calvin Klein jeans. He also had a white bandage across his nose, and both eyes were red and swollen. When Kennedy pulled up, Magenta jerked the back door open and clambered inside with her companion.

"Thank *God* you came back around. I wanted you to *see* this! Say good afternoon to Detective Kennedy and Detective Robinson. Guys, this is Nunzio."

Nunzio was in bad shape, perhaps from his encounter with a Bronx cop last night, perhaps from withdrawal. His nose was running. There was blood on his upper lip. He dipped his head shyly and kept it down. Robinson leaned over the car seat and handed him a Kleenex.

"What's his problem, Magenta? He want to lay a charge against Solarski? Crittenden? Whoever?"

"No, you assholes. What good would *that* do? Anyway, Nunzio doesn't always mind getting slapped around, do you, Nunzio? No. I was talking to him while you were driving around. He's got something you might want to know."

Kennedy and Robinson came to point, like a brace of hounds. "What is it, Nunzio? What do you want to say?"

They let him get himself together. For three minutes they watched him try to speak. This kid should have been in a home, being tended to, being sheltered. But he wasn't. He was out here on Manida, getting fucked up the ass at ten bucks a crack.

When he did speak, it was in the small cracked voice of a child, feminine in its cadence.

"I . . . I have to go to the doctor. I'm sick."

"What kind of sick?" asked Robinson.

The boy was embarrassed. "I have the clap. And stuff. I can't hold my poo anymore. I need to wear a diaper."

Mothering Christ, thought Kennedy. "Okay, we'll do what we can." God, the car seat! "Do you have to go now?"

"No. I have some Pampers on, anyway. But . . ."

There was obviously something more on his mind. Kennedy shot an exasperated look at Magenta. She just put a finger to her lips and motioned him to be still.

"I . . . I have to go to the doctor, right?"

"Yes, you do. You want us to take you? You want a bus? We can call one now." Kennedy held his temper.

"My doctor isn't a real doctor but he takes care of me. Only he's not home. I mean, I don't know if he's home. The Green Ones are all in the way and I can't see."

"The green ones? What? The nurses?"

"So last night I had to see him at the hospital where he lives. He could give me something to fix my nose. And the other stuff. He tells me not to let them fist-fuck me too much. He tells me it's bad for my colon. He's nice to me."

Definite basket boy here. "Yeah? Where is this doctor?"

"The thing is I went there and we were both waiting for him to come back home only he didn't and so this other guy and I we waited together and this guy in the picture comes along and says he's been waiting for *hours*."

Robinson interrupted him. "*This* picture? This guy?"

Nunzio held the shot up in front of his right eye. His left one was badly swollen. "Yes. That was him. I know because when the vice cop was hitting me he was holding this man's picture in front of me so when I saw the same face I knew it was him. It made me frightened all over again."

"Let me get this straight. You saw this guy, the guy in the picture, *after* the cops went through here last night? Is that it?"

Robinson broke in again. "Where does your doctor live?"

"I can't tell you that. If I tell you that then he won't be able to help anybody anymore. He doesn't have his license. They took his license away because he was giving us methadone so we wouldn't be sick. He gives me free methadone so I feel better. I don't need sky if I have my doctor. Anyway, we never went inside. My friend was waiting too and he's the one who went away with this man in the picture. My friend says the man is his new roommate."

Kennedy slammed the back of the seat. "Shit, kid! I don't give a fuck if Christ himself is dealing shit out of the fucking communion bowl! You better tell me something I can use. Is our guy living with *your* guy? Is that it?"

Magenta was outraged. "Eddie! He's *sick*! Don't be a bastard. Anyway, he's talking about Sugar Bowl."

"Sugar Bowl? Where's that?"

"Not where. Who. Azucarero—Sugar Bowl. His real name is George Blanquilla. I know where he lives."

"The doctor, or Sugar Bowl?"

"Sugar Bowl, Eddie! There is no doctor. Nunzio is not all that healthy in the old beaneroonie, if you get my drift. His doctor is any paramedic at the Lincoln Hospital clinic who has the time to talk to him. What he's trying to say is that your guy met with Sugar Bowl last night outside the Lincoln Hospital and that no-body has *seen* Sugar Bowl down here at Hunts Point for almost a week. Figure it out!"

Kennedy and Robinson looked blankly at each other.

"Wait a minute, Magenta. I'm a little confused here. Nunzio doesn't have a doctor. What he's trying to tell us in his own fucked-up brain is that he went to Lincoln Hospital and he met this kid. . . ?"

"Sugar Bowl."

"Sugar Bowl, and that while they are waiting to see some

paramedic, along comes *our* guy, Mokie Muro, *this* guy in the
picture, and . . ."

"Eddie, start the car," said Robinson.

"Where are we going?"

"Where are we going, Magenta?" Robinson asked.

"The Melrose Houses."

"Oh, shit," said Kennedy.

"What?"

"The Melrose Houses are maybe ten blocks from the Blue
Flame bar."

At 1838 hours Kennedy and Robinson were standing on either side of George Blanquilla's flat in the Melrose Houses. Although neither detective had a gun out, there was a certain
tension in the air. Kennedy knocked on the door.

"Yes? Who is it?"

"Mr. Blanquilla?"

"Yes? Who's there?"

"Police, Mr. Blanquilla. We'd like to talk to you."

"Just a minute." There was a sound like a drawer opening.
Both men flattened against the wall far from the door, and now
the guns were out.

"You sure there's no other way out?"

"Yeah. I'm sure."

There was a scrabbling at the door, chains dropping and bolts
turning. It opened about two inches, enough to reveal one dark-
brown eye, quite wide, and a crescent of cheek. "Yes?"

Kennedy held out his shield and ID folder. The eye studied it
for a moment, and then drew back. The door closed and opened
again.

"You want Mokie? He's not home right now."

At 1856 hours they had a Crime Unit on Morris, a van on
Courtlandt, and a couple of Portables in the air shaft. Kennedy
and Robinson were parked outside the Blue Flame bar, drinking
coffee.

"You never worked in the Bronx, did you, Frank?"

"No. I came on in the sixties. They sent me straight to
Harlem. I think they thought I was a nigger. I grew up in
Vancouver. My father worked for Abitibi. I spent the first half of

my life thinking I was perfectly normal. Thank God I got down here and had myself straightened out."

"You Canadian?"

"No. Seattle originally. Nice town. Out there, everybody is my color, only it's not the skin. It's the rain. It rains all year 'round. You don't tan. You rust."

"You must have loved Harlem. Where'd they put you?"

"Where else? The Two-Eight. I did okay. Except for the roaches. I stopped believing in God when I saw my first roach nest. You know, I once calculated that there must be over six billion roaches in Harlem. There are more cockroaches in Harlem than there are people on the planet. It's a good thing they don't vote."

A black woman in tight blue jeans and a satin jacket with a Black Socks logo came out of the Blue Flame bar and jogged along on her stilettos, heading in their direction with no particular ideas showing on her face. When she got even with the car, she made a sudden move, ducking down and slipping into the back seat.

"He's there. He's been there for about an hour. How you want to do this?"

"Well, what is it, Officer. . . ?"

"Peavey, Violet G."

"Yeah. What's the scene in there. Where is he in the bar?"

"Right at the back, in a booth, with his eyes on the front door. Got his back up against the wall. Looks like a tense little shit. You been in there yet?"

Robinson laughed "Only three times today. Anybody with him? Any kind of support in there?"

"No. He's alone as far as I can see. I sat at the bar and had a Coors with Ziggy. Let's be careful with Ziggy, huh? He's a nice guy. One of my best finks. I don't want to see him getting hurt."

Kennedy didn't like that. "You think he'll tip the guy? You know, help out another hard-luck *pachuco*?"

Officer Peavey gave Kennedy an up-and-down. She had just the faintest tint of violet color on her cheeks, and a dusting of gold sparkles in the shadows around her eyes. Kennedy took the chance to look right back at her. Nice-looking woman. He was starting to have a regular obsession about black women: hate them, love them. Say what you want, they sure had the eyes. Kennedy wondered if she'd like his scars. Would he like hers?

"Ziggy knows what the guy's on the hook for. He wants to see you blow his fucking creep head right off. Are you?"

Kennedy said nothing. Robinson smiled over the seat-back at her. "I *hope* so, sweetheart. I sincerely hope so."

"Good," said Officer Peavey.

"Frank, why don't you get on to the units around the Melrose. Tell them they can relax. We'd like a couple of cars in the back here. But for Chrissakes, no noise. Officer Peavey . . . mind if I ask you a personal question?"

"Depends," said Peavey. "What is it?"

"What have you got on under that jacket?"

Peavey's face went through a number of changes.

Robinson's face was closing up. "Eddie—"

"No," said Kennedy. "That's not what I meant."

Violet Peavey was quiet for a moment. Then she smiled.

Officer Peavey reached for her zipper.

CHAPTER 14

THE DOPPLER EFFECT

Kennedy let himself wonder, for just a little while, sitting in his Plymouth outside the Blue Flame bar, how kids like Mokie Muro manage to get along with themselves. How do they cope with somebody's last breath puffing up into their faces? Kennedy had killed one man in his whole career and he hoped never to kill another. So how did Mokie do it, work it around in his mind? Make it come out that the victim really wanted it, or that he had to do it?

Mokie Muro must have been feeling pretty good because he was smiling to himself when the black couple came in the front door. But he noticed there was something strange about them. The satin jacket had been on the woman the last time he'd seen her, standing at the bar. Hadn't it?

Robinson and Peavey never looked his way, not once, but he bolted anyway. He was up and out of that booth and slamming through the kitchen on his way to the back door, smashing through the swinging doors, over the garbage in the slippery hall, slamming a palm against the plaster to keep upright, skittering, hearing the voices shouting behind him, and the heavy feet, and the woman cursing him. He may have tensed up across the back, trying to feel the shot as it punched through. He may even have felt a little self-pity. He probably did. Tinto Olvera was thinking along the same lines yesterday, thinking about how it wasn't fair and he didn't mean to do it and she was just asking for it. Mokie and Tinto, they were both like that. God knows where they

261

thought they were going to run to. People like to put things off as long as they can. It's just human nature. They like to pretend that things will work out okay. Some neurologists suggest that we even have a biological mechanism to help us with it, a denial gland. It's a great concept. Quite liberating, really. With something like that pumping away inside us, who needs a heart? Don't shoot me, Officers, says Mokie Muro, flying down the back hall of the Blue Flame bar. It wasn't my fault. Give me another week, I'll have convinced myself I wasn't even there. Just don't kill me.

And nothing exploded out the front of his chest in a meaty red ball. Nothing smacked its way through the back of his head, through the years of his childhood and his teenage years—what it was like at Spofford, getting his first taste of pussy, his first spike full of crank and the red blood rising in the bulb, the greasy pink thrill of raping. . . . Those memories stayed intact as he cleared the last crate and flew toward the door, and he was still pulling in the air and pushing it out, all systems were go within a foot of that door. . . . He must have thought how sweet it is to be alive. He must have thought: Please, God, don't let them kill me. Because he knew they wanted to kill him and it wasn't his time. *Just let me get to that door and don't kill me please till I get through that door.*

And back of that was the thought that if he got through the door he'd just ask to make it to the next block and there'd be another request when he got there. It was the Doppler effect of a soul on the run, sending back a cry: *Let me get to the door. Let me get to the street. Let me get to paradise still standing on my feet.* Some of us even deserve it. Some of us go just saying *Please let this kid not kill me. Please let this kid not kill my child. Let him just rape me and call it a day.*

Mokie hit that door with the point of his shoulder, in the air, flying, well on his way, his ears full of the crash of it and the hinges tearing and the wood splinters tumbling in the fading light.

Eddie Kennedy put everything he had in that kick, the Chief not even in his hand, Kennedy not wanting to kill him, just kick him in the crotch. You can't always get what you want. But if you try, sometimes, you get to give it.

*   *   *

Kennedy and Robinson rolled back into Manhattan around eight in the evening, into a major thunderstorm rocking and rolling on the Triborough Bridge. They felt the power of the storm in the tires and in the steel of the bridge itself. Through the wrack and shreds of cloud and the lateral rain, midtown and downtown shimmered and wavered, wrapped in a pale aura of slimy light. The East River was a sea of wild black water, showing white along the pilings and foaming in the races. Roosevelt Island and the 59th Street Bridge looked like cruise ships foundering.

Robinson cracked open another Coors, the foam shooting out over the dashboard. Kennedy took his and held it so tight it crackled. The cold hurt to the bone.

"Here's to us," said Robinson. They drank a toast in silence, listening to the wind.

Mokie Muro was under guard at Lincoln Hospital, riding an ice pack like Cowboy Bob, looking a little stretched around the cheeks and eyes. They'd have to go back and get him in the morning. The intern had been critical. There had been talk of ruptures and internal bleeding. He had raised the grim specter of sterility and lawsuits. Kennedy had thanked him, quite sincerely, and walked out to the squad car to wait for Robinson. Stokovich was a happy man, up in Westchester County, with his feet up on a hassock and his wife flipping through *Woman's Day*. "Go home," he said. "Get drunk. Kiss Robinson for me."

"I will," said Kennedy, hearing the wind through the lines.

"So what do you think, Eddie? Think the island will blow away?"

"That? Look at it, Frank. Nothing moves that town."

He looked over at Robinson, watching his face.

"I gotta tell you, Frank. Sometimes it's true. All I can see are your eyes."

"How's the beer? We have three left."

"I'm fine, Frank. You go ahead."

"Tell me something, Eddie. If they're crazy, why do they run?"

There was nothing to say to that. "Don't go all philosophical on me now."

"Yeah? Then tell me something else, Eddie. You popped a guy once, up in the Bronx, isn't that right?"

After a pause, Kennedy said, "Yes. I did."

"A chicken hawk, wasn't it? I heard it was a chicken hawk. Some guy was killing children, wasn't he?"

"Yeah. He was."

"I heard he racked you up, in one of those burnouts in Morrisania. I heard you got pretty fucked up, fell through a hole?"

Kennedy said nothing. What could he say?

"They ever find that kid? The one who went missing?"

"Yeah. They found him. He was dead."

Kennedy ran into traffic on the FDR. Frank turned on the radio, ran through some stations, uptown chatter, midtown swing, a couple of rock channels, until he found somebody willing to play a little slow dancing and shut the fuck up while he did it. Nothing more was said until Kennedy got them down to the 49th Street turnoff. There was more traffic around U.N. Plaza, but the wind was easier.

"I met this cop once, from out of town. A detective. He was telling me about this homicide they caught. It's June, and it's hot, right? Eddie?"

"Hey, I'm here. It's June and it's hot."

"Okay, so they find this kid, he can't be any more than twelve or thirteen. All he's wearing is a pair of shorts and a thin blue T-shirt. He's in a park, on his back, kind of folded up into himself, next to some trees. It looks like somebody has tried to bury him in the grass. But only a couple of inches. Like they tried to push him into the soil and they gave up when it was only half done."

"Are we going somewhere with this, Frank?"

"Yeah. There's a catch. The kid is frozen solid. He is a solid block of frozen flesh. It's June and the kid is lying in the grass, it looks like he's been lying there for a couple of hours, and he's *still* frozen solid."

"Was he dumped from a truck or something? Kept in a freezer and just dumped in the park?"

"No. There were no footprints, no tracks, no sign that anybody had ever stepped on that piece of ground. If somebody had dumped him there, they'd have to have left some sign of it. There was nothing."

"No way. Not possible. They must have missed it."

"Not this guy. He was a sharp cop. If it was there, he'd have found it. It wasn't that the first guys on the scene had just screwed up the sight. There were no marks at all. And the kid was frozen solid."

"No marks? Your guy was sure? Then it's impossible. He's telling you a story."

"No. That's the thing. It wasn't impossible. Can you figure it out?"

Robinson left him alone to try. All the way down Second, Kennedy thought the thing over.

Finally, he got it. "This park. Was it anywhere near a flight path? Was there an airport around?"

"Yes. Right on both counts."

"Was the park close enough to the airport that the planes would be putting their wheels down as they went over it? Over the park?"

"Yes."

"A stowaway. The kid was a stowaway. They find any ID on him?"

"No. Flat broke and busted."

"So he got over the fence, in some rat's-ass airport, in Guadeloupe or Haiti, someplace in the Caribbean. Plans to go to A-may-ree-ca. He hides in the wheel well of some big airliner. It takes off. He freezes to death at thirty thousand feet. The plane comes in to land at the airport. The wheels go down. Out comes the frozen little kid. He drops a couple of thousand feet and ends up, frozen, half-buried, in the middle of your park. With no footprints or tire tracks to explain how he got there."

"Bingo! You got it!"

"Yeah, I got it. So what's your point?"

"The point is, Eddie, that there's no point to it. It's just what it is. You know that as well as I do. You even said it to Wolfie, the other night."

"What are you talking about?"

"He told me about it. He was thumping the drum about Cardillo. Remember? He was all upset about that dipshit Farrakhan, and you said to him—I remember it because Wolfie had written it down—you said—"

"Wolfie wrote it down? Something I said, he wrote it down?"

"Yeah, Eddie. You're the grand old man of the squad. Wolfie looks up to you. He says you make it all fit. You said to him: 'Your only problem is you want justice, and you're not going to get it. So

fuck it. It's ten cents a dance. It's a tango in Roseland. It is what
it is.' "

"I said that?"

"Yeah. And you were right. So you lost a kid. I lost one too.
Doctors lose people every day. People get cut up and the courts
tie themselves in knots trying to see if the guy who did it managed
to squeeze every last drop out of his constitutional rights. And the
victims rot in the dirt, Eddie. The only way to get through it is to
go through it. I'll bet you have dreams. Am I right?"

"Yes. Sometimes."

"Right. So does Wolfie, and Fratelli. I do. I have God's worst
nightmares, sometimes. I wake up and I'm hanging on to Charlotte like she's the last plane out of hell. Stone-cold bitch dreams.
Killers come at me. Bodies get up off the autopsy table. They bury
me in a ditch—I can feel the mud hit my face. The thing is, don't
fight it. It's like Zen. It's a Zen thing—"

"Hey, no mystical bullshit here, hah? I've had a bad week."

"It's just an attitude. You go in there and you see how it
moves and what it moves to. You get inside it, like you get inside
a killer's head. I've seen you do it. And you just . . . dance with it.
No thinking, no answers. Just be still and dance with it. The Zen
tango—that's what it is. That's *all* it is."

"What is?"

"*It* is. It is what it is. This is where I get off."

"Hey, the station's that way."

Robinson got out by a high-rise at the corner of 34th and
Second. The wind was pulling at him, and the rain crawled
sideways across his face as he leaned into the door.

"Charlotte lives here. No way I'm sleeping alone tonight.
Take care, Eddie." And he was gone.

Snakes of rain were coiling on the windshield. Fuck the
regulations, said Kennedy. He turned the squad car around onto
34th Street. First was empty. He was home in fifteen minutes. He
left the car in the street, with the permit on the dash. Even the
brownies were under cover tonight. Calvin was asleep in his
wingback behind the desk. Kennedy stood, dripping, in the dim and
marbled lobby, feeling safe and desolate at the same time.

His apartment was unchanged. The coffee cup stood precisely

where he had left it. He found a Miller behind a moldering loaf of rye. The phone rang.

He let it ring. It stayed ringing. Finally, angry, he snatched it up.

"Yeah? What?"

"Eddie?" A woman's voice. Christ! Elaine Farraday. He was supposed to call her this afternoon. Shit!

"Elaine! God, Elaine, I'm sorry. I meant to call you but I got a little hung up."

"So did I. I thought I'd missed your call. Look, am I disturbing you? Maybe you have some company?"

"Company? I have mold on my dinner. Company I do *not* have." He gave the place a nervous once-over, trying to see it as a guest might. "What are you up to?"

"Tell you the truth, Eddie, I'm up to some company. This is a god-awful night to spend alone. Would you be outraged if I invited myself over? I have some Beck's, and I think there's a steak frozen to the roof of my fridge. I'll pry it off and come over."

"Elaine, I'd be honored. You'd make my day. Want me to come meet you halfway?"

"No, Eddie. I'm a big girl. Give me half an hour."

Kennedy had just managed to put the apartment in order. He even changed the sheets, feeling like a conniving son of a bitch, but it was mostly a matter of form. What he really wanted to do was sit on his couch with her and listen to her talk.

When the phone rang again, he felt it in his chest.

Ring. It's Stokovich. The kid died.

Ring. It's Stokovich. The kid *escaped.*

Ring. It's Elaine. She's changed her mind.

Ring.

Ring. He scooped it up, bracing himself.

"Mr. Kennedy?" A man's voice, but no one he knew.

"Yes."

"Thank goodness! I've been trying to reach you."

Great. An emergency. "Well, here I am."

"Yes, well, it's about your cat, Mr. Kennedy."

Dudley! Kennedy had also forgotten about his cat. What an asshole he was. And then he realized. Dudley was dead. That was the reason for the call. Dudley died. Kennedy felt a cold fire in his cheeks, and the room blurred.

"Yes?"

"Can you come over and get him? He's wrecking the place. He's a maniac! Can you get him in the morning?"

GLOSSARY

ACU   Anti-Crime Unit; precinct-level plainclothes police officers working to counter low-level street crime

ADA   Assistant District Attorney

Alphabet City   Slang term for the area around avenues A, B, C, and D, on Manhattan's Lower East Side

AT&F   Alcohol, Tobacco & Firearms

Banker   Street slang for the person who receives and holds cash paid out for drugs

Barnes man   Street slang for a major drug dealer; originally after Nicky Barnes, a well-known Harlem pusher

Barricaded EDP   An emotionally disturbed person who has barricaded himself in an apartment or refuge

Bernie   After Bernhard Goetz; any victim who might be armed and prepared to use the weapon

Blacktar   Distilled and concentrated heroin; also known as Tootsie Roll, Black Gold, or Shriek

Blue Sky   Street slang for heroin; also known as Liquid Sky

Brownie   Traffic officer

Bug   In police jargon, a criminal with a complete lack of empathic feeling

269

Burnout A ruined tenement building

CATCH Computer Assisted Terminal Criminal Hunt

Catch a stack To rob someone with a lot of money

CD Command Discipline

Chicken hawk A child molester

Chief of Patrol Senior officer commanding all uniform patrol operations for the five boroughs; reports directly to the Commissioner

Citywide NYPD term for a bulletin sent out to police personnel in all five boroughs

C.O. Commanding Officer

Collar Police jargon for a successful arrest

Communications NYPD term for the citywide radio network

CP The Command Post; a center of operations in the field close to a crime scene

CPL Criminal Procedure Law

Crack Distilled and crystallized cocaine

A crew A gang of young boys who have come together to engage in street crime as a unit

CSU Crime Scene Unit; specially trained team of NYPD detectives assigned to gather evidence at the scene of a major crime

DAMP Department of Alternative Management Program

DATF Detective Area Task Force; an NYPD management term for a squad of detectives assigned to investigate all major crimes in a given sector, usually about four precincts. Detective Area Task Forces replaced the old Homicide Zone system.

DCDS Deceased confirmed dead at scene

DEA The Drug Enforcement Administration

Defense cuts Deep slicing wounds usually found in the fingers, the palms, the wrists, and the forearms of a person who has been the victim of a knife attack

Desk officer   NYPD term for the uniform sergeant at the desk of a precinct house; reports to the Operations Coordinator

The Deuce   Forty-second Street between Sixth and Ninth Avenues

Diamond season   Warm weather

DOB   Date of birth

DOI   The Department of Investigations; an elite unit staffed by the NYPD, assigned to investigate civic and corporate corruption

Do-rag   Street slang for a tight head-scarf

Drop a dime   To provide information to the police about a specific crime; originally to make a call to the cops

Drop gun   A junk pistol usually confiscated from a criminal and carried by some police officers as a means of justifying a dubious shooting

DT   Street slang for a detective or a plainclothes cop on a street-crime assignment

Duty Captain   Uniform police captain responsible for all official personnel within a particular borough. Reports to Patrol Borough Commander

EDP   Emotionally disturbed person

Eighty-sixed   Army term for "canceled out" or "removed"

EMS   Emergency Medical Services; an ambulance service

ESC   Emergency Services Central

ESU   Emergency Services Unit; elite NYPD response team trained in special weapons and tactics (SWAT), rescue procedures, and other emergency police crises

Executive Officer   Second in command to the Precinct Commander

FATN and FINEST   NYPD terminology for the teletype network that links the precincts and the various departmental branches citywide

Fiend   To throw a choke hold on a victim

First Officer   Homicide term for the first uniform patrol officer to arrive at a crime scene

Five by five   "You are coming in loud and clear."

Five Charlie   Typical NYPD radio code for a squad car assigned
                    to a precinct patrol sector in Lower Manhattan

Fixer   Any location where a P.O. remains in permanent atten-
            dance, usually in a booth

Flak jacket   A bullet-resistant vest made of a Du Pont fabric
                  called Kevlar, a tight weave of Fiberglas mesh

Front   To back down from a fight

Gash   A white woman who has been raped

Get busy   To rob someone

Get fresh   To buy new clothes

Get paid   To commit a successful robbery; street slang

Getting fast   Slang term for cheating a partner out of money or
                   goods

GFY   Go fuck yourself

Give it up   To hand over one's valuables peaceably

Green Book   A large green clothbound ledger in which a chrono-
                 logical record is kept of every homicide case reported
                 in a given Detective Area

Grounders   NYPD term for a homicide case that can be solved with
                relative speed and simplicity

Gun run   NYPD radio term for a radio call involving firearms

A head   A victim

Home boy   Someome from the home blocks, the neighborhood

Hose job   Street slang for oral sex

Hot shot   An unexpectedly potent and therefore lethal hit of heroin

IAD   Internal Affairs Department; division of the NYPD assigned
          to investigate crimes committed by serving officers within the
          NYPD

Information   A verified written accusation by a person with knowl-
                  edge of the circumstances surrounding a crime or
                  eyewitness experience of a crime

IPSC   International Practical Shooting Competition; street-simulated combat scenarios for handgun users

Jakes   Uniform police officers

Keepers   Arrests that result in a prisoner being held and formal charges being laid against him at Central Booking

Knocked   Slang for getting arrested

Lajaras   Hispanic slang for a policeman; after O'Hara

Landline   NYPD jargon for the telephone

Latent print   An invisible print created by natural oils on the skin surface when the finger comes into contact with smooth or polished surfaces

Lividity   Also known as post-mortem lividity; bruiselike marking of the skin on a cadaver due to settling of the blood after death

'Ludes   Quaaludes, a soporific, also known as the Breakfast of Losers

Maggot   Street slang for anyone white

Maricon   Hispanic slang for a homosexual

Marielitos   Slang term for Cubans who were ejected by Castro from Mariel Harbor in 1980

Maytag   Prison slang for a weak male unable to protect himself from homosexual rape in the cell blocks; also used as a verb

M.E.   Medical examiner

MHR   Manhattan Human Resources

MOS   Member of Service; a member of the NYPD

My way   Back home in the neighborhood

Mysteries   NYPD term for homicide cases that prove difficult if not impossible to solve

No further   No more units need respond to this call.

NSU   Neighborhood Stabilization Unit; controversial training method used to introduce new recruits to a precinct area without having them come into too close contact with supposedly cynical older cops. Recruits are assigned in groups of three to a squad car and overseen by an experienced sergeant or lieutenant.

NYSIIS Criminal Identification numbers

OEEO Office of Equal Employment Opportunity

Operations Coordinator Assistant to the Precinct Commander; also called Ops Coordinator

Patrol Borough Commander Assistant to Chief of Patrol in all borough police operations

PCP Phencycladine phosphate, a horse tranquilizer that causes severe perceptual and psychological distortions in the user.

PEP Preventative and Enforcement Patrol; now-defunct forerunner of the citywide SNAP units; used in Harlem

Perps NYPD slang for "perpetrators," or criminal suspects

PG Patrol Guide

PI Police identification form

Piece A firearm or a woman

Plastic prints Classification term for a type of fingerprint found on a soft surface such as clay, wet paint, soap, wax, oil, or grease

Pocket man Similar to a banker; the one assigned to hold the cash from a robbery or other crime

Pocket prints An obvious wallet or roll of bills visible through the material of a victim's clothing

Poppy love Elderly Jewish male

Portables Foot patrol officers

Precinct Commander Commanding officer of a precinct

PW NYPD slang for a policewoman

Racket   NYPD slang for a private police party

Ratboy   Street slang for a man skilled in testing the strength of various illegal drugs; also, a gunman.

Recorder   In Homicide terms, a police officer responsible for noting the names and badge numbers of all officials attending at a crime scene

Red flag   A method of injecting heroin; the needle is inserted and the bulb allowed to expand until blood shows in the works. This insures that the hit will go straight into a vein and not be dissipated in flesh or muscle. It also allows the drug to be injected in tiny amounts, to prolong the rush.

Reds   Spansules or gelatin capsules; usually Dexedrine

Rigor   Rigor mortis; transitory hardening of the muscles after death

RMP   Radio Motor Patrol car; a squad car in the NYPD

Rodman's Neck   Location of the NYPD firearms training range

SCU   Street Crime Unit; detectives assigned to target muggers, pickpockets, and smash-and-grab thieves

Secretors   Medico-legal term for someone whose blood type can be determined from his physiological fluids

Semi-wadcutter   Standard police cartridge; a modified wad-cutter slug which is still flat at the tip but has rounded shoulders to insure the best combination of in-flight stability and energy transference to the target material; usually a .38 Special

Shine   NYPD slang for a useless bureaucrat, from the shine on the seat of his pants

Shitcan   NYPD slang for a homicide case that is unlikely to be solved for various reasons

The shooter   Street slang for the person who actually holds the street packet of a drug, and who turns it over to the person who has bought it

Short-eyes   A man who has a sexual fixation on young girls

Short-timer   U.S. Army term for a soldier whose combat tour is almost complete

Size the vic   To examine a potential victim from a distance

Skells   NYPD slang for criminals

Slash   Any attractive white woman

Slicks   Vietnam combat term for Medevac chopper; used in the NYPD to imply the arrival of a bunch of shines whose job it is to cover up a departmental mistake and to protect the bosses at One Police Plaza

SNAP   Street Narcotics Apprehension Program; a unit of plain-clothes officers assigned to fight street-level drug trafficking

SNU   Street Narcotics Unit

South Frank   Typical NYPD radio code for a particular squad car assigned to a precinct patrol sector in Manhattan

Spike   Slang term for a heroin user's needle

Stick   U.S. Army in Vietnam custom; a short-timer kept track of his remaining combat time by marking the days off on a small wooden stick.

The stressor   An event that triggers a murder

Swain talk   "Iz" added to the first syllable of a word; for example, some street blacks call a Jewish male a "zi-Iz-ip tee-ZOP."

Suitcased   A method of concealing capsules of a drug inside a condom or balloon inserted in the anus or the vagina

Suit   A young, college-educated cop clearly marked for advancement to Headquarters

Ten code   NYPD radio number code used to provide security for broadcast calls which may be monitored, and to save air time by speeding the exchange of information

Ten 2   "Call in to the base, please."

Ten 4   "I hear and will comply."

Ten 5   "Say again, please."

Ten 6 "Shut up; you're jamming the airwaves."

Ten 7 Out of the car for lunch

Ten 11 "An audible alarm is ringing in my sector."

Ten 13 NYPD radio code call for "Officer needs assistance"; most urgent police call, instantly responded to by all nearby units

Ten 17 "On the way to your location."

Ten 22 Theft in progress

Ten 30 Violent assault in progress

Ten 33 Police emergency in progress

Ten 53 Vehicular accident has taken place in sector

Ten 59 "A fire alarm has been triggered in my area."

Ten 62 "I'm off the air temporarily."

Ten 85 "Meet me at this location."

Ten 90, X, Y, or Z Car is clear of an assignment, with a notation on the Communications computer about the call.

Ten 98 Car is clear of an assignment and ready for other duty.

Throwaway Shirt or jacket worn by a mugger during an assault and discarded immediately afterward to confuse the pursuit

Toot Cocaine; also known as White Lady, Sleep, or Ice

Visible prints Type of fingerprint created when feet, palms, or fingers which are tinted or soiled come into contact with clean surfaces and leave a visible print

Word up Pay attention

Works Heroin user's drug equipment

Yoke Army slang for a choke hold

Zip top Street slang for anyone Jewish

Zone Commander Operations and Personnel supervisor for a particular borough; works primarily at One Police Plaza in a bureaucratic function